# The Mini**FARMING**™
# Handbook

# The
# Mini**FARMING**™
# Handbook

### Brett L. Markham

Skyhorse Publishing

10 9 8 7 6 5 4 3 2

Library of Congress Cataloging-in-Publication Data is available on file.

ISBN: 978-162914-197-8

Printed in China

# Table of Contents

# Introduction

**One of the** most common questions I've been asked is "What is Mini Farming, and how does it differ from gardening?" The simple answer is that Mini Farming is a lot like gardening, except that it is seen from the perspective of economics in terms of money and time. Like all simple answers, it doesn't tell the whole story, and many essentials are missing. To fill in the blanks requires an understanding of the origin of the idea and the needs it sought to meet.

I am not sure how things are going in other parts of the world, but in the United States anyway, people are getting squeezed economically. In 2007, before the most recent recession, the Economic Policy Institute reported that, with the exception of a brief period in the late 1990's, real wages for median and low-wage workers had remained stagnant from 1973 to 2007 despite impressive gains in productivity.[1]

Though worker productivity had increased more than 20% from 2001 to 2007, in terms of buying power, wages had remained relatively stagnant, even for college educated workers. The trend reported in 2007 is still alive and well in 2013. USA Today reports that despite stock markets and corporate profits breaking records, wages remain stagnant.[2]

Meanwhile, as I was formulating the conceptions of Mini Farming in 2005 and 2006, I had noticed a substantial rise in the number of home foreclosures. In fact, from 2000 to 2006, the foreclosure rate had more than doubled.[3] I saw this as very troubling given that the period from 2001 to 2006 was widely reported as an economic recovery, rather than a recession. Ultimately, there were 470,000 foreclosures in 2000, but a staggering 2.3 million annual foreclosures by 2012.

Also, during that time, I observed that the price of gas and home heating oil had tripled between 2000 and 2006. It's even higher now.[4] Though many factors contribute to high energy prices, in researching the matter I discovered that no matter how much politicians may play it down, our own Government Accountability Office is predicting massive economic dislocations and widespread starvation due to a peak and decline in global oil production at some point in the relatively near future.[5] But even without that factor, oil prices indirectly affect the price of nearly everything else in our economy and directly affect most budgets for commuting and heating.

---

[1] Bernstein J, Mishel L (2007) Economy's Gains Fail to Reach Most Workers' Paychecks, Economic Policy Institute, Briefing Paper # 195
[2] Davidson P, Waggoner J (2013) Profits don't flow through to wages, USA Today, May 6, 2013
[3] Statistics Brain, Home Foreclosure Statistics, retrieved 11/1/2013
[4] Gas Buddy Website
[5] Crude Oil: Uncertainty about future oil supply makes it important to develop a strategy for addressing a peak and decline of oil production, Government Accountability Office, report to Congress, February 2007.

So the first need I sought to address with Mini Farming is a distinctly economic one. Even though big picture issues such as oil prices, foreclosure rates and wage stagnation over a period of decades are adversely affecting millions of people, those matters are well beyond my ability to fix. But for any given household, the effect of those factors can be reduced dramatically by growing your own food in an economically sensible way. In other words, instead of worrying about things I can't change, I instead focused on things that I can change, such as helping people grow their own food.

"Gardening" is a hobby because the way most people go about it, by the time you account for the costs of transplants, seeds, fertilizer and pesticides, it only manages to break even economically. The value of the food grown approximates the cost of the inputs. Alternatively, Mini Farming methods create food with greater value than the cost of elements that go into it. The net economic positive in offsetting food bills has the same economic effect on the family as a very large tax-free raise.

This also has the effect of turning the home from a very high priced hotel into an income producing asset. The typical suburban home is mainly a place where people sleep and watch television. Though it may appreciate over time, the cold hard reality is that as of this writing, more than seven million home owners actually owe more on their home than it is worth.[6] Mini Farming looks at the yard around your home as a source of valuable products. Your home is transformed from a place of consumption into a center of production that pays you every week. This transformation makes a home substantially more affordable because the food it produces to offset grocery bills can be worth enough to pay the mortgage.

---

[6] Glink I, (2013) Millions of Homeowners Still Underwater Despite Price Gains, CBS News Moneywatch, 9/12/2013

Another issue I wanted to address is nutrition. Everybody knows most Americans don't eat enough fruits and vegetables, and that this has unfortunate long-term implications for health. Several studies have indicated that on a dollars-per-calorie basis, the fresh fruits and vegetables we need are quite expensive compared to items in the cookie, cracker and snack aisle. In fact, healthy low-calorie foods are roughly ten times as expensive as the unhealthy calorie-dense foods available.[7] Dr. Adam Drewnowski, commenting on a study conducted for the University of Washington stated that "Vegetables and fruits are rapidly becoming luxury goods."[8]

Even for people who can regularly afford fruits and vegetables, the depletion of trace nutrients in agricultural lands over the decades has led to a steady decline in the nutritional content of the vegetables we buy. Commodity agriculture does not reward production of nutritionally superior products because it draws no distinctions based on nutritional value. Because of this, fertilizer regimens are focused only on minerals necessary to make a product that looks good. Of the 50 or more minerals humans need in their diet, only 13 are regularly replenished in commodity agriculture. As a result, though the specifics vary with the crop, the content of elements such as copper in our foods has dropped by as much as 96% since the 1930s.[9] Research by the Nutrition Security Institute correlates declining mineral content with increased risk of a host of chronic diseases.[10]

Mini Farming methods use organic amendments rich in trace minerals as well as composting and biochar to retain those minerals.

---

[7] Kish, S. (2008) Healthy Low-Calorie Foods Cost More on Average, USDA Cooperative State Research, Education, and Extension Service

[8] Parker-Pope T. (2007) A High Price for Healthy Food, *New York Times*, December 5, 2007

[9] Thomas D. A study on the mineral depletion of the foods available to us as a nation over the period 1940 to 1991. Nutr Health. 2003;17(2):85-115.

[10] Wallin J, Marler J, Human Health, the Nutritional Quality of Harvested Food and Sustainable Farming Systems, Nutrition Security Institute

Of course, food raised at home is more fresh than food from the supermarket, which results in a higher vitamin content as well. On the scale of a Mini Farm, sustainable organic methods not only produce the most nutritious food, but they are the most economically productive as well. Mini Farming combines intensive agricultural methods with organic sustainable methods and up-to-date soil and pest management practices to give you amazing production of nutritious and delicious food at a net profit.

So the major objectives of Mini Farming pertain to economics and nutrition, and those objectives are achieved through sustainable and intensive methods.

Of course, in the modern world, people are pressed for time. Commuting times are longer, work hours are longer and many times our employers expect us to be glued to smart phones even while we sleep. A harried parent who is struggling to pick up children from daycare after work doesn't have eight hours a day to dedicate to food production. So Mini Farming methods are optimized for time. As a result, the time investment amounts to about an hour a day when averaged over a year, in exchange for netting 80% of the food needed for a family of four.

Mini Farming also has some minor goals. The social realities of the American family are causing key self-sufficiency skills to be lost. According to CDC statistics, more than 40% of children are born to unmarried mothers. Of those born to married couples, 50% of the children will see their parents divorce. This means that in aggregate, 70% of children born are winding up in homes missing a parent. These circumstances necessitate schedules and lifestyles that are usually incompatible with parents passing on skills they learned from their own parents. Those skills might include sewing, fishing, cooking, gardening, canning, cheese-making, wine-making, pruning apple trees and more. The opportunity to pass along these skills simply doesn't exist, and so over the past few generations they have become increasingly rare.

Skills such as raising chickens, canning and gardening raise the standard of living above what one's paycheck could normally afford. A couple of weeks ago I noticed whole organic chickens at the supermarket for nearly $30. Most people would buy the conventional whole chicken for $7 instead because their budgets simply don't allow dumping $30 on meat for a single meal. When you raise your own organic free-ranging chicken and put it in your freezer, it costs less than $7, but is worth more than $30. But out of 100 people that you meet, how many of them could confidently process a chicken as food? Without that skill, you're stuck with the $7 chicken infused with antibiotics, but if you have that skill you get to eat as though you made enough money to buy $30 chickens, while spending less than you would on a $7 chicken.

This same reasoning applies to numerous home skills. Cooking food yourself at home gives you a superior product when compared to eating out, and costs a lot less. Lobsters at my local supermarket usually cost $3.99/lb, but getting them at a local restaurant costs nearly $30. If you learn how to prepare lobsters at home, you get to eat a $30 meal for only $3.99. When this logic is applied to food you grow yourself, you save even more. Asparagus at a restaurant costs a fortune, but asparagus from my long-established bed costs practically nothing and tastes better.

Obviously, there are points of diminishing return, and I am certainly not arguing that we should go back to weaving our own cloth or threshing wheat. Many commodity items, including clothing, can't be produced at home in a time-efficient manner that makes the endeavor worthwhile. But my key point is that the skills that many of us never learned whether due to lack of interest, parents who were too busy or changing social dynamics are in fact quite valuable in economically measurable ways. The value of those skills stretches paychecks and gives a higher standard of living.

Given the trends of wage stagnation that have persisted for decades and are unlikely to change, the loss of these skills effectively reduces the standard of living for people who, lacking the skills to do things for themselves, must rely on others whom they pay, do without, or settle for inferior food. With economic security being so precarious for so many people, and with families being splintered so that extended family doesn't provide the safety net that it used to, the disappearance of these skills is a serious problem.

Throughout the Mini Farming series of books I have endeavored to teach skills that my paternal grandparents took for granted. Whether it is growing your own transplants, saving your own seeds, canning your own pickles, processing your own chickens or making your own wine from the apple tree out back, the Mini Farming series of books empowers you with know-how that will let you take charge of your own food supply. When you can take charge of your own food supply in this environment of economic uncertainty, you rightly feel empowered and your family is better off both financially and nutritionally.

One final goal of the Mini Farming series is to help people reconnect with something *real*. So much of what we see today is a form of mediated and "spun" reality that has no true substance. Whether it be an income tax code whose rules are so convoluted they could fool a CPA, focus-group-tested words used to describe products or the airbrushed models gracing the cover of a magazines, we get diverted into assigning what is essentially an artificial world more value and a higher priority than the real world. Nothing is more real than matching yourself to the rhythm of the seasons, planting seeds and digging into the earth to harvest crops. For myself, anyway, it is like meditation. While I am weeding my garden beds I am not worried about a new change in the dress code at work or whether I need some expensive cream to look handsome. It's just me, the beds, the crops and the weeds under a blue sky.

Likewise, it is very hard to Mini Farm alone. Though a lot of it can be done alone, when it comes time to harvest and save food, you'll find that the active cooperation of the whole family is necessary. Everyone in the family comes together in a joint enterprise from which all benefit, but the time spent together where you have to be completely present in the moment is a way to reestablish connections that become frayed in a world of omnipresent communication with third parties and pressing schedules.

I worked intimately with Jenn McCartney, my editor at Skyhorse Publishing, to formulate the content of this book. I read all of the reviews of my books that I could find, so I could see which sections of the books people found most useful. This book is a compilation from the other five books I have written on Mini Farming and it encapsulates the best of everything you need to be food self-sufficient on ¼ acre or even less. It contains everything you need to know to grow and preserve your own food, along with raising and processing chickens and even making your own wine. It includes skills that were well known to my grandparents but are sadly unfamiliar to many who could really use them today. I am really pleased with it, and I believe you'll be pleased with it too.

I am most happy that this book meets my objectives for Mini Farming. It will help you economically while increasing the nutritional quality and availability of the best foods for your family. It closes the generational gap in self-sufficiency skills, and it will help you reconnect with your food, nature, and loved ones in an intimate and healthy way, continuing a sacred chain that goes back to the very beginning.

Brett Markham, 2014

# Raised Beds

# 1

**Raised beds and** properly constituted soil make mini-farming practical. Modern people in the industrialized world have a lot less spare time and a lot less available land than their ancestors.

Raised beds offer so many advantages over row gardening that it is hard to imagine why everyone except big agribusiness cartels isn't using them. Especially in northern climates, raised beds can help gardeners lengthen their growing season because they can raise soil temperature by 8 to 13 degrees compared to ground soil temperatures.

By raising the level of the soil, farmers and gardeners can start their crops earlier because excess moisture drains easily so the cold spring rains won't overwhelm new crops. Raised beds are also easily fitted with attachments, such as cold frames.

A raised bed is essentially a bottomless and topless box laid on the ground and filled with soil. The boxes can be built from wood, plastic boards, cement, and other materials. Raised beds can be made from mounded earth, but surrounding them with a box structure limits erosion of the carefully prepared soil of the bed.

⊗ Raised beds extend the season and reduce problems related to excess water.

# Material Choices

**The frames of** raised beds are in constant contact with damp earth and can be subject to rotting. Ordinary lumber will last two or three years before replacement is needed. This can be delayed by carefully painting all exposed surfaces of the frames with a water-based exterior latex paint and allowing them to dry thoroughly before putting them to use. Do not use oil-based paints or paints containing antimildew ingredients or else you'll poison the soil in your beds. Because of the weight of the soil, boards used should be at least 1.5 inches thick to avoid bowing, and opposite sides of long runs should be tied together every eight feet or so. The biggest benefits of lumber lie in its easy availability and easy workability.

Ordinary concrete blocks are inexpensive and easy to use. They are readily available, durable, and heavy enough to hold the soil in a raised bed without need for mortar. They can be picked up and moved around to relocate or expand beds, and they can be reused almost indefinitely. The only downside is their weight—45 pounds for each. That means that in spite of their compact size, only 22 at a time can be hauled in a pickup truck rated to haul a half ton. Since each block is eighteen inches long, a pickup-sized load gives only 33 linear feet.

Boards made from recycled plastic used for decks and other outdoor structures have become more available in recent years and combine the assets of the easy handling of traditional lumber with the durability of concrete block. Several raised-bed kits are on the market that use plastic boards, and these may be a good idea if you plan on doing a small amount of gardening, but because of the expense of the kits, they don't make sense on the scale needed to feed a family. For a mini-farm, save expense by buying the plastic boards at the lumber store and cutting them to the right size yourself.

It is true that more modern pressure-treated lumber uses less toxic components than it used to, but the components are still toxic, and they can leach into the soil of the growing bed, so they are best avoided.

Many other materials can be used, ranging from landscaping timbers to poured concrete forms. Just let imagination, cost, durability, and the potential toxicity of anything you might use guide the decision. Keep in mind that using materials that leach poisons into the growing beds completely defeats the purpose of the home garden or mini-farm because consuming the products grown in those beds can be extremely hazardous. (The arsenic in pressure-treated wood, for example, is both directly toxic and highly carcinogenic.)

⊗ Raised beds can be made from a variety of materials. This one is made with cinder blocks and landscape timbers.

# Shape and Orientation of Raised Beds

**The most common** and useful shape for raised beds is rectangular. Certain planters for flowers are circular, and this works fine as long as the diameter is not so great that the gardener has to step into the bed. Another common shape is a 4-foot square. This works well for casual vegetable-only gardening on a small scale, but at the scale of providing all the needs of a family, it becomes wasteful of space and material.

I recommend a rectangular shape because it makes maximum use of space and minimal material while making it easy to add standardized structures like hoop houses.

Any rectangular bed is going to be longer than it is wide. To give maximum sun to crops and avoid shading, ensure that the long sides face north and south. Any trellising for vining crops should be established along the north edge to get the advantage of sunshine without shading other crops.

# Size of Raised Beds: Width

**Everyone has an** opinion on the proper size of raised beds. The Grow Biointensive method favors a width of 5 feet and a length of 20 feet to establish a "microclimate" for intensive agriculture. Square Foot enthusiasts advocate a maximum width of 4 feet, because it is easy to reach into a bed that is 4 feet wide from either side and get to whatever is in the middle. Many experienced organic farmers use even narrower raised beds.

The five-foot width advocated by Ecology Action requires, for many people, stepping into the bed onto a board intended to more widely distribute the weight and minimize damage to the soil structure. But stepping into the garden bed at all, even using a board, defeats the purpose of careful management of the soil structure by compacting the soil. The board would need to be set up so it can be laid across the sides of the bed structure and be rigid enough that it won't bend when someone is standing on it. (This would be impossible using the complete Grow Biointensive method since, in that method, the raised beds are only mounded soil without structural sides. My method uses structural sides instead.)

The 4-foot width is narrow enough that most people can reach into the garden from both sides since only a 2-foot reach is needed. This will not work, however, when trellised crops that grow food on both sides of the trellis are grown against one of the long sides of the bed. In that case, picking pole beans, for example, requires a 4-foot reach, which most people don't have. My wife and I did this with a 4-foot-wide bed one year, and watching my wife balance on one of the frame boards while reaching for the beans with one hand and holding on to me with the other was a sure sign that I would need to make some changes the following year!

For reasons of experience and convenience, then, I recommend that beds should be four feet wide if they aren't going to be used for tall vines like pole beans. They should be three to three and a half feet wide otherwise.

# Size of Raised Beds: Length

**We already know** that beds need to be rectangular for economic reasons and three to four feet wide for convenience—but how long can they be? Technically, they can be as long as the farmer wants, but there are some aspects of length worth considering.

One of the biggest causes of insect and disease problems is growing the same plants in the same space year after year. Bacterial, fungal, and viral diseases often have preferred host plants—and sometimes won't even grow in plants of an unrelated genus. Since these pathogens are competing against more beneficial microbes in compost-enriched soil, they can survive for only a limited period of time—usually three years or less—in soil that doesn't provide a suitable host.

Insect pests (some of which spread diseases) are quite similar. They have a particular appetite—a particular niche—such as cabbage. Such pests not only eat cabbage and infect it with diseases but also lay their eggs in the soil around the cabbage so that their offspring will emerge right next to their favorite food. One important way of foiling such pests is to make sure that when their offspring awaken in spring, they find plants that aren't appetizing.

Limiting the length of raised beds so that you have more room to create several of them makes it easy to practice crop rotation because the soil in one bed is isolated from the soil in the others. Making sure the same crop isn't grown in the same bed for three years solves a lot of problems in advance. In my own mini-farm, beds range in length from 8 to 24 feet.

# Start at the Right Time and Grow Slowly

**The time between** when the soil can first be worked in the spring and when the early spring crops need to be planted is about three weeks. This is simply not enough time to create enough raised beds.

Ultimately, for total food self-sufficiency, you will need about 700 square feet per person. If you plan to raise market crops, you'll need even more. That will require a lot of beds. The number will depend on the length you choose.

Assuming the creation of beds that are 4-feet × 25-feet, that means you'll need at least seven beds per person or 21 beds for a family of three. Using 4-feet × 8-feet beds, that would be 22 beds per person or 66 for a family of three. In practice, depending on dietary preferences, chosen crop varieties, climate, and other factors, a larger or smaller number of beds could actually be used.

Initial creation of raised beds takes a considerable amount of time and is very labor intensive, but once they've been created, they require very little work to maintain. Raised beds can be created in a number of ways, but even the most time-efficient methods will take a few hours per bed. If you have limited time, getting all the beds made in spring will be physically impossible.

Therefore the best time to embark upon mini-farming is *the summer or fall before* the first growing season. This way the beds can be prepared in a more leisurely fashion and then sowed with cover crops for overwintering. In the spring, you only have to cut the cover crops and put them into the compost pile, cultivate existing beds, and start planting. (Cover crops are explained in the next chapter.)

It may be best to start mini-farming slowly—say, by initially creating enough beds for just a single individual's food—and then keep adding beds as time and materials allow until the required number has been established. This is because of the trade-off between time and money. If the prospective farmer has the time to establish all of the required beds initially, that's great. But if time is lacking, the only way to shortcut the system is to pay for heavy equipment and truckloads of compost.

I don't want the fact that fall is the best time to get started to discourage you from starting in either the spring or summer if that is when you want to start. It is always better to start than to delay because even just a couple of raised beds can produce a lot of food. If you get started in the spring or summer, just keep in mind that you'll want to add new beds in the fall as well.

# Creating the Beds

**For reasons of** economy and productivity, I recommend creating the beds initially by double-digging. Lay out the area to be dug using stakes and string, then once it is dug, surround that area with the material you have chosen to create the box for the bed. Because the process of double-digging will loosen the soil, the level of the dug area will be between four and six inches higher than the surrounding soil.

Double-digging has been a standard agricultural practice for soil improvement in various places around the world for untold generations, and it is what I recommend because it is the most effective for the money required. The idea behind double-digging is that plants send their roots deeply into the soil, and making sure there are nutrients and aerated soil two feet deep provides ideal growing conditions. Up where I live in New Hampshire, any attempt at digging, no matter how modest, can be difficult because of the large number of rocks encountered. Did you ever wonder where all those picturesque rock walls in New England came from? Yep—they came from farmers getting rocks out of their fields.

My grandfather never double-dug anything but his asparagus beds. But, then again, he had 96 acres of land, horse teams, plows, tractors, four sons, and three daughters, so he wasn't trying to squeeze every ounce of productivity out of every square foot like a modern mini-farmer either. Nevertheless, the asparagus grown in a double-dug bed was far superior to any other.

Although many plants, especially grasses, can send roots several feet deep, the majority of a plant's root system exists in the top six inches of the soil. That's why Mel Bartholomew's Square Foot gardening system, which uses only six inches of soil, works. But in spite of the fact that six inches of perfectly prepared soil can be adequate, there can be no doubt that two *feet* of soil will necessarily hold a greater reservoir of nutrients and water.

As my father would say, with my apologies to our beloved cat, Patrick, in advance, "there's more than one way to skin a cat." Meaning, of course, that double-digging is not the only suitable way to prepare soil for mini-farming. There are actually three ways of digging the beds.

# Digging Methods

**The old-timers where** I grew up never used the term *double-digging*. In the United States and Great Britain, that practice has been historically known as "bastard trenching" to differentiate it from full or "true" trenching. Most modern texts don't mention it, but there are actually three sorts of trenching that are useful under different circumstances. All three types of trenching are brutally hard work, particularly in areas with a lot of large rocks or with soils composed mainly of clay, but they offer benefits worth the effort. These three types of trenching are *plain digging, bastard trenching*, and *trenching*.

Plain digging relies on using a garden spade to dig into and turn over the soil to the depth of a single spade. The area to be dug is laid out using string or other marking, and a garden spade is used to remove the soil one-spade wide and a single-spade deep across the width of the bed, and that soil is placed into a wheelbarrow. Then a couple of inches of compost is added to the bottom of the first trench, and the soil from the next parallel trench is added on top of the compost in the first trench. This process continues until the last trench is dug and compost added to the bottom, and then the soil saved from the first trench is added to the hole left by the last trench.

The only difference between plain digging and double-digging (a.k.a. bastard trenching) is that in the latter, after a trench is dug a single-spade deep and before the compost is added, a digging fork is

⊗ The garden fork and digging spade are indispensable tools for double-digging.

worked into the soil at the bottom of the trench to lift and break up the soil. Finally, more compost is added on top and mixed with the top six inches of soil. I perform this last step after I've built the form around the dug area.

Both plain digging and double-digging can be useful for newly created beds and can be especially useful for an area that is covered with grass as the spits of dirt (the dirt that makes up a spade-full is known as a "spit") can be turned grass-side down in the adjacent trench as they are dug. It is extremely useful in either case, where the land to be used for farming was previously weeds or lawn, to sift through the soil to remove wireworms and grubs as you go along. When I use either of these trenching methods, I not only put compost in the bottom of the trenches but add some across the top of the finished bed and mix it in as well.

True or full trenching is serious work, but it is appropriate for regenerating soil in beds that have been previously double-dug or where the soil can be worked deeply without using a backhoe. A properly maintained bed should never need regeneration, but true trenching can be useful when dealing with land that was previously overfarmed using conventional methods since it exchanges the subsoil with the top soil. In true trenching, the first trench is dug a single-spade deep and the soil from that set aside, and then the same trench is dug another spade deep and that soil is set aside as well, separately from the soil from the top of the trench. Then a digging fork is used to break up the soil in the bottom as deep as the tines will go, and compost is added.

When the second adjacent trench is dug, the spits from the top are added to the bottom of the first trench, then the spits from the bottom are added to the top of that. In this way, the topsoil is buried, and the subsoil is brought to the top. Continue in this way until the last trench is dug, at which time the top spits from the first trench are put into the bottom of the last trench, and then those spits are topped with those that remain.

Because true trenching exchanges the topsoil with the subsoil, and subsoil tends to have far less organic matter, generous amounts of aged compost should be added to the top layer, worked in thoroughly, and allowed to sit for a couple of weeks before putting the new bed to use.

In any of the three trenching methods, you will be using hand tools to move, literally, thousands of pounds of soil for each bed. This can be grueling work, and you should always use spades and digging forks that have been either bought or modified to accommodate your height. The correct height of a spade or fork (plus handle) can be judged by standing the tool vertically next to you, then seeing how high it reaches on your body. The top of the handle should fall somewhere between your elbow and the middle of your breastbone.

Digging forks and spades can be purchased with either straight or "D" handles. You should get the "D"-handled versions, as they will lessen the amount of required back twisting. When using the tools, keep your back straight, and avoid both twisting and jerky movements. Work at a comfortable pace, and take breaks when needed. This way you get an excellent and safe aerobic workout that improves your strength and flexibility while improving the soil.

# Illustrated Double-Dig

**Every year I** expand my mini-farm a little by adding a few raised beds. The beds in my farm vary in size depending on the materials I had available at the time of construction, but most of them are 3-1/2 feet wide and 8 feet long. In the spring of 2006, I added a few beds and had my wife take pictures of the process so I could include them for your reference.

1    Mark off the area to be dug. In my case, I just laid out the boards where I would be digging. Notice a completed bed in the foreground and boards marking where the new bed will be in the background.

⊗ Boards are used to mark off the new bed. You could just as easily use string or chalk.

⊗ Loosening the soil.

⊗ First row dug.

⊗ Adding compost.

2   Dig the first row across the width of the bed one-spade deep, and put the dirt from that row in a wheelbarrow.

3   Loosen the soil in the bottom of the trench with a digging fork.

4   Add compost to the bottom of the trench.

5   Dig the second trench parallel and adjacent to the first one.

6   Because, in this instance, I am digging an area that was covered with grass, I turn the spits from the second trench upside down in the first trench.

7   Work some additional compost into the top few inches of the finished bed.

⊗ Digging the second trench. Beware the author's stylish footwear!

⊗ Putting spits in the trench upside down.

⊗ Working compost into the top few inches of the new bed.

As you can see from the photo tutorial, preparing raised beds by double-digging is a pretty straightforward and very physical process. It is great exercise and loosens the soil to a depth of two feet, placing organic material throughout the entire depth. The yields from beds that I work like this are phenomenal!

# What about "No-Dig" Beds?

**In my experience,** I have found nothing that competes, in terms of sheer productivity, with properly double-dug raised beds. However, this can be a lot of work, and folks without a lot of time or with physical disabilities might not want to undertake the effort. You can still get very good results, though, using a no-dig method that I've tested.

Save up old newspapers—just the black-and- white portions, not the glossy parts. In the fall, build your frame out of 2 × 4 lumber right on the ground. Lay down the newspaper several layers thick, and then fill the bed completely with finished compost. Don't skip the newspapers because their purpose is to smother the grass underneath. If the grass isn't smothered, and if you are using only 2 × 4 lumber, you'll end up with a lot of grass growing in the bed.

When spring rolls around and the ground thaws, just use the digging fork to fluff it up a little; then plant, and you are done.

For no-dig beds it is particularly important to keep them planted with cover crops when fallow during the off-season because you are depending on the action of plant roots to mix the soil and keep it loose.

Because seeds don't always germinate well in compost, I'd recommend using the bed for transplanted crops for the first year, and then a good soil builder like beans the next year. In all other respects, you can treat this just like a regular raised bed. If fresh compost is added yearly, after three years the productivity will be the same as for a double-dug bed.

# Trellising for Raised Beds: Flexible Trellising System

**Trellises are necessary** for certain crops and can be a valuable adjunct for others. Because raised beds don't provide much room for sprawling plants such as cucumbers or pole beans, adding a trellis makes growing these crops more practical and space efficient.

Many crops are more productive in vining versions than bush versions. This includes beans, peas, cucumbers, tomatoes, and more. Pole beans, for example, can yield almost twice as much product per square foot as bush beans. This means that a row of pole beans grown on a

⊗ Electrical conduit makes a sturdy and versatile trellis.

trellis along the north side of an 8-foot bed using only 8 square feet of space can produce nearly as many beans as 16 square feet of bush beans. This same calculation applies to other vegetables.

As mentioned earlier in the chapter, beds will ideally be located with the long sides facing north and south. Trellises should be established on the north side. If, for some reason, this orientation isn't convenient, the second-best choice is to have the long side upon which trellises will be established on the north west or, in the worst case, west side. Don't establish trellises on the south or east sides of a bed or they will shade crops during the times of day that are most sunny.

There are as many ways to erect trellises as there are farmers, and I've used many different methods over the years. In the past few years, my preferred method of trellising uses rebar, electrical conduit, and conduit fittings. Electrical conduit comes in lengths 10 feet long. By cutting it to strategic lengths and using appropriate fittings, you can vary its height and length. By fitting it over rebar driven into the ground, you can lift it off the rebar easily in the fall for storage, and moving it to a different bed is a snap.

Because lumber used to create the beds is eight feet long, the longest you need the conduit to be is eight feet. This is for the horizontal piece on top. Meanwhile, trellis heights can range all the way from two feet for peas to four feet for tomatoes to even six feet for pole beans. A trellis height of more than six feet isn't a good idea, as reaching the top would be tiring or—even worse if a stool is required—dangerous.

The easy way to get a flexible system is to buy 10-foot lengths of conduit six pieces at a time. Three are cut into an 8-foot and a 2-foot piece, two are cut into a 6-foot and a 4-foot piece, and the final length of conduit is cut into two 4-foot pieces and one 2-foot piece. When done, you have three 8-foot horizontals, two 6-foot verticals, four 4-foot verticals, and four 2-foot verticals. In addition to these, for every six pieces of conduit, you will need six 90-degree elbows, four screw couplings, and six pieces of 2-foot rebar. (You can find rebar already cut to length and bundled at Home Depot and similar stores.)

Once the rebar is hammered into the ground on either end of the beds, you can completely assemble or disassemble a trellis of any height from 2-foot to 8-foot in two-foot increments using only a screwdriver.

⊗ Driving the rebar into the ground.

⊗ Placing an upright over the rebar.

# Complete Trellis Creation, Step-by-Step

1    Hammer 2-foot pieces of rebar into the ground at either end of the raised bed, leaving 6 inches protruding above the ground.

⊗ Attaching the horizontal to the bend.

⊗ Deck screws drilled into the edge and protruding ⅜ inch.

Deck Screws

2   Slip your vertical piece of conduit over the rebar. Repeat for the other side.

3   Attach a 90-degree elbow to each vertical piece of conduit, and then secure the horizontal conduit to the elbows.

4   Put deck screws into the side of the raised bed along the trellis every 6 to 12 inches. Leave them protruding about a quarter of an inch.

5   Run string between the horizontal bar on top and the deck screws in the side of the raised bed.

6   Now you have a completed trellis!

⊗ Run string between the horizontal and the deck screws.

⊗ Completed trellis.

# 2

# Soil Composition and Maintenance

**The productivity and** fertility of the farm and plant resistance to pests and disease depend on the quality of the soil. Soil quality can be enhanced and outside inputs reduced through proper tillage, compost, cover cropping, and crop rotation. These are crucial to maintaining the high level of fertility required for the close plant spacing in a mini-farm without spending a lot of money on fertilizer.

When French Intensive gardening was developed, horses were the standard mode of transportation, and horse manure was plentiful and essentially free. This explains the reliance on horse manure as a source of soil fertility. According to the Colorado State University Cooperative Extension Service, the average 1,000-pound horse generates 9 tons—18,000 pounds—of manure occupying nearly

⊘ Horse manure should be composted and not added directly to the bed.

730 cubic feet per year.[11] The sheer volume, smell, and mess of such quantities of manure often mean that places that board horses will give it away for the asking to anyone willing to haul it away.

Horse manure is good food for crops as well. According to the same source, horse manure contains 19 pounds of nitrogen per ton, 14 pounds of phosphate, and 36 pounds of potassium. This works out to about 1% nitrogen, 0.7% phosphate, and 1.8% potassium.

There's no such thing as a free lunch, and horse manure is no exception. Raw horse manure can spread a parasitic protozoan called giardia and E. coli as well as contaminate water sources and streams with coliform bacteria. Raw manure can also contain worm eggs that are easily transmitted to humans, including pinworms and various species of ascarid worms. Horse manure is high in salts, and if used excessively, it can cause plants grown in it to suffer water stress, even if well watered. The highest permissible rate of application of horse manure assuming the least measurable salinity is between two and three pounds of manure per square foot per year.[12] In addition to the above objections, horse manure doesn't have a balanced level of phosphorus, meaning that it should be supplemented with a source of phosphorus when used.

Straight horse manure is also in the process of composting. That is, the process has not yet finished. Unfinished compost often

[11] Davis, J. G., Swinker, A. M. (2004) *Horse Manure Management* Retrieved Jan 29, 2006, from http://www.ext.colostate.edu/pubs/livestk/01219.html

[12] Ibid

contains phytotoxic chemicals that inhibit plant growth. For horse manure to be directly usable as a planting medium, it must first be well rotted, meaning it either should be composted in a pile mixed with other compost materials such as plant debris or should at least sit by itself rotting for a year before use. The former method is preferable since that will conserve more of the manure's valuable nitrogen content. The potential problems posed by horse manure are eliminated through composting the manure with other materials first and then liberally applying the resulting compost to beds. The composting process will kill any parasites, dilute the salinity, and break down phytotoxins.

Making perfect soil from scratch, on a small scale, works quite well. The Square Foot gardening method gives a formula of 1/3 coarse vermiculite, 1/3 peat moss, and 1/3 compost by volume plus a mix of organic fertilizers to create a "perfect soil mix."[13] My own testing on a 120-square-foot raised bed confirms that the method works beautifully. For small beds, the price of the components is reasonable. A six-inch-deep 4-foot × 6-foot bed would require only four cubic feet of each of the components. Coarse vermiculite and peat moss currently sell for about $18 for a four-cubic-foot bale. Assuming free compost, the cost of making perfect soil mix comes to $1.50 per square foot of growing area. This works quite well on a small scale, but when even 700 square feet are put into agricultural production, the cost can become prohibitive.

Double-digging was covered in the previous chapter, and it is what I recommend for mini-farming. Although it is more difficult in the beginning, it affords the best opportunity to prepare the best possible soil for the money invested. No-dig beds, also described in the previous chapter, are a second option.

---

[13] Bartholomew, M. (2000) *Ca$h from Square Foot Gardening*

# Water-Holding Capacity and pH

**Few soils start** out ideal for intensive agriculture or even any sort of agriculture. Some are too sandy, and some are too rich in clay. Some are too acidic, and others are too alkaline. Many lack one or more primary nutrients and any number of trace minerals.

Soil for agricultural use needs to hold water without becoming waterlogged. Sandy soils are seldom waterlogged, but they dry out so quickly that constant watering is required. They make root growth easy but don't hold on to nutrients very well and are low in organic content or humus. (There is some dispute among experts on the exact definition of *humus*. For our purposes, it can be defined as organic matter in the soil that has reached a point of being sufficiently stable that it won't easily decompose further. Thus, finished compost and humus are identical for our purposes.) Clay soils will be waterlogged in the winter and will remain waterlogged as long as water comes to them. As soon as the water stops, they bake and crack, putting stress on root systems. Clay soil is clingy, sticky, and nearly impenetrable to roots. Loam soil is closest to the ideal, as it consists of a mix of sand and clay with a good amount of humus that helps it retain water and nutrients in proportions suitable for agriculture.

Both sandy and clay soils can be improved with vermiculite. Vermiculite is manufactured by heating mica rock in an oven until it pops like popcorn. The result is a durable substance that holds and releases water like a sponge and improves the water-holding characteristics of practically any kind of soil. Because it is an insoluble mineral, it will last for decades and possibly forever. If the soil in your bed isn't loamy to start with, adding coarse or medium vermiculite at the rate of four to eight cubic feet per 100 square feet of raised bed will be very beneficial. (Vermiculite costs $4 per cubic foot in four-cubic-foot bags at the time of this writing.)

If you can't find vermiculite, look instead for bails of peat moss. Peat moss is an organic material made from compressed prehistoric plants at the bottom of bogs and swamps, and it has the same characteristic as vermiculite in terms of acting as a water reservoir. It costs about the same and can also be found in large bales. It should be added at the same rate as vermiculite—anywhere from four to eight cubic feet per 100 square feet of raised bed. Keep in mind that peat moss raises the soil's pH slightly over time and decomposes, so it must be renewed.

The term *pH* refers to how acidic or alkaline the soil is and is referenced on a scale from 0 to 14, with 0 corresponding to highly acidic battery acid, 14 to highly alkaline drain cleaner, and 7 to neutral distilled water. As you might imagine, most plants grown in a garden will perform well with a pH between 6 and 7. (There are a few exceptions, such as blueberries, that prefer a highly acidic soil.) pH affects a lot of things indirectly, including whether nutrients already in the soil are available for plants to use and the prevalence of certain plant disease organisms such as "club foot" in cabbage.

On the basis of a pH test, you can amend your soil to near neutral or just slightly acid, a pH of 6.5 or so, with commonly available lime and sulfur products. To adjust the pH up 1 point, add dolomitic limestone at the rate of 5 pounds per 100 square feet of raised bed and work it into the top two inches of soil. To adjust the pH down 1 point, add iron sulfate at the rate of 1.5 pounds per 100 square feet of raised bed and work it into the soil. To adjust the pH by half a point, say from 6 to 6.5, cut the amount per 100 square feet in half.

⊗ Vermiculite enhances the water-holding capacity of the soil.

pH amendments don't work quickly. Wait 40 to 60 days after adding the amendments, and then retest the soil before adding any more. If amendments are added too quickly, they can build up in the soil and make it inhospitable for growing things.

# Fertilizers

**The fertility of** soil is measured by its content of nitrogen, phosphorus, and potassium, and fertilizers are rated the same way, using a series of numbers called "NPK." The N in NPK stands for nitrogen, the P for phosphate, and the K for potassium. A bag of fertilizer will be marked with the NPK in a format that lists the percentage content of each nutrient, separated by dashes. So, for example, a bag of fertilizer labeled "5-10-5" is 5% nitrogen, 10% phosphate, and 5% potassium.

A completely depleted garden soil with no detectable levels of NPK requires only 4.6 ounces of N, 5 ounces of P, and 5.4 ounces of K per 100 square feet to yield a "sufficient" soil. In the case of root crops, less than 3 ounces of N are needed.

Inexpensive soil tests are available to test the pH, nitrogen, phosphorus, and potassium content of soil. A couple of weeks after the soil in the bed has been prepared and compost and/or manure have been worked in, you should test the soil's nutrient content and amend it properly. The most important factor in the long-range viability of your soil is organic matter provided by compost and manures, so always make sure that there is plenty of organic matter first, and then test to see what kind of fertilization is needed.

You can buy a soil test kit at most garden centers, and most give results for each nutrient as being depleted, deficient, adequate, or sufficient. The latter two descriptions can be confusing because in ordinary English, they have identical meaning. For the purposes of interpreting soil tests, consider "adequate" to mean that there is enough of the measured nutrient for plants to survive but not necessarily thrive. If the soil test indicates the amount to be "sufficient," then there is enough of the nutrient to support optimal growth.

The Rapitest soil test kit is commonly available, costs less than $20, and comes with enough components to make 10 tests. The LaMotte soil test kit is one of the most accurate available and can currently be purchased via mail order for less than $55. When preparing a bed, I recommend adding enough organic fertilizers to make all three major nutrients "sufficient."

Organic fertilizers are a better choice than synthetic ones for several reasons. Organic fertilizers break down more slowly so they stay in the soil longer and help build the organic content of your soil as they break down. Synthetics can certainly get the job done in the short term, but they also carry the potential to harm important microbial diversity in the soil that helps to prevent plant diseases, and they also hurt earthworms and other

◉ The LaMotte soil test kit is very accurate.

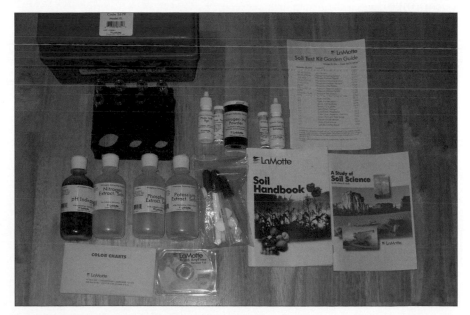

beneficial soil inhabitants. For these reasons, I strongly discourage the use of synthetic fertilizers.

Organic fertilizers, like synthetics, are rated by NPK, but because they are made from plant, animal, and mineral substances, they contain a wide array of trace minerals that plants also need. Probably the biggest argument in favor of using organic fertilizers is taste. The hydroponic hothouse tomatoes at the grocery store are grown using exclusively synthetics mixed with water. Compare the taste of a hydroponic hothouse tomato with the taste of an organic garden tomato, and the answer will be clear.

There is one thing to keep in mind with organic fertilizers: Many of them are quite appetizing to rodents! One spring, I discovered that the fertilizer in my garage had been torn open by red squirrels and eaten almost entirely! Ever since, I store organic fertilizers in five-gallon buckets with lids.

There are a number of available sources for organic fertilizers. Some come premixed, or you can make them yourself from individual components.

Making your own premixed fertilizer is easy. For N, you can use alfalfa meal, soybean meal, or blood meal. For P, bone meal and rock phosphate work well. For K, wood ashes, greensand, and seaweed will work. The foregoing list is far from exhaustive, but the materials are readily available from most garden or agricultural stores.

Table 1 contains two numbers notated as either "leaf" or "root" because root crops don't need as much nitrogen as leafy vegetable crops. In fact, too much nitrogen can hurt the productivity of root crops. There's also no reason to formulate a fertilizer for depleted soil since that shouldn't happen after the first year, and maybe not even then if adequate compost has been added. If it does, just add triple or quadruple the amount used for adequate soil. Looking at these tables, it should be pretty easy to formulate a couple of ready-made fertilizers.

## *Table 1:* **Nitrogen Sources**

| Nitrogen Source | %N | Ounces per 100 sq. ft. for depleted soil | Ounces per 100 sq. ft. for adequate soil |
|---|---|---|---|
| Alfalfa meal | 2.50 | 184 leaf/120 root | 52 leaf/34 root |
| Soybean meal | 6.00 | 76 leaf/50 root | 21 leaf/14 leaf |
| Blood meal | 12.00 | 38 leaf/25 root | 10 leaf/7 root |

## *Table 2:* **Phosphorus Sources**

| Phosphorus Source | %P | Ounces per 100 sq. ft. for depleted soil | Ounces per 100 sq. ft. for adequate soil |
|---|---|---|---|
| Bone meal | 21.00 | 23 | 6 |
| Rock phosphate | 39.00 | 13 | 4 |

## *Table 3:* **Potassium Sources**

| Potassium Source | %K | Ounces per 100 sq. ft. for depleted soil | Ounces per 100 sq. ft. for adequate soil |
|---|---|---|---|
| Wood ashes | 7.00 | 77 | 21 |
| Greensand | 5.00 | 108 | 30 |
| Seaweed | 5.00 | 108 | 30 |

A "high nitrogen" fertilizer for vegetative crops like spinach could consist of a mix of 10 ounces of blood meal, 6 ounces of bone meal, and 21 ounces of wood ashes.

As long as you keep the proportions the same, you can mix up as much of it as you like to keep handy, and you know that 37 ounces of the mixture are required for each 100 square feet. Just a tad over two pounds.

A "low nitrogen" fertilizer for root crops like parsnips could consist of a mix of 34 ounces of alfalfa meal, 4 ounces of rock phosphate, and 30 ounces of greensand.

Just as with the first formulation, as long as you keep the proportions the same, you can mix up as much as you'd like, and you know that 68 ounces are required for each 100 square feet—a hair over four pounds.

Your actual choice of fertilizers and blends will depend on availability and price of materials, but using a variety of components guarantees that at some point practically every known nutrient—and every unknown nutrient—finds its way into your garden beds. Wood ashes should be used no more often than once every three years because of the salts they can put into the soil and because they can raise the soil pH.

Fertilizers should be added to the soil a couple of weeks before planting and worked into the garden bed; any additional fertilizer should then be added on top of the ground as a side dressing, perhaps diluted 50/50 with some dried compost.

The reason for dilution is that some organic fertilizers, such as blood meal, are pretty powerful—as powerful as synthetics—and if they touch crop foliage directly, they can damage plants.

Liquid fertilizers are worth mentioning, particularly those intended for application directly to leaves. These tend to be extremely dilute so that they won't hurt the plants, and they are a good choice for reducing transplant shock.

In some cases, liquid fertilizers can be a lifesaver. One year, I planted out cabbage well before last frost in a newly prepared bed. Having added one-third of the bed's volume in compost of every sort imaginable, I made the mistake of assuming the bed had adequate nutrients. What I had forgotten is that plants can't use nitrogen when the soil is too cold. A couple of days after the cabbage plants were planted, they turned yellow, starting from the oldest leaves first, which is a classic symptom of severe nitrogen deficiency.

⊗ Popular organic liquid fertilizers.

As an experiment, I added a heavy side-dressing of mixed blood meal, bone meal, and wood ashes and watered it in on all the cabbage plants, but for half of them, I also watered the leaves with a watering can containing liquid fertilizer mixed according to package directions. The result was that all of the plants watered with the liquid fertilizer survived and eventually thrived, while a full half of the plants that received only a side-dressing died.

Now, I use liquid fertilizer—specifically Neptune's Harvest—whenever I transplant, especially in early spring.

# Soil Maintenance

**Believe it or** not, soil is a delicate substance. More than merely delicate, it is quite literally alive. It is the life of the soil, not its sand and clay, that makes it fertile and productive. A single teaspoon of good garden soil contains millions of microbes, almost every one of which contributes something positive to the garden. The organic matter serves as a pH buffer, detoxifies pollutants, holds moisture, and serves to hold nutrients in a fixed form to keep them from leaching out of the soil. Some microbes, like actinomycetes, send out delicate microscopic webs that stretch for miles, giving soil its structure.

The structure of soil for intensive agriculture is maintained through

- cover crops (explained later in this chapter) to maintain fertility and prevent erosion;
- regularly adding organic matter in the form of left over roots, compost, and manures;
- crop rotation; and
- protecting the soil from erosion, compaction, and loosening.

Once the soil in a bed has been prepared initially, as long as it hasn't been compacted, it shouldn't need more than a fluffing with a broad fork or digging fork yearly and stirring of the top few inches with a three-tined cultivator. Digging subsequent to bed establishment is much easier and faster than the initial double-dig.

It was noted earlier that you shouldn't walk on the garden beds. An occasional unavoidable footprint won't end life on earth, but an effort should be made to avoid it because that footprint compacts the soil, makes that area of soil less able to hold water, decreases the oxygen that can be held in the soil in that area, and damages the structure of the soil, including the structure established by old roots and delicate microbial webs. Almost all species of actinomycetes are aerobic—meaning that they require oxygen. Compacting the soil can deprive them of needed oxygen.

The microbial webs in soil are extremely important in that they work in symbiosis with root systems to extend their reach and ability to assimilate nutrients.[14] Damaging these microbial webs—which can stretch for several feet in each direction from a plant—reduces the plant's ability to obtain nutrients from the soil.

My wife thought I was overreaching on this point and insisted on occasionally walking in the beds to harvest early beans, so I did an

---

[14] Howard, D. (2003) Building fertile soil *Mother Earth News*, Issue 198, June/July 2003

experiment. I planted bunching onions from the same packet of seeds in places where she had walked in the beds and in places where she hadn't. The results? Total yield per square foot, measured in pounds, was 20% lower in the places where my wife had walked. She only weighs 115 pounds! The lesson is plain: Maximum productivity from a raised bed requires avoiding soil compression.

Some gardeners favor heavy duty tilling of agricultural land at least yearly and often at both the beginning and end of a season. The problem with such practices lies in the fact that the very same aspects of soil life and structure that are disrupted by compaction are also disrupted by tilling, particularly deep tilling.

Soil amendments, such as compost and organic fertilizers, should be mixed with the soil—no doubt. But this doesn't require a rototiller. A simple three-tined cultivator (looks like a claw), operated by hand, is sufficient to incorporate amendments into the top couple of inches of soil. Earthworms and other soil inhabitants will do the job of spreading the compost into deep soil layers.

## The Amazing Power of Biochar

Most of us are used to thinking of charcoal as an indispensable aid to grilling, and that it certainly is! But less well-known is its equally beneficial effect when added to ordinary garden soil. The standard charcoal you buy at the grocery store may be impregnated with everything from saltpeter to volatile organic compounds intended to aid burning, so it may not be a good choice. There are some "all natural" or even organic charcoals out there that can be used, such as Cowboy Brand Charcoal, though. In addition, some companies make charcoal specifically intended for agricultural use, such as Troposphere Energy.

Of course, if you have access to hardwood, making your own charcoal isn't terribly difficult. In fact, for agricultural use, you don't even need hardwood—just any old vegetable matter—and you can make the charcoal that is trendy nowadays to call "biochar."

The benefits of biochar mixed in the soil are many and were first discovered by the peoples inhabiting the Amazon basin in pre-Columbian times. They discovered that turning their vegetable matter into charcoal, pulverizing it, and adding it to the soil enhanced the soil's productivity. Soil scientists have now discovered that charcoal, previously thought to be inert in soil, lowers the soil's acidity; creates a haven for the beneficial bacteria that live in symbiosis with the root hairs of crops; helps to keep fertilizers in the soil instead of letting them be washed out, thus decreasing the need for fertilizer; and helps to loosen tight soils. In addition, it helps to sequester carbon from the atmosphere, thereby reducing global warming. More benefits are being discovered all the time.

The easiest way to add this incredible fertilizer to your garden beds is to make it right where you want it used: in your beds. Use a hoe to make a couple of one-foot-wide and six- to nine-inch-deep trenches running the

❯ The three-tined cultivator is a workhorse for raised beds.

length of the bed. Place dried branches, leaves, and other vegetable matter neatly, but not too tightly packed, in the trenches. Then, light them on fire in several places. (Avoid using chemicals such as charcoal lighter or gasoline as these could seriously poison the soil.) Once the material is burning well and the smoke has turned gray, cover with the mounded-up soil on the sides of the trenches to deprive it of oxygen, and let it smolder until the pieces are no larger than a deck of cards. Then, douse the embers with plentiful quantities of water. If you do this every fall with garden refuse and other vegetable matter, you will soon have soil that, taken together with the other practices here, will have astonishing levels of productivity.

# Cover Crops and Beneficial Microbes

**Today we know** a lot more than our great- grandparents did about the relationship between plants and microorganisms in the soil. It turns out that the microorganisms in soil are not merely useful for suppressing diseases but actually an integral part of a plant's root system.[15] Up to 40% of the carbohydrates that plants produce through photosynthesis are actually transported to the root system and out into the soil to feed microorganisms around the root system. In turn, these microorganisms extend the plant's root system and make necessary nutrients available.

Friendly microorganisms grow into the roots themselves, setting up a mutually beneficial cooperation (symbiosis) and respond with natural production of antibiotics when needed to protect their host. Planting cover crops will serve to keep these critters fed through the winter months and protected from environmental hazards such as sun

---

[15] Ibid.

and erosion. This way they are healthy and well fed for the next planting season.

For these reasons, harvesting should be considered a two-part process in which the task of harvesting is followed as soon as possible with the sowing of cover crops, which can also be known as green manures.

Green manures are plants grown specifically for the role they play in sustaining soil fertility, but they also reduce erosion and feed beneficial microbes outside the growing season. The benefits of green manures on crop yield are far from merely theoretical. In one study, for example, the use of hairy vetch (a common legume) as a green manure and mulch increased tomato yields by more than 100%.[16] Green manures are generally either grains or legumes; grains because of their ability to pull nutrients up into the topsoil from a depth of several feet,[17] and legumes because of their ability to take nitrogen out of the air and fix it in nodules in their roots, thereby fertilizing the soil. They are either tilled directly into the ground once grown or added to compost piles. Legumes use up their stored nitrogen to make seed, so when they are used as green manures, they need to be cut just before or during their flowering. During the summer growing season, green manures should be grown in beds that will be followed by heavy-feeding plants, such as cabbage, as part of a crop rotation plan.

An important aspect of making a mini-farm economically viable is the use of green manures to provide and enhance soil fertility and reduce dependence on purchased fertilizers. To that end, cover crops should be grown over the winter to start the spring compost pile and should also be planted in any bed not in use to prevent leaching of nutrients and promote higher fertility. The careful use of green manures as cover crops and as specific compost ingredients can entirely eliminate

---

[16] Abdul-Baki, A., Teasdale, J. (1993) A no tillage tomato production system using hairy vetch and subterranean clover mulches *Horticultural Science* 28(2) pp. 106–108

[17] Jeavons, J. (2002) *How to Grow More Vegetables*

*Table 4:* **Cover Crops/Green Manures and Nitrogen Yields**

| Name | Sow | Harvest | N Yield | Notes |
|---|---|---|---|---|
| Hairy vetch | Spring or fall | Fall or spring | 160 lbs/ acre | Sow in August– September, can become a weed if followed by grains, don't follow with lettuce |
| Red clover | Spring or fall | Fall or spring | 105 lbs/ acre | Sow in August for winter cover, good choice under fruit trees, shade tolerant |
| Field peas | Spring | Summer | 100 lbs/ acre | Won't overwinter north of Maryland, good for interplanting with brassicas |
| Cereal rye | Fall | Spring | None | Sow in early fall, wait four weeks after cutting in spring before sowing subsequent crops because rye suppresses germination of other plants |
| Alfalfa | Spring | Summer | 130 lbs/ acre | Prefers well-drained soils, highest N fixation |
| Barley | Spring | Summer | None | Doesn't work in acid soils |
| Oats | Spring | Summer | None | Established quickly |
| Winter wheat | Fall | Spring | None | High in protein |

the need for outside nitrogen inputs. For example, alfalfa makes an excellent green manure during the growing season in that it leaves 42 percent of its nitrogen in the ground when cut plus provides biologically fixed nitrogen to the compost pile. I recommend

⊗ Hairy vetch is an excellent cover crop.

that 25 to 35 percent of a mini-farm's growing area should be sown in green manures during the growing season, and all of it should be sown in green manures and/or cover crops during the winter.

Green manures interplanted with crops during the growing season can form a living mulch. Examples include sowing hairy vetch between corn stalks at the last cultivation before harvest or planting vegetables without tilling into a bed already growing subterranean clover.[18] On my own mini-farm, I grow white clover between tomato plants.

Cover crops aren't a cure-all, and they can cause problems if used indiscriminately. For example, using a vetch cover crop before growing lettuce can cause problems with a lettuce disease called sclerotina.[19] Because the increased organic matter from a cover crop can cause a short-term increase in populations of certain pests such as cutworms, it is important to cut or till the cover crop three or four weeks before planting your crops.[20] Legume green manures, such as peas, beans, vetch, and clovers, also need to be covered with the correct type of bacterial inoculant (available through seed suppliers) before they are sown to ensure their health and productivity.

Given these complications, how does a farmer pick a cover crop? Cover crops need to be picked based on the climate, the crop that will be planted

[18] Sullivan, P. (2003) *Overview of Cover Crops and Green Manures*
[19] Thomas, F. et al. (2002) *Cover Cropping in Row and Field Systems*
[20] Ibid

afterward, and specific factors about the cover crop—such as its tendency to turn into an invasive weed. Legumes and grains are often, though not always, sown together as a cover crop. Some cover crops, like oats and wheat, can also serve as food. If this is anticipated, it might be worthwhile to investigate easily harvested grains like hull-less oats. However, keep in mind that the choice of green manures will be at least partially dictated by climate. Many crops that grow fine over the winter in South Carolina won't work in Vermont.

# Crop Rotation

**Crop rotation is** one of the oldest and most important agricultural practices in existence and is still one of the most effective for controlling pest populations, assisting soil fertility, and controlling diseases.

The primary key to successful crop rotation lies in understanding that crops belong to a number of different botanical families and that members of each related family have common requirements and pest problems that differ from those of members of other botanical families. Cabbage and brussels sprouts, for example, are members of the same botanical family, so they can be expected to have similar soil requirements and be susceptible to the same pest and disease problems. Peas and beans are likewise part of the same botanical family; corn belongs to yet another family unrelated to the other two. A listing of the botanical names of most cultivated plant families with edible members follows:

**Amaryllidaceae**—leek, common onion, multiplier onion, bunching onion, shallot, garlic, chives

**Brassicaceae**—horseradish, mustards, turnip, rutabaga, kale, radish, broccoli, cauliflower, cabbage, collards, cress

**Chenopodiaceae**—beet, mangel, Swiss chard, lamb's quarters, quinoa, spinach

**Compositae**—endive, escarole, chicory, globe artichoke, jerusalem artichoke, lettuce, sunflower

**Cucurbitaceae**—cucumber, gherkin, melons, gourds, squashes

**Leguminosae**—peanut, pea, bean, lentil, cowpea

**Solanaceae**—pepper, tomato, tomatillo, ground cherry, potato, eggplant

**Umbelliferae**—celery, dill, carrot, fennel, parsnip, parsley

**Gramineae**—wheat, rye, oats, sorghum, corn

**Amaranthaceae**—grain and vegetable amaranth

**Convolvulaceae**—water spinach, sweet potato

Some plants will do better or worse depending on what was grown before them. Such effects can be partially canceled by the use of intervening cover crops between main crops. Thankfully, a large amount of research has been done on the matter, and while nobody is sure of all the factors involved, a few general rules have emerged from the research.

- Never follow a crop with another crop from the same botanical family (e.g., don't follow potatoes with tomatoes or squash with cucumbers).
- Alternate deep-rooted crops (like carrots) with shallow-rooted crops (such as lettuce).
- Alternate plants that inhibit germination (like rye and sunflowers) with vegetables that don't compete well against weeds (like peas and strawberries).
- Alternate crops that add organic matter (e.g., wheat) with crops that add little organic matter (e.g., soybeans).
- Alternate nitrogen fixers (such as alfalfa or vetch) with nitrogen consumers (such as grains or vegetables).

The most important rule with crop rotations is to experiment and keep careful records. Some families of plants have a detrimental effect on some families that may follow them in rotation but not on others. These effects will vary depending on cover cropping, manuring, and composting practices, so no hard and fast rules apply, but it is absolutely certain that an observant farmer will see a difference between cabbage that follows carrots as opposed to cabbage that follows potatoes. Keeping careful records and making small variations from year to year while observing the results will allow the farmer to fine-tune practices to optimize quality and yields.

A three-bed rotation applicable to where I live in New Hampshire might give you an idea of how crop rotation with cover cropping works. We'll start with the fall.

*Table 5:* **Example Three-Bed Rotation with Cover Cropping**

|  | *Bed 1* | *Bed 2* | *Bed 3* |
|---|---|---|---|
| *Fall Year 1* | Rye | Hairy vetch/rye | Hairy vetch/oats |
| *Spring Year 2* | Peas | Tomatoes | Corn |
| *Midsummer Year 2* | Broccoli/cabbage | White clover is sown between plants | Pole beans are sown between stalks |
| *Fall Year 2* | Hairy vetch/rye | Hairy vetch/oats | Rye |
| *Spring Year 3* | Tomatoes | Corn | Peas |
| *Midsummer Year 3* | White clover is sown between plants | Pole beans are sown between stalks | Broccoli/cabbage |

# 3

# Time and Yield

**Most of the** United States, even the northern plains, has a growing season long enough to allow for multiple plantings of many crops. Moreover, well-orchestrated timing allows harvests to be timed either to allow a little at a time to be harvested for daily use or marketing—which is useful for crops like lettuce—or to allow multiple large harvests for the purpose of preservation and storage. Many crops are frost hardy, and second plantings will allow harvests to continue for as long as a month after the first fall frost, without using anything to extend the season. For example, two crops of broccoli or spinach can be raised in the same area as one crop, doubling production per unit area.

# Succession Planting

**This is a** technique for maximizing productivity of garden space by having a new crop ready to plant as soon as an earlier crop is harvested. An example is planting a second crop of broccoli in the same space where a first crop of broccoli was harvested at midsummer. Another example is sowing spinach early and then planting beans where the spinach used to be as soon as the spinach is harvested.

Crops that work well for the early planting in a succession are anything from the cabbage family, spinach, peas, radishes, turnips, beets, and onions from sets. ("Sets" are the miniature onions for planting that you can buy in a mesh bag at the garden center. They aren't the same as supermarket onions.) The foregoing crops are usually harvested no later than the middle of July. Crops that can be planted in mid-July for a late summer or fall harvest include bush beans, lettuce, spinach, carrots, turnips, beets, parsnips, and anything in the cabbage family.

# Timed Planting

**Timed planting means** spreading out harvests by staggering the planting dates for a particular crop across a few weeks rather than planting it all at once. The result is a steady supply of a particular crop for market or a continual harvest that can be frozen, eaten, or canned in small sessions.

The easiest way to do this is to take the total number of plants intended for a given crop and divide it by three. Sow the first third on the first sowing date for that crop, the second third a week later, and the final third two weeks later. This will give the same total harvest as planting the whole crop at once but will spread out the harvest over a two-week period.

The next aspect of timed planting is replanting. Take carrots, for example; if carrots were planted in four sessions, each two weeks apart, when the first planting is harvested, that area can be replanted with more carrots so the space never sits idle. By the time the final crop of carrots is ready for harvest, you are only two weeks away from yet another first harvest.

Succession planting and timed planting both provide a little insurance so if serious weather hits early or late, there's still a harvest. All that you need to know to successfully use succession and/or timed planting is the days to maturity for the crop under consideration and its frost hardiness.

# Interplanting

**Interplanting is used** in two ways. It is used to give green manures a head start on the winter and to maximize the amount of food that can be harvested from a given area. Carefully chosen, interplanted crops can save on fertilizer as well, as when a nitrogen producer such as beans or clover is interplanted with a nitrogen consumer such as tomatoes or corn.

⊗ Interplanting crops creates synergies.

There are some practical considerations to interplanting, and chief among them are overcrowding and shade. Plants that require a lot of space or sunlight, such as tomatoes, could have difficulty if planted in an established stand of corn. If planted before the corn has germinated, the tomatoes would shade the seedlings. On the other hand, white clover works well with most plants, as do beans.

Perhaps the most famous example of successful interplanting is the so-called Three Sisters of the Native Americans—corn, beans, and squash, which they grew together. In this case, the pole beans and squash vines used the corn stalks for support.

# Fall Gardening

**Frost hardy crops** and biennials kept alive over the winter for seed production (called "overwintering") can be planted first in the spring, harvested in the summer, and then replanted for a second fall or early winter harvest. Late harvests can be achieved for many crops without going to the trouble of using season extension structures. Overwintering crops, so they can be used either as needed or for seed production, is more problematic. In the South or Pacific Northwest, it can be done outdoors. In the upper Midwest or Northeast, such plants have to be brought indoors for the winter or else protected with, at minimum, an unheated greenhouse or cold frame.

For purposes of fall gardening, crops can be divided into three categories: tender, semihardy, and hardy. Tender crops are damaged by a light frost. Semihardy crops will tolerate a light frost, and hardy crops will tolerate hard frosts.

The best bets for fall gardening are semihardy and hardy crops. Some hardy crops, like broccoli and spinach, often taste better when grown in the fall rather than in the spring. Semihardy crops should be timed for harvests within 28 days after the first frost, and hardy crops should be timed within 56 days after the first frost. For this, the time to harvest needs to be known. Each variety of a given crop has slightly different dates of maturity, and those dates are indicated in seed catalogs and on seed packets. Because growth is slower in the

*Table 7:* **Crop Hardiness**

| Tender | Semihardy | Hardy |
|---|---|---|
| Beans | Beets | Broccoli |
| Corn | Carrot | Brussels sprouts |
| Cucumber | Cauliflower | Cabbage |
| Eggplant | Celery | Kale |
| Melon | Chard | Onion |
| Okra | Lettuce | Parsley |
| Pepper | Parsnip | Peas |
| Squash | Potato | Spinach |
| Sweet potato | | Turnip |
| Tomato | | |

fall, 10 days should be added to the maturity date, so plant 10 days earlier for fall harvests.

# Using Seedlings for a Head Start

**Some crops, such** as cucumbers, can be directly seeded in the garden or transplanted. Transplanting seedlings gives the plants a head start and can allow maximum production from the number of growing days in the season.

Winter squash, requiring 80 or more days to harvest, is a good candidate for transplanting seedlings, particularly in the northern half of the United States where there are often fewer than 90 frost-free days in a row in the growing season. Since squash shouldn't be direct seeded until 14 days after the last frost, leaving fewer than 80 remaining growing days, growing transplants instead will increase the amount of squash harvested without requiring the farmer to use season extension devices.

The same applies for crops in the fall garden. In the late season, broccoli can be direct seeded, but giving it a four-week head start by growing seedlings inside and then transplanting them will accelerate the harvest.

One place where I have used this technique to good effect is with a crop that most authors will tell you not to transplant: corn. Grown on the agribusiness scale, seed for sweet corn is usually coated with a fungicide to keep it from rotting in the ground. Seed corn is prone not just to rot but to being eaten by wire worms. In addition, it doesn't all germinate at the same time. On a very large scale, this all evens out. But on a small scale—say growing 48 plants in a 4-foot × 8-foot raised bed—it can be a problem. Transplanting seedlings is an ideal solution.

What I do is start 64 seedlings indoors about two weeks before the first frost-free date. It's important to not try any longer than two weeks because corn grows a taproot, and after that, transplant shock can be too great. After two weeks, some may not have germinated, and some will be taller than others. What I do is pick the 48 most uniform plants and transplant them into the bed. I keep the others handy for a week just in case cut worms or some similar pest strikes.

You can use this technique for most crops outside of root crops. By starting from seed indoors, you gain an advantage of anywhere from two to six weeks.

# Example Timeline

**The following table** is part of the calendar for my own mini-farm in New Hampshire, so the exact dates may not work for you. Nevertheless, the examples given should be helpful.

*Table 8:* **Example Activity Schedule**

| Date | Activity | Date | Activity |
|------|----------|------|----------|
| 02/11 | Start onion and leek seeds inside | 05/06 | Start cucumber, melon, and squash inside |
| 02/18 | Start broccoli, cabbage, and kale inside | 05/07 | Sow radish and salsify seeds outside |
| 02/25 | Start cauliflower inside | 05/13 | Sow 1/2 of carrots, beets, parsnips, and turnips; cut cover crops and add to compost pile |
| 03/01 | Start lettuce inside | 05/27 | Plant tomato and pepper transplants outside |
| 04/01 | Start tomatoes and peppers inside | 05/28 | Sow corn seed and second 1/2 of carrots, beets, parsnips, and turnips |
| 04/15 | Start marigold, nasturtium, pyrethrum, and dill seeds inside | 06/03 | Harvest radishes and plant cucumber, melon, and squash transplants where the radishes were |
| 04/22 | Transplant broccoli, cabbage, and kale outside | 06/23 | Harvest broccoli and kale and replant with new transplants for a second crop |

| Date | Activity | Date | Activity |
|------|----------|------|----------|
| 04/23 | Plant potatoes and peas outside, covered with hoop house | 07/07 | Harvest cauliflower and replant with new transplants for a second crop |
| 04/29 | Start new broccoli seedlings inside for second planting | 07/20 | Harvest potatoes and carrots, prepare potato area, and sow with carrots and spinach |
| 05/06 | Plant cauliflower transplants outside | 07/24 | Pull up pea plants and add to compost pile, sow area with lettuce |

# 4

# Pest and Disease Control

**Pest and disease** problems are an unavoidable fact of life for the mini-farmer. Sometimes, they are barely noticeable and cause no significant problems. But at other times they can cause major crop losses.

There are, unfortunately, hundreds of pests and diseases that affect vegetable crops. Going into the detail of identifying these is beyond the scope of this book, so instead I'll refer you to *The Organic Gardener's Handbook of Natural Insect and Disease Control,* published by Rodale and edited by Barbara Ellis and Fern Bradley. This 500-page book is loaded with color pictures and extensive explanation for every disease or pest you are likely to encounter, including specific details of organic methods for dealing with problems. What follows in this chapter is an overview that concentrates more on principles than details, along with my own unique passive-active-reactive pest management strategy developed specifically for the needs of mini-farms.

Since the old adage that "an ounce of prevention is worth a pound of cure" is true, mini-farming focuses automatically on passive prevention by giving plants what they need. Active prevention is used when experience or reliable data indicate that a particular pest or disease is likely to be a problem. Active reaction is employed when the value of likely crop damage will exceed the costs of active reaction methods.

Passive prevention is the application of good farming practices: well-composted and appropriately amended healthy soil, adequate sunshine, proper watering, crop rotation, and sufficient airflow. In essence, this simply means to give plants growing conditions that are as close to optimal as possible. This will make them healthier and thus less susceptible to diseases and less attractive to pests.

Active prevention uses active measures to prevent diseases or repel insect pests. Examples include applying repellent garlic or hot pepper sprays on plants to deter pests, installing physical barriers, putting out traps, or spraying the plants periodically with a fungus preventative. Sometimes, for certain types of pests, poisons that are usually used as a reactive measure may be required as active prevention.

Active reaction occurs when preventative measures fail and a problem already exists. Active reaction will often employ the same methods as active prevention, only with greater intensity, but it will also include, in most cases, the application of natural botanical or synthetic poisons or fungicides.

Pest management needs to be viewed holistically, as part of a bigger picture, to minimize crop damage while simultaneously protecting the long-range viability of the mini-farm. As part of this view, it is good to establish a threshold for what constitutes an acceptable level of damage before reactive, as opposed to preventative, measures need to be taken. This threshold is established economically, considering that the time,

⊗ Potato beetles are a common garden pest.

costs, and risks associated with active pest control measures will diminish the net grocery savings. So the threshold of acceptable damage for a given crop, in terms of percentage crop loss, is the level at which the value of the lost crop portion exceeds the cost of active control measures.

# Passive Prevention

**Passive prevention gives** the biggest bang for both your time and money because the focus lies mainly in performing ordinary farming chores. Soil, water, sunshine, and crop rotations are the foundation of pest and disease control; all of these create an environment inhospitable to the persistence of pests and disease.

A healthy, living soil with plenty of nutrients allows for vigorous growth so that crops can outgrow problems. In addition, healthier plants are less attractive to pests and less susceptible to disease in most cases. Healthy soil plays host to various portions of the life cycles of many beneficial insect populations, along with beneficial microbes that compete with nasty pathogens for nutrients and generate antibiotics to eliminate them. It is no mistake that forests thrive independent of human intervention, and the more closely a farmer's garden approximates naturally optimal conditions for a crop, the less susceptible it will be to pest and disease problems.

An important aspect of healthy soil, particularly with intensive agriculture, is compost. Merely using compost in your soil can significantly reduce pest and disease problems.

Proper watering is another important aspect of disease control. Plant diseases spread most easily when plant tissues are wet; both excessive watering and overhead watering can increase the likelihood of disease problems. However, adequate moisture is also important because drought-stressed plants become more attractive to pests.

Crop rotation is impossible to over emphasize. Just like there are viruses and bacteria that affect some mammals but not others—such as feline leukemia—there are numerous plant diseases that affect one family of vegetables but not others. Since these microbes need a host hospitable to their reproduction to complete their life cycles, depriving them of the host they need through crop rotation is extremely effective at controlling many diseases. The same applies to insect pests, so the same crop should not be grown in the same bed two years in a row. Ideally, crop rotation will prevent crops of the same family from growing in the same bed any more often than once every three years.

Specific plant variety selection is another important preventative. Notwithstanding the economic benefits of using open-pollinated seeds (described in the next chapter), some hybrids carry disease- and pest-resistance genes that can make them a better choice if certain diseases or pests become a repetitive problem. On my farm, for example, I now grow hybrid cucumbers that are resistant to bacterial wilt disease.

Finally, never discount the power of the sun. The same UV rays that make excessive sunshine a risk factor for skin cancer also scramble the genetic code in bacteria and viruses, rendering them incapable of infection. Sunshine sanitizes.

Attracting beneficial insects is also useful. Most beneficial insects

⊗ Dill is a common attractant of beneficial insects.

feed on or invade pest species at some point in their life cycle, but they also require certain plants for their well-being. Providing these plants in the garden will give beneficial insects a base of operations they can use to keep pest species controlled.

A small planting of early, intermediate season, and late-blooming beneficial insect attractors in each garden bed will help stack the deck in the farmer's favor. Ladybugs love to eat aphids; dandelion, marigold, and hairy vetch will attract them. Tachanid flies help keep cabbage worms and stink bugs in check; a planting of parsley or pennyroyal will give them a home. Beneficial insect attractors that bloom early include sweet alyssum, columbine, and creeping thyme. Intermediate bloomers include common yarrow, cilantro, edging lobelia, and mints. Late bloomers include dill, wild bergamot, and European goldenrod. An easy plan is to plant a few marigolds throughout the bed, a columbine plant, a bit of cilantro, and some dill.

You should familiarize yourself with the properties of beneficial plant attractors before planting them in your beds. Don't just run out and plant mint in the garden bed directly, for example, because it will take over the entire bed. Instead, plant mint in a pot and then bury the pot in the garden soil so that the upper edge sticks out of the soil 1/2 inch or so.

You may also want to choose some plants that you will already use in some other way—such as mint for tea, dill for pickling, and cilantro for salsa. That way you are making maximum use of limited space. There is nothing wrong with growing goldenrods just because they are pretty!

Another valuable addition to the garden and yard, once the seeds have sprouted and the plants are growing well, would be chickens or guineas. Both types of birds, but guineas particularly, wreak havoc on bugs, especially bugs like ticks that nobody wants around anyway. Such livestock can effectively keep many sorts of garden pests from

*Table 12:* **Preventative Plantings**

| Beneficial Insect | Controlled Pests | Plants to Provide |
|---|---|---|
| Parasitic wasps | Moth, beetle, and fly larvae and eggs, including caterpillars | Dill, yarrow, tansy, Queen Anne's lace, parsley |
| Hoverflies (syrphid flies) | Mealybugs, aphids | As above, plus marigold |
| Lacewings | Aphids, mealybugs, other small insects | Dandelion, angelica, dill, yarrow |
| Ladybugs | Aphids | Dandelion, hairy vetch, buckwheat, marigold |
| Tachanid flies | Caterpillars, cabbage loopers, stink bugs, cabbage bugs, beetles | Parsley, tansy, pennyroyal, buckwheat |

reaching the critical mass of population necessary to be threatening to crops.

# Active Prevention

**Active prevention is** often necessary when a particular pest or disease problem is a practical certainty. In such cases, the active prevention is tailored to the expected problem and can often encompass methods used for both passive prevention and intervention. For example, you may notice your garden is regularly infested with earwigs. Once the bugs are noticed inside a cauliflower plant, they've already done a lot of damage. A weekly spraying with pyrethrin (a natural insecticide) or hot pepper wax (a repellent) will increase the usable harvest significantly.

The materials and techniques most often used for active prevention include traps, immune boosters, compost extracts, imported beneficial insects, and application of repellents, fungicides, and pesticides. (The latter is particularly important with certain fruit trees.)

## Lures and Traps

Many insect pests can be caught in traps. In commercial operations, traps are usually used to monitor pest populations to determine the optimal timing for the application of pesticides. In a mini-farm, because of the smaller land area involved, it is often practical to employ enough traps to completely eradicate a particular pest (or one of the sexes of that pest) in the garden without resorting to poisons. Examples of pests easily trapped are codling moths, Japanese beetles, and apple maggots. Traps can also be employed for cucumber beetles, white flies, and a number of other pests, but they tend to be less effective. The time when various insects emerge varies from area to area. Because the lures used in traps often have limited lifespan, the timing of their deployment can be important. This is something you'll learn from keeping notes, and within a couple of years you'll have no trouble with the timing of traps.

## Immunity Boosters and Growth Enhancers

One immune booster for plants on the market at the moment is marketed by Eden Bioscience in the form of harpin protein. Harpin protein, which is produced naturally by the bacterium that causes fire blight in apples and pears, elicits a broad immune response from vegetables that makes them more resistant to a wide array of pests and diseases while enhancing their growth. Eden Bioscience uses this discovery in a product called Messenger that is nontoxic and relatively inexpensive at my local agricultural supply store.

A company called Vitamin Institute sells a product called Super-thrive that is advertised to improve the growth rate of plants and whose primary ingredient is thiamine. I have done some side-by-side testing, and the results have been ambiguous.

On the other hand, I have found a growth enhancer called Root Boost to live up to its advertising. It is not a fertilizer but rather an enhancer that is primarily based on kelp extract with the addition of humic acids. This product, when used as directed, really does enhance the soil and the plants that depend on it.

## Compost Extract and Compost Tea

Compost extract is the most well-known and most widely studied homemade disease preventative. It is exactly what it sounds like: a shovel of properly aged compost in a water-permeable sack immersed in a bucket of water and steeped for 7 to 14 days.

As the chapter on composting pointed out, compost extract contains a cocktail of microbes and the chemicals that they produce. Compost extract contains a mix of beneficial bacteria and fungi that, when sprayed onto plants, eats the food substances that would otherwise be eaten by disease-causing organisms. As a result, the disease-causing organisms get starved out. A biweekly spray of compost extract is a good idea, and numerous studies attribute properties to the substance that are nothing short of miraculous. It can help prevent diseases such as black spot and powdery mildew. Best of all, it's free.

The next step up from compost extract is compost tea. Compost tea differs from an extract in that it is the result of an active attempt to increase the amount of fungi and bacteria in the solution through aeration. Still water (as used in compost extract) doesn't have much dissolved oxygen in it, and the beneficial microbes in compost require oxygen. So, actively aerating the water in which the compost is steeped will serve to boost populations of beneficial microbes from the compost. This can be done inexpensively by putting a fish tank aerator and air pump in the bottom of a container containing the water and compost. Some reasonably priced and favorably reviewed commercial options are also available through Keep It Simple, Inc. (www.simplici-tea .com) or Alaska Giant (www.alaskagiant.com).

## Importing Beneficial Insects and Nematodes

Imported beneficial insects have their greatest applicability in greenhouses because, being quite mobile, when applied outdoors they are prone to fly away. Even outside they can be useful though, particularly when applied to crops infested with their favorite pest species and also provided with their favorite plants. Table 12 (earlier in this chapter) lists which beneficial insects to use for what problem and what sorts of plants should be established in advance of their arrival so they will stay in the garden.

Beneficial nematodes are extremely small worms that wait underground for a chance to work their way into pest insects and kill them. Beneficial nematodes are harmless to plants and pollinators and shouldn't be confused with pest nematodes such as root knot nematodes. Once inside the host, the nematodes release their gut bacteria, *Xenorhabdus luminescens*, into the insect's interior, where the bacteria multiply and the nematodes feed on them. The pest species eventually dies from infection. There are two commonly used species of nematodes, listed in Table 13. Beneficial nematode products often contain both species to be as broadly useful as possible.

Beneficial nematodes require extreme care in their handling and are usually shipped by overnight courier in a refrigerated package. They are stored in the refrigerator until they are used. It is best to wait until ground temperatures are above 50 degrees, the ground is damp,

*Table 13:* **Beneficial Nematodes**

| Species | Pests Controlled | Notes |
|---|---|---|
| Steinernema spp | Webworms, cutworms, vine borers | Not effective against grubs |
| Heterorhabditis spp | White grubs, vine weevils, root weevils | |

and a light rain is falling. Then put the nematodes in a pump-style sprayer and apply them to the ground where you want them. The reason for this is that beneficial nematodes are very prone to dehydration, and the falling rain helps them get into the soil. If you live north of Maryland, you'll need to apply them yearly because they can't survive the winter. If you live in a more southerly clime, the nematodes will probably survive, so a second application may not be needed.

## Pest Repellents

Organic repellent mixtures are not 100% effective, but they serve as a valuable part of an integrated strategy for pest management. One repellent mixture is simple hot pepper. Capsaicin, the active ingredient in hot peppers, repels onion, carrot, and cabbage maggots. Simply finely chop up a cup of hot peppers, and steep it for a day in a gallon of water to which a single drop of dish soap has been added. Another repellent mixture is garlic, manufactured the same way. One thing that I do, with great success, is make hot pepper and garlic mixtures in a coffee maker that has been set aside for agricultural use only. There are some commercial repellent preparations worth noting as well, including CropGuard and Hot Pepper Wax.

There is *some* evidence that certain plants can repel pest insects. According to numerous sources, for example, nasturtiums and radishes repel cucumber beetles. I have experimented extensively with this practice and found no difference in cucumber beetle populations between cucumber plants surrounded by radishes and intertwined with nasturtiums and cucumber plants grown on their own. On the other hand, I have found that onion family crops repel wireworms, so I interplant leeks with my parsnips. A number of sites on the Internet list repellent plants, so I encourage you to experiment with the reputed properties of repellent plants and keep notes to see what works best for your garden.

# Active Reaction

**Even the most** conscientious farming practices and most vigilant preventive measures will often fail to prevent pest and disease problems. Once these problems become apparent, reactive measures are in order.

Reactive measures will often include some of the same materials and methods as passive and active prevention. For example, many fungal infections can be eradicated by the timely application of compost tea, neem oil, or garlic oil. (Neem oil is an oil extracted from a tree in India.) Most often, though, reactive measures will involve the use of fungicides and/or natural or synthetic pesticides. Because these reactive measures use substances with greater potential to harm people or the environment, I don't recommend their application unless the farmer is certain that a likelihood exists that failure to apply them will result in an unacceptable level of crop loss.

Another tip to make active measures most effective is to take a cue from doctors treating HIV and tuberculosis: Never treat an insect or disease problem with only one active agent at a time. Using only one active agent increases the odds of survivors living to convey immunity to that agent in the next generation. When you mix two or more active agents, you increase the odds of success while decreasing the odds of creating resistant organisms. So, for example, I routinely apply neem oil mixed with a microbial insecticide or garlic and hot pepper repellents mixed together.

## When Disease Prevention Fails

Plant diseases fall into four broad categories: bacterial, viral, protozoan, and fungal. Usually, these are impossible to distinguish by the naked eye except through experience with their symptoms. (See also the Rodale book recommended earlier in this chapter.) All such diseases present the problem that once a plant is infected, it becomes a storehouse of infective particles that can be spread to other plants via insects, wind, or handling. The longer an affected plant remains in the garden, the greater the odds that it will infect other plants. Diseases caused by viruses, bacteria, and protozoans are seldom treatable, but sometimes you can save a plant by pruning out the affected portions. Many fungal diseases, though, *are* treatable through a combination of pruning and spraying.

When a plant infection of any sort is first noticed, you may be able to save the plant by applying compost tea and/or Messenger. These products can stimulate an immune response that helps the plant overcome the infection. Their usefulness in that regard varies depending on the plants and diseases involved, so try it and keep notes of the results. A number of spray fungicides can also be used. Common fungicides include copper sulfate, Bordeaux mix (a mixture of copper sulfate and lime), baking soda, garlic oil, and neem oil. Baking soda is mixed two table-spoons per gallon of water with one ounce of light horticultural oil added, and the others are mixed according to label directions.

Some less well-known antifungal agents can have surprising results. I had a problem with powdery mildew on my lawn last spring (we had an especially wet spring), and I eliminated the infection by spraying with a mix of neem oil and fixed copper.

If saving the plant is either unsuccessful or inadvisable, then the plant should be removed from the garden immediately. Removing an infectious plant can be problematic since it can be covered with microscopic spores that will spread all over the place if the plant is disturbed. The solution is to spray the plant with something that will hold any spores in place and inactivate as many as possible before attempting removal. A good spray for this is made of two tablespoons of castile soap, one tablespoon of copper sulfate, one tablespoon of lime, and one tablespoon of light horticultural oil all mixed together in a gallon of water. The soap and oil will make the plant sticky so that spores can't escape, while the copper sulfate and lime serve to actually kill many infectious organisms. Spray the plant thoroughly with this (though not until it is dripping), and then cut it out and remove it, being as careful as possible to avoid letting it touch any other plants.

When dealing with plant diseases, you should consider your hands and tools to be a mode of disease transmission. When handling known diseased plants, it makes sense to handle *only* the diseased plants before hand washing and also to immediately sterilize any tools used on the diseased plants with bleach. A suitable sanitizing solution is one tablespoon of bleach per quart of water.

Diseased plant materials can be thermophilically composted with minimal or no risk as long as proper retention times are observed. If the farmer uses mesophilic composting instead, then diseased plant debris should be burned or placed in the curbside trash. It is also very important not to grow the same family of plant in the same area the next year. If a variety of the plant that resists that disease can be found, it would be a good idea to switch to that variety for at least a year or two, if not permanently.

# When Pest Prevention Fails

The best soil management and prevention mechanisms will not be 100% effective against insect pests. For example, naturally attracted beneficial insects exist in balance with pest insects. If the beneficial insects were to eat all of the pest species, then the beneficial insects would starve or move somewhere else, and the pest species would experience a resurgence in the absence of its natural enemies.

Reactive control measures include anything used in the preventive stages, along with importing beneficial insect populations, applying microbial insecticides, and using substances that actually kill insects directly, such as soaps, oils, and natural or synthetic insecticides. Synthetic insecticides should be reserved as a last resort since they would reduce the healthfulness of the crop (as described later in this chapter) and would make it impossible for you to sell your produce as organic for several years if you wish to do so.

Both natural and artificial insecticides can also harm beneficial helpers, such as necessary pollinators and earthworms, and disrupt the life of the soil and thus harm fertility in the long run, so they are best employed only when absolutely necessary. Because natural insecticides don't last as long in the garden, they have less potential to do unintended damage.

# Microbial Insecticides

Microbial insecticides are microbes (or toxins produced by microbes) that are deadly to pest insects but harmless to beneficial insects and humans. They have the advantage of being relatively benign but the disadvantage of being fairly species specific. For example, *Bacillus popilliae* is deadly to Japanese beetle larvae but harmless to other white grubs that infest lawns. They aren't contact poisons, and they must be eaten by the insect to be effective. Microbial insecticides have become increasingly popular, even among conventional farmers, and are readily available at agricultural stores.

## Soaps and Oils

Plain old soap (not detergent, but soap) kills a number of insects by dissolving a waxy coating that they need to breathe and preserve moisture. Specialized insecticidal soaps can be used, or else a pure castile soap (such as Dr. Bronner's), mixed two tablespoons per gallon of water. Insecticidal soap will effectively control aphids, white flies, scale, spider mites, and thrips. It needs to be reapplied fairly frequently—about weekly—to interrupt the life cycle of the target pest.

Light horticultural oils are highly refined mineral oils that control the same insects as insecticidal soap by covering and smothering the pest and its eggs. Mix and apply according to label directions.

*Table 14:* **Common Microbial Insecticides**

| Microbe | Pests Controlled | Notes |
|---------|------------------|-------|
| *Bacillus thuringiensis* var. *kurstaki* | The caterpillar stage of a wide variety of moths | Will not control codling moths |
| *Bacillus thuringiensis* var. *israelensis* | Mosquito, black fly, fungus gnat | |
| *Bacillus thuringiensis* var. *san diego* | Colorado potato beetle | |
| *Nosema locustae* | Grasshoppers | Because of grasshopper mobility, may not work for small yards |

Both oils and soaps should be tested on a single plant first, then wait a day, because they can be toxic to certain plants. (Their degree of toxicity to plants varies with heat, sunshine, humidity, general plant health, and other factors. Most often, they won't cause a problem, but it never hurts to test first.)

## Natural Insecticides

The fact that something is natural doesn't mean that it is harmless. Ebola, smallpox, and strychnine are all 100% natural, for example. Natural insecticides fall under the same category and thus require care in their use. Natural insecticides can be purchased, or they can be grown and made at home. From a cost standpoint, the latter approach is preferable, though certain natural insecticides aren't practical for home manufacture.

Pyrethrin is a contact insecticide that controls most aphids, cabbage loopers, stinkbugs, codling moths, and white flies among other pests. It does not affect flea beetles, imported cabbage worms, or tarnished plant bugs.

To make your own pyrethrin, grow pyrethrum daisies (*Tanacetum cinerarifolium*) somewhere in the garden. Cut the flowers when they are in full bloom for the highest concentration of poison, and hang them upside down in a cool, dry, dark place to dry. Once they are dried, take a quart jar of the dried flowers and grind them up using an old food processor or blender that you pick up at a yard sale and that *you will never use for food again.* Mix it with one gallon of water and two drops of dish liquid, and allow it to steep for three days, stirring every once in a while. When done, filter it through cheese cloth that you will throw away afterward, store in a tightly capped bottle in a cool dark place, and label it appropriately as a poison so nobody drinks it accidentally. You dilute this for use by mixing one quart of the poison with three quarts of water, shaking, and applying via a sprayer. (I cannot stress strongly enough that all bottles containing poisons of any sort be labeled appropriately. Not far from where I live, a child died tragically a couple of years ago because of an unlabeled container of insecticide.)

Other natural insecticides are widely available, including neem. These can be purchased at most garden centers or via mail order and should be used with as much care and caution as synthetics, because they can be toxic to humans.

## Synthetic Pesticides

While this book focuses on organic methods, synthetic pesticides available to home gardeners bear mentioning. Ideally, because of a combination of growing conditions, attraction of natural predators, and other factors, pests won't be a problem so no pesticides will be needed—synthetic or otherwise. But that's the ideal. Reality can be far different, especially when first beginning a mini-farm. Even the most careful planning won't completely eliminate pest problems.

As a mini-farmer, you are trying to put a lot of food on the table, and you are trying to put *safe* food on the table. Perhaps, like me, you are an organic purist. But what happens when the theory of being an organic purist runs into the reality of a pest problem that threatens an entire crop? In my case, since I sell my produce as organic at 200% higher rates than conventional produce, it is actually better for me to lose a crop entirely than use synthetic pesticides. But what if my operation were strictly oriented toward putting food on the table? In that case, *maybe* I would use them, albeit cautiously and as a last resort, because some research shows that the synthetic pesticides available at the hardware store can be just as safe as botanical insecticides—and more effective—when used properly.

Please note that I said "maybe," "cautiously," and "as a last resort" for a reason. First off, in a mini-farm established using the methods in this book, economically threatening insect problems should be rare, and insect problems that won't respond to natural remedies even more rare. In fact, I have had only *one* pest problem where synthetics would have possibly been the better short-term solution.

Second, the government agencies charged with ensuring the safety of foodstuffs, drugs, and insecticides have a poor track record. For example, an article in *USA Today* disclosed that in 55% of FDA meetings regarding drug approvals, over half of the participants had financial conflicts of interest serious enough tonote.[21] According to the same article, committees approving such things are actually *required by law* to include officials representing the industry in question. This is not exactly a recipe that would inspire confidence in most objective observers and perhaps explains the dozens of chemicals (including various insecticides and drugs) approved by government agencies and subsequently recalled after people have been harmed or killed.

Finally, studies indicate that synthetic pesticides make food less healthful by reducing the ability of plants to create antioxidants.[22] This explains my caution regarding synthetic pesticides. If you are nice enough to buy my book, should I repay your kindness by giving you advice that could hurt you without totally disclosing the facts as I know them? Government agencies have a poor track record, and research in universities is often funded by self-interested parties. The extent to which this affects the results and conclusions of research is impossible to tell. So I am going to give you information on two synthetic

---

[21] Couchon, D. (2000) Number of drug experts available is limited *USA Today*, Sept 25, 2000

[22] Asami, D., Hong, Y., Barrett, D., Mitchell, A. (2003) Comparison of total phenolic and ascorbic acid content of freeze-dried and air-dried marionberry, strawberry and corn grown using conventional, organic and sustainable agricultural practices. *Journal of Agricultural Food Chemistry*, Feb 26, 2003

insecticides, understanding that the research I have available says they are safe but that it could be discovered later that you shouldn't touch them with the proverbial 10-foot pole.

The use of natural insecticides like pyrethrin is perfectly acceptable under the National Organic Program, but in practical terms these substances are every bit as toxic as commonly available synthetics while being less effective in many instances. The main difference is that the natural insecticides break down into nontoxic compounds very quickly under the influence of heat, sunshine, wind, and rain so they won't make it into your food supply if used properly, whereas the synthetics are specifically formulated to be more persistent.

Let's take pyrethrin as an example. Pyrethrin is a natural neurotoxin that insects quickly absorb through the skin. Once it is absorbed, the race is on between the insect's enzymes that detoxify the pyrethrin and the pyrethrin's toxic effects. Many insects, if they receive a sublethal dose, will pick themselves up and dust themselves off less than an hour after apparently being killed! Synthetic pyrethrins approach this problem by mixing the product with a substance like piperonyl butoxide that delays the insect's ability to make the enzymes to detoxify the pyrethrin, thus lowering the threshold considerably for what would constitute a lethal dose. Moreover, semisynthetic pyrethrins, such as allethrin, are often more toxic to insects while being less toxic to mammals (such as humans) than their natural counterparts.

So a semisynthetic pyrethrin spray combined with piperonyl butoxide would require less poison to be used and be more effective, and the type of pyrethrin being used would be less toxic to humans.[23]

According to a metabolic study, neither natural nor synthetic pyrethrins accumulate in the body or show up in breast milk because

---

[23] Extoxnet (1994) *Pyrethrins* from http://pmep.cce.cornell.edu/profiles/extoxnet/pyrethrins-ziram/pyrethrins-ext.html. Retrieved May 20, 2006,

they are quickly detoxified in the human body.[24] Any allethrin consumed by a human is rapidly transformed into something less toxic and eliminated.[25] In addition, allethrin is broken down into nontoxic compounds through the action of air and sunlight within a few days,[26] though not as quickly as natural pyrethrin.

The piperonyl butoxide used to increase the effectiveness of pyrethrins is a semisynthetic derivative of safrole—an oil found in the bark of sassafras trees. It works by inhibiting enzymes that detoxify the pyrethrins in the insect's body. Safrole is a known carcinogen, but the status of piperonyl butoxide as a carcinogen is disputed. Unlike allethrin, piperonyl butoxide is stable in the environment and doesn't break down easily.[27]

Given current information, the allethrin doesn't worry me much, but I am sufficiently uneasy about the persistence of piperonyl butoxide in the environment that I wouldn't personally use it. Either way, synthetic pyrethrins and those containing piperonyl butoxide should be used according to label directions and never be used on crops within a week of harvest; even then harvested crops should be well washed.

Carbaryl (also known as "Sevin") is another common synthetic insecticide used in home gardens. There is no clear evidence that carbaryl is carcinogenic or causes birth defects, and 85% of carbaryl is excreted by humans within 24 hours.[28] Carbaryl has a half-life of 7 to 14 days in sandy loam soil, and the manufacturer (GardenTech)

---

[24] Elliot, M. et al. (1972) Metabolic fate of pyrethrin I, pyrethrin II and allethrin administered orally to rats *Journal of Agricultural Food Chemistry 20*

[25] Kidd, H., James, D. (eds) (1991) *The Agrochemicals Handbook, Third Edition*

[26] Napa County Mosquito Abatement District (2006) Retrieved June 12, 2006, from www.napamosquito.org/Pesticide/pesticide.htm

[27] New York State Health Department (2000) Retrieved March 13, 2006, from http://www.health.state.ny.us/nysdoh/westnile/final/c3/c3summry.htm

[28] Extoxnet (1996) (Extoxnet is a government-funded database of toxic substances located at http://extoxnet.orst.edu)

states that it is not absorbed by the plant.[29] Therefore, if used according to label directions, and produce is carefully washed, it should be safe. According to numerous studies, "Carbaryl breaks down readily and experience shows it readily decomposes on plants, in soil and water to less toxic byproducts. Accumulation in animal tissues and biomagnification of residues in food chains with carbaryl and its metabolites does not occur."[30]

Certainly, the preponderance of science says that carbaryl is perfectly safe when used according to label directions. It definitely takes care of cucumber beetles much more effectively than my organic approaches. Nevertheless, common sense and the fact that it is a neurotoxin that takes a lot longer than most botanical insecticides to break down would dictate that it be used only as a last resort. All in all, if I were to use a synthetic insecticide, I would use carbaryl in preference to the others available. And, in fact, that is what I used before switching to organic gardening.

# Animal Pests

**So far, in** this chapter, when discussing pests we've largely been talking about insects. But one ignores larger pests, such as raccoons, rabbits, and deer, at his or her farm's peril. For many years, my farm ran along just fine with only minor damage from moles who ate strawberries and ripe tomatoes, and raccoons who occasionally stole an ear of corn. But one year, my entire crop of beans, sweet potatoes, and Brussels sprouts was wiped out in just one night by a herd of hungry deer. And they kept coming back to nibble at the sad remains. Clearly, action was needed.

---

[29] GardenTech (2006) Retrieved July 5, 2006, from http://www.gardentech.com/sevin.asp
[30] Hock, W. *Sevin (Carbaryl): A Controversial Insecticide*

Moles can be a bit of a nuisance in my garden. They are there, primarily, to eat grubs. If you get rid of the grubs by applying Milky Spore or beneficial nematodes, you will dramatically reduce the mole population. For faster relief, there are a number of castor oil products on the market that put castor oil into the dirt. When the moles dig, they get the castor oil on their fur, and they lick it off. This gives them diarrhea, and they move on within a couple of weeks. I've found this quite effective. A number of companies sell a battery-powered spike that generates noise that is supposed to deter moles. These may work for you, but I've found them ineffective.

Rabbits are only an occasional problem and don't usually do much damage on the farm. What I do is mix a hot pepper product with anything else I happen to be spraying and use it to wet the leaves. This serves as sufficient deterrent.

Deer are another matter entirely. I tried all the standard tricks. Bars of soap, hair clippings, urinating around the property line, and similar homespun remedies did nothing. Spraying the plants with hot pepper wax was inadequate and only marginally effective. I have found only three things that really work. The first is quite expensive: an impenetrable physical barrier in the form of a fence eight-feet tall. The second is a product called Deer Scram, which is a deterrent scent that is sprinkled around the area to be protected. The third is the use of a baited electric fence.

A baited electric fence is a regular electric fence that has been baited with peanut butter wrapped in aluminum foil. Deer adore peanut butter, so they put their mouth right on the aluminum foil and get zapped. This works incredibly well and requires only a single strand of fencing about four feet off the ground where pets are safe. This same trick works for raccoons if you add another strand about 18 inches off the ground.

⊗ Products for deterring furry pests.

# 5

# Seed Starting

**It is a** good idea to learn to start seedlings for three reasons. The first reason is economic: Starting seedlings at home saves money. The second reason is variety: Starting seedlings at home vastly increases the range of crop choices because certain varieties may not be available at your local garden center. Finally, since seedlings grown at home were never in a commercial greenhouse, you'll have a known-good product that is unlikely to be harboring pests.

Starting seeds is simple: Place seeds in a fertile starting medium in a suitable container; provide water, heat, and light; and that's it. Many seeds—such as grains and beets—are sowed directly in a garden bed, but others such as tomatoes, broccoli, and peppers, must be either started in advance or purchased as small plants ("seedlings") and then transplanted.

# Timing

**Seedlings need to** be started indoors anywhere from 2 to 12 weeks before transplant time, depending on the particular crop. Transplant time is reckoned in weeks before or after the last predicted frost of the year for spring and summer crops and in weeks before the first predicted frost for fall and winter crops. The timing of transplanting is dictated by the hardiness of the particular crop. Broccoli is pretty hardy, so it is often planted 6 weeks before the last predicted frost, whereas cucumber is very tender, so it is planted 1 or 2 weeks after.

So the most important information that you will need for starting seeds is the date of the last frost for your geographic region. This can be found from the Cooperative Extension Service or from an Internet search in most cases. The National Climatic Data Center maintains comprehensive tables on the Internet that give the statistical likelihoods of frost on a given date along with the probabilities of the number of frost-free days, broken down by state and city. Weather. com also provides data relevant to gardening.

Once you've determined the average date of your last spring frost, determine the date for starting seeds and transplanting seedlings into the garden by adding or subtracting a certain number of weeks from the date of the last frost, depending on the crop (see Table 15).

If my average last spring frost is June 1st, then I would start my tomato plants seven weeks before June 1st and set them out on that date. Cabbage would be started 13 weeks before June 1st and set out in the garden 5 weeks before June 1st. Eggplant would be started 8 weeks before June 1st and set out 2 weeks after June 1st.

*Table 15:* **Spring and Fall Planting Guide**

| Crop | Start Spring and Summer Seedlings Relative to Last Spring Frost | Transplant Spring and Summer Seedlings Relative to Last Spring Frost | Start Fall Seedlings Relative to First Fall Frost | Transplant Fall Seedlings Relative to First Fall Frost |
|---|---|---|---|---|
| Broccoli | −12 weeks | −6 weeks | Transplant date −42 days | Frost date +32 days −days to maturity |
| Brussels sprouts | −12 weeks | −4 weeks | | |
| Cabbage | −13 weeks | −5 weeks | Transplant date −56 days | Frost date +25 days −days to maturity |
| Cantaloupe | −2 weeks | +2 weeks | N/A | N/A |
| Cauliflower | −12 weeks | −4 weeks | Transplant date −56 days | Frost date +18 days −days to maturity |
| Celery | −13 weeks | −3 weeks | Transplant date −70 days | Frost date +11 days −days to maturity |

| Crop | Start Spring and Summer Seedlings Relative to Last Spring Frost | Transplant Spring and Summer Seedlings Relative to Last Spring Frost | Start Fall Seedlings Relative to First Fall Frost | Transplant Fall Seedlings Relative to First Fall Frost |
|------|------|------|------|------|
| Collards | –12 weeks | –4 weeks | Transplant date –56 days | Frost date +18 days –days to maturity |
| Cucumber | –3 weeks | +1 week | N/A | N/A |
| Eggplant | –8 weeks | +2 weeks | N/A | N/A |
| Kale | –13 weeks | –5 weeks | Transplant date –56 days | Frost date +25 days –days to maturity |
| Lettuce | –8 weeks | –2 weeks | Transplant date –42 days | Frost date +4 days –days to maturity |
| Okra | –4 weeks | +2 weeks | N/A | N/A |
| Onions | –12 weeks | –6 weeks | Transplant date –42 days | Frost date +32 days –days to maturity |
| Peppers | –6 weeks | +2 weeks | N/A | N/A |
| Pumpkins | –2 weeks | +2 weeks | N/A | N/A |

| Crop | Start Spring and Summer Seedlings Relative to Last Spring Frost | Transplant Spring and Summer Seedlings Relative to Last Spring Frost | Start Fall Seedlings Relative to First Fall Frost | Transplant Fall Seedlings Relative to First Fall Frost |
|---|---|---|---|---|
| Squash (summer) | −2 weeks | +2 weeks | N/A | N/A |
| Squash (winter) | −2 weeks | +2 weeks | N/A | N/A |
| Tomatoes | −7 weeks | +0 weeks | N/A | N/A |
| Watermelon | −2 weeks | +2 weeks | N/A | N/A |

Anything that can be planted in the garden before the last spring frost can also be grown as a fall crop. For fall cabbage, if my average date of the first fall frost is on September 6th, and my cabbage requires 65 days to mature according to the seed package, then I would transplant my cabbage seedlings on July 28th. This is computed by adding 25 days (from the table) to September 6th then subtracting 65 days for the days to maturity (from the seed package). I can tell when to start my cabbage from seed by subtracting 56 days (from the table) from the transplant date. So I should start my cabbage seedlings for fall on June 2nd.

# Starting Medium

**Gardening experts have** many varied opinions on the best starting medium. To confuse matters, seed catalogs try to sell all kinds of starting mediums for that purpose, and the number of choices can be confusing.

Whatever is used as a seed-starting medium should be light and easy for delicate roots to penetrate, and it should hold water well and not be infected with diseases. It should have some nutrients but not too heavy a concentration of them. Commercial seed-starting mixes are sold for this purpose and work fine, as do peat pellets of various shapes and sizes. At the time of writing, commercial seed-starting mixes cost about $3 for enough to start 150 plants, and peat pellets cost about $5 per 100.

Compared to the cost of buying transplants from a garden center, the price of seed-starting mixes or peat pellets is negligible. But for a farmer growing hundreds or even thousands of transplants, it may be economical to make seed-starting mixes at home. Most seed-starting mixes consist mainly of finely milled peat moss and vermiculite. The Territorial Seed Company recommends a simple 50/50 mix of vermiculite and peat moss,[31] but some authorities recommend adding compost to the mix because it can suppress diseases.[32] Some farmers also add a little clean sand. If these latter two ingredients are added, they shouldn't constitute more than 1/3 of the soil volume in aggregate. Don't use garden soil, and don't use potting soil. It is extremely important that any compost used to make seed-starting mix be well finished so that it contains no disease organisms or weed seeds. (Garden soil can be used as an ingredient if it is first sifted through a 1/4-inch mesh screen and then sterilized. Instructions for sterilizing are given later in this chapter. Potting soil can be used under the same conditions—if it is sifted then sterilized.)

A little compost or worm castings mixed into seed-starting mixes is fine and can be helpful in warding off diseases. But even organic

---

[31] http://www.territorial-seed.com/stores/1/March_2001_W133C449.cfm retrieved on 2/27/2006
[32] Coleman, E. (1999) *Four Season Harvest*

fertilizer in too great a concentration will create an environment ideal for the growth of various fungi that will invade and harm the seedlings. An indoor seed-starting environment is not like the great outdoors. Wind movement, sunshine, and other elements that keep fungi at bay are greatly reduced in an indoor environment. As a result, the teaspoon of solid fertilizer that does so much good outdoors can be harmful to seedlings.

Another reason for keeping the nutrient content of seed-starting medium low is the lower nutrient concentrations cause more aggressive root growth. Improved root growth leads to a transplant that will suffer less shock when it is planted outdoors.

Here is my own recipe:

- Finely milled sphagnum peat moss, 4 quarts
- Medium vermiculite, 1 pint
- Well-finished compost passed through a 1/4-inch screen made from hardware cloth, 1 pint
- Worm castings (available at any agricultural store), 1 pint

Again, the simple 50/50 mix of peat moss and vermiculite recommended by the Territorial Seed Company and most commercial seed-starting mixes work perfectly fine. Feel free to experiment!

Because the starting medium used for seeds is deliberately nutritionally poor and provided in insufficient quantity to meet a seedling's nutritional needs, it will become necessary to fertilize seedlings periodically once their first "true" leaves appear. The first two leaves that appear, called the cotyledons, contain a storehouse of nutrients that will keep the plant well supplied until the first true leaves emerge. (Plants can be divided into two categories—those with two cotyledons, called "dicots," and those with one cotyledon, called "monocots." The first true leaves look like the leaves that are distinctive for that plant.) Adding solid fertilizer to the cells of a seedling tray would be both harmful and impractical, so liquid fertilizer will need to be used.

Seedlings are delicate, and full-strength fertilizer is both unneeded and potentially harmful. A good organic kelp, fish, or start-up fertilizer diluted to half strength and applied every two weeks after the first true leaves appear should work fine.

# Containers

**Mini-farming is not** a small hobby operation. The average mini-farmer will grow hundreds or perhaps thousands of seedlings. The best methods for starting seeds on this scale include cellular containers like those used by nurseries, peat pellets, and compressed soil blocks.

The use of undivided flats is advocated in the Grow Biointensive method. In this method, a rectangular wooden box of convenient size and about 2 inches deep is filled with starting medium, and seeds are planted at close intervals. The seeds are kept moist and warm, and once the cotyledons have appeared, the seedlings are carefully picked out and transplanted into a new flat with a greater distance between seedlings. This process is repeated again when the growth of the plant makes it necessary, and the final time the plant is transplanted, complete with a block of soil, it goes straight into the garden. The most obvious benefit of this method is that it is inexpensive. The largest detriment is that it is extremely time-consuming. Grow Biointensive publications also state that this method produces a beneficial microclimate and stronger transplants, but my own experiments have shown no appreciable difference between seedlings grown this way and seedlings grown exclusively in soil blocks or peat pellets. Certainly, this technique works well, and in a situation where the farmer is rich in time but poor in cash, it is a very good option.

The commercial growers who make the small six-packs of transplants for the garden center use plastic multicelled containers. These containers cost money, of course, but also save on labor costs and are easily transplanted. These units have a hole in the bottom of every cell, fit into rectangular plastic boxes that provide for bottom watering, and can be picked up at most agricultural stores for around $2 or $3 for a tray and eight 6-pack containers. The price of these works out to about $6 per 100 plants, which isn't expensive considering that the containers can be reused year to year as long as they are well washed between uses so they don't spread diseases. If you sell seedlings, as I do, you will want to take the cost of these containers (and labels) into account in setting your price. In practice, once acquired, the economics of using these is sound since the per-plant cost drops dramatically after the first year, and they save a lot of time compared to using undivided flats.

The disadvantage of multicelled containers is that each cell contains only two or three cubic inches of soil. This means that the soil can't hold enough nutrients to see the seedling through to transplanting time, so bottom watering with liquid fertilizer is required. Also, because of the small amount of space, roots grow to the sides of the cell and then wind around and around, contributing to transplant shock. Finally, because of the small soil volume, multicelled containers can't be left unattended for more than a couple of days because their water supply is depleted rapidly. Even with these disadvantages, they are the method of choice for producing seedlings for sale because of their convenience.

**⊗ Broccoli seedlings destined for market.**

Peat pellets have a significant advantage over multicelled containers when it comes to transplant shock. Taking a transplant from a multi-celled pack and putting it directly into garden soil can set the plant back for a few days as it acclimates to the new soil conditions. Peat pellets get around this problem because transplants are put into the garden without being disturbed, and roots can grow right through them into the soil. This allows for gradual acclimatization and virtually eliminates transplant shock.

Peat pellets cost about $5 per 100 and can be purchased at agricultural supply stores and occasionally at places like Walmart. They come as compressed dry wafers and are expanded by placing them in warm water. Once the pellets expand, the seeds are placed in the center and lightly covered, then the pellet is bottom watered as needed until time to plant in the garden. In the case of peat pellets, the seed-starting mix of a peat pellet is essentially devoid of nutrients altogether, making liquid fertilizer a must. If you use peat pellets, be sure to carefully slit and remove the webbing at transplanting time so it doesn't bind the roots.

Peat pots suffer from the same disadvantages that affect multi-celled containers because of their small soil volume, plus they don't break down well, and they constrain root growth in many cases, so I don't recommend them. When I worked some compost into my beds last spring, I dug up perfectly intact peat pots that had been planted a year earlier.

⊗ Peat pots often fail to break down quickly.

Compressed soil blocks, while not aesthetically acceptable for commercial sale, are the best available choice for the farmer's own seedlings. That's because a compressed soil block contains 400% more soil volume than a peat pellet or multicelled container, meaning it will contain more nutrients and moisture. Seedlings raised in compressed soil blocks using a properly constituted soil mix may require no liquid fertilizer at all. Because roots grow right up to the edge of the block instead of twisting around, and the block is made of soil so decomposition

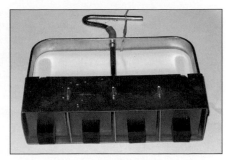

⊗ A standard 2-inch soil blocker with rectangular inserts.

isn't an issue, transplant shock all but disappears. They are also the least expensive option when used in volume.

Compressed soil blocks are made with a device called a "soil blocker" into which a soil mix is poured, and the mix is then compressed.

A standard mix for the soil used in the blocker contains 30% fine peat moss, 30% good finished compost, 30% sterilized garden soil and 10% fine sand.[33] A balanced organic fertilizer such as Cockadoodle DOO is added to the mix at the rate of 1/2 cup per four gallons of soil mix, and the pH is adjusted with lime if necessary to fall between 6.2 and 7.0. My own mix is 50% peat moss, 40% worm castings, and 10% coarse vermiculite with a bit of balanced fertilizer. (Garden soil can be sterilized by spreading it no more than 1-inch thick on a baking pan and baking in the oven at 200 degrees for 20 minutes. Don't use a good pan!) It is important that the ingredients used in a soil mix be sifted so large twigs don't interfere with the operation of the soil blocker.

Even though the devices for making soil blocks cost about $30 each, they are made of steel and will last many years, so they will save

---

[33] Patry, S. (1993) *Soil Blocks Increase Space Utilization and Plant Survival* Retrieved March 7, 2006, from http://www.eap.mcgill.ca/MagRack/COG/COG_H_93_02.htm

⊗ Use 1/4-inch hardware cloth to screen out debris.

many times their cost compared to multicelled containers. I bought mine from Peaceful Valley Farm Supply over the Internet.

One particular technique for using soil blockers merits attention. An insert can be purchased for the 2-inch soil blocker that makes a 3/4-inch cubic indentation in the block to accept 3/4-inch soil blocks. This is a great idea because it allows germination to be accomplished in smaller soil blocks that are then transplanted into the larger ones. That way you aren't taking up a large soil block with seed that won't germinate.

⊗ Soil blocks with sprouted lettuce seedlings.

# Light

**Plants evolved with** needs for light intensity that match the output of the sun, which provides light that is so intense that merely looking at it can permanently damage the eye. Naturally, seedlings grown inside also need an intense light source that can provide enough light without also making so much heat that plants get burned.

With the exception of certain flowers, most plants do not need light to germinate. In fact some plants, like those in the brassica family, may have their germination inhibited by light. But once the first plant parts emerge above the ground, all plants need light to grow. In most of North America and Europe, there is not enough sunshine coming through even a south-facing window to adequately start seedlings during the winter months when most seed starting takes place, so a source of artificial light is required. Selecting an artificial light source should be based on an understanding of the plants' requirements.

Plants require light of various wavelengths or colors for various purposes. Red wavelengths, for example, regulate dormancy, seed production, and tuber formation, whereas blue wavelengths stimulate chlorophyll production and vegetative growth. Violet wavelengths affect plants' tendency to turn toward a light source. The best light sources for starting seedlings, then, should generate a wide spectrum of light wavelengths that encompass both the blue and the red ends of the spectrum.

There is a growing number of options for artificial lighting; unfortunately, most of these are quite expensive. Following is my particular approach that inexpensively meets the light needs for seedlings.

All sorts of special carts costing anywhere from $200 to $1,000 are sold for this purpose, but with a little ingenuity you can create a suitable contrivance, made like the one illustrated, at very low cost.

This device is made from a simple wire rack sold in the hardware department of Walmart for $50. Three racks hold up to four large seed trays each, and two 48-inch shop light fluorescent light fixtures are hung over each rack using simple adjustable chains from the hardware store. This way, the lights can be independently raised and lowered to keep them the right distance above the plants as they grow. The six lights (or fewer if you don't need them all) are plugged into an electric outlet strip that is plugged into a timer. Each light holds two 40-watt 48-inch fluorescent tubes.

⊗ A homemade rack for seedlings works great and costs little.

The fluorescent tubes need to be selected with the needs of plants in mind. Cool white fluorescents put out more blue light, and warm white fluorescents put out more red light. Combining the two in the same fixture gives a perfectly acceptable mix of wavelengths. It's what I use, and a good many farmers use it successfully.[34] There are also special tubes for fluorescent light fixtures that are specifically designed for growing plants or duplicating the sun's wavelengths—and these work well too but at a cost roughly six times higher than regular tubes and at a reduced light output. The thing to watch for with fluorescent lighting generally is light output, because plants need a lot of it. Go with the highest light output tubes that will fit in a 48-inch shop light fixture.

---

[34] Murphy, W. (1978) *Gardening under Lights*

Because the lights are used approximately five months out of the year, the tubes need to be replaced only every other year. Replace them even if they look and work fine, because after being used for two years, their measurable light output will have declined.

The intensity of light decreases in inverse proportion to the square of the distance from the source. In other words, the further away the lights are, the less light the plants will get. Fluorescent tubes need to be set up so that they are only an inch or two above the seedlings for them to get enough light. Because plants grow, either the height of the lights or the bottom of the plants needs to be adjustable.

Plants need a combination of both light and darkness to complete their metabolic processes, so too much of either can be a bad thing. Because even closely spaced florescent lights are an imperfect substitute for true sunshine, the lights should be put on an inexpensive timer so seedlings get 16 hours of light and 8 hours of darkness every day.

Don't forget: Once seeds sprout, shine the light on them!

# Temperature

**Many publications provide** various tables with all sorts of data about the optimum temperatures for germination of different garden seeds. For starting seeds in the house, almost all seeds normally used to start garden seedlings will germinate just fine at ordinary room temperatures. The only time temperature could become an issue is if the area used for seed starting regularly falls below 60 degrees or goes above 80.

If seed-starting operations get banished to the basement or garage where temperatures are routinely below 60 degrees, germination could definitely become a problem. The easiest solution for this situation is to use a heat mat (available at any agricultural supply store) underneath your flats that will raise the soil temperature about 20 degrees higher than the surrounding air.

⊗ A heating mat is especially useful for peppers and tomatoes.

# Water

**Seedlings should be** bottom watered by placing their containers (which contain holes in the bottom or absorb water directly) in water and allowing the starting medium to evenly water itself by pulling up whatever water is needed. Seedlings are delicate and their roots are shallow, so top watering can disrupt and uncover the vulnerable roots.

It is important that the starting medium be kept moist, but not soaking, for the entire germination period. Once the germination process has begun and before the seedling emerges, allowing the seed to dry out will kill it. Most containers used for seedlings are too small to retain an appreciable amount of water; for this reason seedlings should stay uniformly damp (though not soggy) until transplanted.

Unfortunately, dampness can cause problems with mold growth. Often, such mold is harmless, but sometimes it isn't, and telling the difference before damage is done is difficult. If gray fuzz or similar molds appear on top of the seedling container, cut back the water a bit, and place the container in direct sunlight in a south-facing window for a few hours a day for two or three days. This should take care of such a problem.

Another cause of mold is the use of domes over top of seedling flats. These domes are advertised to create an environment "just like a greenhouse." In reality, they create an environment extremely conducive to mold, even in moderately cool temperatures. No matter how clean and sterile the starting medium, anytime I have ever used a dome on top of a seed flat, mold has developed within two or three days. I recommend that you do not use domes.

# Fertilizer

**As mentioned earlier,** once seedlings have their first set of true leaves, they should be bottom watered with a half-strength solution of organic liquid fertilizer once every two weeks in addition to regular watering. Since starting medium is nutritionally poor, some fertilizer will be a benefit to the seedlings, but anything too concentrated can hurt the delicate developing root system and cause problems with mold. The only exception to this is soil blocks, which can contain enough nutrients that liquid fertilizer isn't needed because of their greater soil volume.

# Hardening Off

**A week or** two before the intended transplant date, you may wish to start the process of "hardening off" the transplants; that is, the process of gradually acclimating the plants to the outdoor environment.

This generally means bringing the seedlings outside and exposing them to sun and wind for an hour the first day, progressing to all day on the last day of the hardening-off period, which lasts about a week before transplanting. The process of hardening off serves to make the transplants more hardy.

In my experience, hardening off makes little difference with plants that are transplanted after the last frost, but it does have an effect on the hardiness of plants that are transplanted before the last frost. It should be done with all transplants anyway, because there is no way to know with absolute certainty if an unusual weather event will occur. I've seen no case in which hardening off transplants has been harmful and numerous cases in which it has helped so it is a good general policy for a mini-farm in which maximum yields are important.

# 6

# Fruit Trees and Vines

**Fruit trees and** vines can provide an enormous amount of food compared to the effort invested. Many fruit and nut trees produce, literally, bushels of fruits or nuts, and some blackberry variants produce gallons of berries per vine. Unfortunately, even though berries may even produce in their first or second season, full-sized fruit and nut trees take several years to come into production and may produce nothing at all for the first few years. Dwarf trees will normally produce fruit within three years, but the volume of fruit they produce is lower.

To offset this problem, diversify! If possible, in the year preceding the start of your mini-farm, plant a small section with berry and perhaps some grape vines for the next year's harvest. Along with these, plant dwarf fruit trees and some full-sized nut trees. In this way, the harvest starts modestly with berries the first year and expands to include dwarf cherries the next year, dwarf apples the year after that, and so on. Within seven years, the farmer is producing enough fruit and nuts for the family plus some surplus.

Fruits are full of idiosyncrasies in terms of disease and pest problems, pruning requirements, suitable climate, and so on. This is particularly true of vinifera grapes, apples, peaches, and other popular fruits. I recommend reading as widely as possible about the fruits you plan to grow and selecting hardy varieties specific to your area, using a reputable nursery, and trying to purchase varieties that are resistant to expected diseases.

I recommend St. Lawrence Nurseries in Potsdam, New York, but there are other reputable nurseries as well. An invaluable Internet resource at the time of this writing is Garden Watchdog, at www.davesgarden.com. Garden Watchdog has a listing for almost every company in the gardening business and a list of feedback from customers along with ratings. Check out any mail-order nurseries with Garden Watchdog before ordering.

In addition to ordering high-quality trees that are likely to be less susceptible to problems, you should work proactively to keep pest problems minimal by making sure plants that attract beneficial insects are already established where the trees will be planted. Most notably, this means clover. Clover attracts insects that feast on the most tenacious pests of apple-family trees and fruits such as codling moths, apple maggots, and plum curculios. The exact type of clover to be planted will vary with the condition of the soil, expected temperatures, and expected precipitation. A good resource for selecting the right variety of clover is a comprehensive organic gardening catalog like that from Peaceful Valley Farm Supply.

Plant trees in the spring, and spray them for the first time in the fall with dormant oil that smothers and controls overwintering insects.

The following spring spray the trees with a lighter horticultural oil in spring when the buds have swelled but not yet blossomed. Also spray them with either a lime sulfur or organic copper-based fungicide according to label directions every spring after their first year. Traps for common problem insects such as codling moths or apple maggots should be set out and maintained at a high enough density to trap out all of the males of the species.

Fruits and nuts often have specific pollination requirements that make it necessary to plant more than one tree. Sometimes the trees have to be of slightly different variants because trees of the same variety were propagated by grafting and are therefore genetically identical and self-sterile. A few nurseries sell trees propagated from seed rather than grafting, and these trees will pollinate each other without issue even if the same variety. Be sure to pay attention to catalog information and ask questions of the nursery staff to avoid later disappointment!

Pruning will be necessary to maximize the productive potential of the trees. There are many schools of thought on the subject of pruning, and numerous weighty tomes have been written, but the basics are easily described.

# Blackberries and Raspberries

**Cane fruits, like** raspberries and blackberries, grow long and heavy enough that the tips of the canes touch the ground—where they then set a new root and grow more new canes. This isn't necessarily desirable, as it leads to an ever-expanding impenetrable thorny mess, so it is best to trellis the canes to prevent this. The easiest trellising for cane fruits is a four-foot-tall "T" at each end of the row of canes with galvanized wire run from each end of the T along the length of the row. The wire holds up the canes so they don't touch the ground, and new canes are trained to stay behind the wire. This makes the berries easy to pick as well.

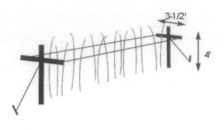

Blackberries are pruned by distinguishing between *primo-canes* and *floricanes.* Primocanes are canes in their first year that bear leaves but no flowers or fruit.

❷ This sort of T-trellis is easily made and works well.

Floricanes are those same canes in their second year, when they bear flowers and fruit. After a cane has fruited, it slowly dies, so fruiting canes should be cut out and removed once their fruiting season has passed. Primocanes should be *topped* during their first year of growth, meaning they should have their tops cut off just about 4 inches above the trellis. This will cause them to send out lateral shoots so that when they bear fruit the next year, they will bear more abundantly.[35] The lateral shoots should be trimmed to 12 inches to 18 inches.

The same general technique applies to raspberries, with some minor changes. Yellow and red raspberries shouldn't be topped, and the later-

als that form on purple and black raspberries should be trimmed to just 10 inches. Ever-bearing raspberry varieties fruit in the late summer of the primocane stage and then again in the early summer of the floricane stage. After the early summer fruiting, the floricanes should be removed. The easiest way to distinguish floricanes in ever-bearing raspberries

❷ Raspberries are nutritious and easy to grow.

---

[35] Strik, B. (1993) *Growing Blackberries in Your Home Garden* Oregon State University

is that the first-year fruit is on the top of the cane and the second-year fruit is at the bottom.[36]

# Grapes

**Grapes can be** divided into three general varieties: European, American, and muscadine. European grape varieties (*Vitis vinifera*) are vulnerable to a nasty pest called phylloxera, which is a tiny louse-like insect that causes all sorts of problems, especially in the eastern United States. Muscadine grapes, native to the southern United States, can be successfully grown

⊗ Properly pruned grape vines yield good crops.

only south of Maryland because of their climate requirements. Other American grape varieties are naturally resistant to phylloxera and can be grown practically anywhere in the continental United States. For varietal wine production, scion wood of European grape varieties is often grafted onto American variety root stocks to reduce their vulnerability to phylloxera.

Since grape vines are expensive and can last for decades, it is important to pick a grape variety appropriate for your local climate. Check a reputable vendor for recommendations. All grape varieties can be used to produce jams, jellies, raisins, and wines for home use. Grapes do best in *moderately* fertile soil because soil as fertile as that in a vegetable garden will cause the leaves to grow so quickly and in

---

[36] Lockwood, D. (1999) *Pruning Raspberries and Blackberries in Home Gardens*

such volume that the fruit will be shaded by the leaves, which will keep them damp and increase the likelihood of disease.

It is possible to start a grape vine in the fall, but odds of success are far greater if it is started in the spring because that gives the transplant more time to get established and store energy in its root system for overwintering.

When you first bring home a grape vine, it will likely have numerous shoots coming out of the root system. Cut off all of the shoots but the strongest one, then cut that one back to only three or four buds. Plant the vine in well-drained soil in a locale with plenty of sun, and water thoroughly. Pretty soon new shoots will emerge at the buds, plus some more from the roots. Cut off the ones that emerge from the roots, and once the new shoots from the buds have grown to about 12 inches, select the best and strongest of these and cut off the others. The best shoot will be pretty much upright. Drive a strong stake into the ground close to the plant, and throughout the summer keep the shoot tied nice and straight to that stake.

Meanwhile, set up your training and trellising system. There are many types, but about the easiest is the Kniffin system using two horizontal galvanized steel wires at three feet and six feet from the ground tied to two strong posts secured in the ground.

The first spring a year after planting, take the chosen shoot (which should have grown to a length somewhat taller than the bottom wire), and select the two strongest lateral shoots and tie those to the bottom wire while continuing to tie the growing trunk vertically to the stake.

Later in the season, once the growing trunk has grown to slightly below or slightly above the top wire, cut it off there and select the two strongest lateral shoots to tie to the top horizontal wires.

Occasionally, the chosen shoot that will serve as the trunk won't put out lateral shoots the first year. If that occurs—it's no big deal. Grape vines are vigorous and forgiving, so if a mistake is made in one year, it can always be corrected the next year. Just take the main shoot that serves as the trunk once it is slightly above the first wire, and tie it to one side of the wire and trim it back to three or four buds. These will form shoots. Select the two strongest of these—one of which will be run horizontally in the opposite

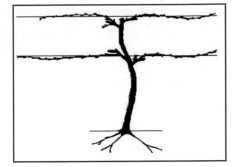

⊗ The Kniffin system is one of the easiest for training grapes.

direction on the wire, and the other of which will be run vertically up the stake and handled as detailed previously.

Ongoing pruning will be important to maintain fruit production because grapes produce on the shoots that come from one-year-old wood. So any shoots that arise from wood that is more than one year old won't bear fruit. That means that the horizontal shoots selected the first year should be removed for the second year and new shoots from the trunk trained along the wires.

The foregoing is not the final word on grape pruning and training, as many other systems are available to those desiring more information—but this should be enough to get you started.

Grapes are prone to black rot and botrytis fungus, as well as birds and deer. Because of the rot and fungal problems, it is important to avoid sprinkler irrigation of grapes and practice good sanitation by consistently removing old fruit and leaves at the end of each season. A copper-based fungicide applied at bloom time is most effective against rot and fungus.[37]

On a small scale, birds and deer can be foiled with netting; on a larger scale, some creativity (such as noisemakers and fencing) will be

[37] Baugher, T. et al. (1990) *Growing Grapes in West Virginia*

required. I grow my grapes far away from everything else, and the birds and deer haven't found them so far!

# Strawberries

**Very few fruits** are as prolific and easy to grow in limited space as strawberries. Moreover, because of their delicate nature, they are expensive to ship long distances, so they sell well in season if you decide to market them. Beds are easy to establish and require minimal maintenance on the scale of a mini-farm.

Strawberries come in three basic types: spring-bearing, ever-bearing, and day-neutral. The spring-bearing variety produces a single crop; the ever-bearing variety produces crops in spring, summer, and fall; and the day-neutral strawberry produces fruit throughout the season. Spring-bearing varieties can be early season, middle season, or late season, meaning that through careful selection of more than one spring-bearing variety, it is possible to extend the length of harvest substantially. Consider the intended use of the strawberries—preservation or fresh eating—in selecting varieties for either a continuous small crop or one or more larger harvests.

Strawberry plants can be spread either through seeds or through plants and runners. The best bet in most cases is to buy strawberry plants of known characteristics and then let them spread by runners. Runners are a long stem that emerges from the crown of the strawberry plant and establishes a new crown and root system wherever it contacts suitable earth.

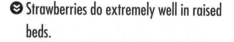

◉ Strawberries do extremely well in raised beds.

Simply place the runners where they will fill in the gaps in your planting—no more than four strawberry plants per square foot.

Strawberries should be well fertilized with compost and any needed organic amendments and be mulched with straw or fallen leaves after the last frost. They occasionally fall prey to botyritis blight, a gray mold that can grow on the berries. To keep this controlled, keep the beds clear of debris, make sure strawberries are harvested when ripe or slightly underripe, and spray with an organic fixed-copper fungicide as needed.

# Apples and Pears

**Apples and pears** are the quintessential home fruit trees and can be grown in almost any part of the United States. A wide selection of modern and heirloom varieties are available that are suitable for fresh eating, preservation, and pies.

Apples and pears offered in nurseries are usually produced by grafting the scion wood of the desired variety onto a more hardy compatible rootstock, such as that of flowering crab. The original rootstock can produce shoots below the graft (known as "suckers"), and these should be trimmed as soon as they are spotted.

Apples and pears should be pruned and trained when they are quite young or else they will become difficult to manage and produce inferior fruit. The objective of training the tree is to provide optimal air circulation and sunlight while keeping the fruit low enough to the ground so that it can be picked without a crane.

It is easiest for a mini-farmer is to select dwarf or semidwarf trees from the beginning. This will reduce pruning requirements and make maintenance easier and safer. Ideally, the tree will be pruned so that the shape is similar to a Christmas tree, which will allow maximum penetration of sunlight and easiest spraying while keeping the greatest

⊗ Pears are a bit easier than apples to keep pest free.

bulk of the fruit closest to the ground.

A large number of articles on the specifics of pruning and training pomme fruits are available, but it isn't hard to master if a few rules are followed. (Apples, pears, and quinces are collectively referred to as *pomme fruits*. The word *pomme* comes from the French word for *apple*.)

When the young tree is first planted, tie it to a straight, eight-foot-long stake driven at least three feet into the soil for strength, cut off any limbs that are larger than 50% of the diameter of the trunk, and trim the trunk back to a height of three feet. Branches are strongest when they leave the trunk at an angle between 60 and 75 degrees, so when the branches are young, it is easy to bring them back to that angle by tying them with string or inserting small pieces of wood between the branch and the trunk. The branches on trees will tend to grow toward the sun, so that tendency will have to be countered the same way because you want the tree to grow straight and well balanced.

Subsequent pruning is best done in late winter or very early spring. The first spring after planting, remove any limbs closer to the ground than two feet and any limbs that are larger than 50% of the diameter of the trunk. If the tree has developed more than seven limbs, select the seven best distributed around the tree to be saved, and prune the rest. It is important when a limb is pruned that it be pruned back all the way to the trunk, otherwise it will sprout a bunch of vertically growing wood and create troubles. Once the pruning is done, limbs that need it should be tied or fitted with spacers to get the right angle to the trunk.

Beware of cutting off just the tips of the remaining limbs, because this can delay fruiting. Once the tree has been fruiting for a couple of years, such cuts can be used sparingly for shaping, but it is better to solve shading problems by removing entire limbs.

For all following years use the same rules by aiming for a well-balanced upright tree without excessive shading.

# Stone Fruits

**Stone fruits include** cherries, apricots, peaches, plums, and nectarines. Because most stone fruits are native to warm climates and are thus susceptible to problems from winter injury or frost killing the flowers in the spring, it is important to carefully select varieties suitable for your area by consulting with a knowledgeable seller with a good reputation. No matter what cultivar is selected, it should be planted in an area protected from wind and with good sunshine and drainage. It is best to select a one-year-old tree five or six feet tall with good root growth.

Like apples and pears, stone fruits can be grafted onto dwarfing rootstocks. Unfortunately, none of the dwarf varieties grow well north of Pennsylvania.[38] The good news is that a number of hardy stone fruit varieties native to North America are available. The bush cherry (*Prunus besseyi*), American wild plum (*Prunus americana*), and American beach plum (*Prunus maritima*) can be grown throughout the continental United States, and Indian blood peach (Prunus persica) can be grown south of Massachusetts. All of these are available in seed form from

---

[38] Pennsylvania State University (2001) *Small Scale Fruit Production: A Comprehensive Guide* http://ssfruit.cas.psu.edu/chapter5/chapter5h.htm

⊗ Nectarines are easy to grow and easy to can or freeze.

Bountiful Gardens (www.bountifulgardens.org) and are also available from a number of nurseries.

Almost all nursery stock is grafted rather than grown from seed for a number of reasons, but the effect of this is that if two trees of the same type and variety are selected, they may be genetically the same exact plant and thus incapable of pollinating each other, causing low fruit yields. More than one of any stone fruit should be selected to aid in pollination, and it is important to consult with knowledgeable nursery personnel about exactly what varieties need to be grown to ensure proper pollination. Space nectarines, peaches, plums, and apricots anywhere from 15 to 20 feet apart, and space cherries anywhere from 20 to 30 feet apart for best pollination and fruit yields.

Stone fruits should be planted in early spring by digging a hole big enough to accommodate the entire root system without bunching it up or looping it around and deep enough that the graft union is about two inches above the ground. Once the soil is filled back into the hole, the area should be watered thoroughly to help the soil settle around the roots. Stone fruits should be fertilized in early spring only (using a balanced organic fertilizer) and never later in the summer. Fertilizing in late summer will cause vigorous growth that the root system hasn't grown enough to support so the tree could be harmed and have difficulty overwintering. By fertilizing in the early spring, the tree has a chance to grow in a balanced way across the entire growing season so it will overwinter properly.

A good fertilizer can be made by mixing together 1 pound of bone meal, 1/2 pound of dried blood, and 3 pounds of dried kelp or greensand. Apply 1/2 pound to the soil surface around the drip line of the tree (the "drip line" is the area on the ground just under the widest branches) by using a crowbar to make four to eight holes six inches deep in a circle around the plant and sprinkling some of the fertilizer in each hole. Use 1/2 pound the first year, then an additional half pound every year thereafter until, in the ninth and subsequent years, 5 pounds are being used each spring. Stone fruits prefer a pH of 6.0 to 6.5, and if a soil test shows amendment to be needed, that can be done in the spring as well. Keep in mind, however, that lime can take several months to work, so don't overlime and raise the pH above 6.5.

The following pruning directions are equally applicable to both dwarf and full-size trees. Because all stone fruits are susceptible to brown rot, they should be trained to an open center rather than a central leader (a single main trunk that reaches all the way to the top of the tree) like an apple tree. This will allow maximum light and air penetration to keep brown rot problems under control.

When the tree is first planted, cut off any branches closer than 18 inches to the ground, and cut the central leader at 30 inches above the ground. This will force branches to grow out at 18 to 30 inches above the ground, which will yield branches at the right height when the tree is mature. Select three or four good branches that are growing evenly spaced around the trunk, and prune back the others all the way to the trunk, then prune back the central leader to just above the topmost selected branch. These selected branches will be the main *scaffolds* of the tree, referring to their structural importance. Stone fruit branches are strongest when they leave the trunk at an angle between 60 and 90 degrees, so now is the time to establish those angles and the direction of growth using a combination of ropes and wooden spacers inserted between the branch and the trunk.

Stone fruits should not be pruned in winter because of susceptibility to winter injury and because of a disease called cytospora canker. Rather, they should be pruned between the time they bloom and the first week after the flower petals have fallen.

The first pruning after planting should occur just after blooming in the early spring of the next year. At that time, any branches that are broken and diseased should be removed, and the main scaffolds should be cut back half their length to an outward facing bud. Any vertically growing shoots should likewise be removed, and spacers or ties for maintaining branch angles should be checked and adjusted as necessary.

The second pruning after planting will occur at the same time the next year. By this time, the main scaffold branches will be developing new branches on them. Select three or four sublimbs on each main scaffold to be preserved. These should be on opposite sides of the scaffolds, not growing straight up or bending down, and be at least 18 inches away from the main trunk. The main scaffold branches should then be cut back by 1/3 to an outward-facing bud, and all limbs but the selected sublimbs should be cut back to the branch or to the trunk as appropriate.

Subsequent pruning simply needs to maintain the open center by removing vertical limbs and limbs that grow inward toward the center. Limbs and sublimbs should be headed back to an outward-facing bud each year to make sure new fruiting wood is growing each year, and limbs should be pruned as needed to maintain the desired shape and size of tree and to avoid broken limbs.

# Nut Trees

**Compared to fruit** trees, nut trees are easier to prune and care for. The only downside is that, except for filberts, they grow to be quite large and thus require as much as 50 feet between trees. Walnuts and, to a lesser extent, pecans and hickories produce a chemical called juglone in their root systems that inhibits the germination of other plants, so they shouldn't be planted close to a garden. A number of trees are unaffected by juglone, including cherries, oaks, pears, and most cone-bearing trees, among others. The only vegetables unaffected by juglone are onions, beans, carrots, corn, melons, and squash.

⊗ Chestnuts, walnuts, and other nuts are highly nutritious.

Most nut trees aren't self-fruitful and therefore must be planted in pairs. The same caveat applies to nuts as to fruits in that many nut trees are made by grafting and thus are genetic clones. For this reason, two different varieties of the same nut will need to be planted unless those trees were grown from seed, in which case two trees of the same variety will work fine.

Nut trees can be grown from seed as long as the requisite period of cold stratification is met to break dormancy. (Cold stratification means exposing the seed to a period of subfreezing temperature for a period of time. Many seeds for trees require this or they will never sprout.) If you plant the seed in the fall and protect it from rodents, it will sprout in the spring. Plant it about two feet deep and mulch with hay over the winter, then remove the mulch in early spring.

The tree should be transplanted into a hole big enough to handle the entire root system. About 2/3 of the soil should be carefully shoveled around the roots and then well watered and the remaining soil shoveled in and tamped down. The area around the tree should then be mulched to reduce competition with weeds and the trunk protected with a circular hardware cloth protector to keep deer and other critters from eating the bark. (Hardware cloth is available at any hardware store at minimal cost.)

Because nut trees have a long taproot that grows slowly, they need to have about half of their top growth pruned back during transplanting, leaving several buds. This balances the upper and lower portion of the tree to enhance survivability. New vertical-growing shoots should emerge from the buds left behind, and when they are 8 to 12 inches long, the most vigorous should be selected as the tree's new central leader, and the remainder cut off even with the trunk.

From that point forward, you are mainly aiming for a balanced tree, so prune to keep the tree balanced. Conduct all pruning in late winter or very early spring, and remove all dead or damaged branches. At the same time, progressively shorten the lowest limbs a little each year until the tree is about 20 feet high, at which point all limbs lower than 6 feet should be removed flush with the trunk. This preserves the food-making ability of the lower limbs until it is no longer needed.

Growing distance/productivity for such large trees can be troublesome on a small lot, but there are ways to get around the problem. Table 17 gives the ultimate distance that the trees should be from each other when fully grown.

Keep in mind that nut trees produce nuts long before reaching full size and that nut wood is some of the most expensive, so selling it could net a nice bundle. If you wish to do so, plant the nut trees about 10 feet

*Table 17:* **Nut Tree Planting Distance**

| *Type of Nut Tree* | *Distance between Trees* |
|---|---|
| Black walnut, hickory, pecan, and hican | 50 feet in all directions |
| English and Persian walnut | 35 feet in all directions |
| Chestnut (Chinese, most American chestnuts succumbed to the chestnut blight) | 40 feet in all directions |
| Filberts | 15 feet in all directions |

apart and then selectively harvest them for wood as their branches come close to touching. In the end, you have properly spaced highly productive nut trees and hopefully a wad of cash.

# Diseases and Pests

**There's no such** thing as a free lunch—or even free fruit! Fruit and nut trees are prone to numerous pest and disease problems. Thus, they require a regular schedule of sanitation and spraying to keep them healthy and productive, and they can pose a challenge to mini-farmers, particularly if they are committed to raising fruit without synthetic pesticides. This is more of a problem with fruits than with nuts, but it can be made manageable through advanced planning and a thorough understanding of the requirements. Pomme fruits such as apples and pears share common pests and diseases, as do stone fruits such as cherries, plums, and peaches. No matter what fruits you grow or what diseases are prevalent, meticulous cleanup of debris around the trees and vigilant pruning of diseased tissues will provide the proverbial "ounce of prevention."

The difficulties of raising apples and pears explain the high concentrations of toxic contaminants in nonorganic varieties. Therefore you should carefully consider if some other fruit might be more suitable given the amount of time you will need to spend if you wish to produce organic apples and pears. According to the Agricultural Sciences department at Pennsylvania State University, as many as 6 to 10 pesticide applications might be required yearly to produce reasonably appealing apples, though as few as 2 or 3 applications are feasible with scab-resistant varieties. Spraying is simplified, and pomme fruits are more practical if dwarf varieties are selected.

Scab is a fungal disease of apples and pears. The spores mature over a four- to six-week period of wet weather in the spring that corresponds with the wet weather required for the release of the spores. The spores take up residence on the leaves of the tree where they grow and produce more spores, starting a cycle of reinfection that infects the fruit as well, causing ugly, misshapen fruit. If all debris (apples/pears and leaves) is removed before the spores can be released, and a good antifungal agent (such as fixed copper or Bordeaux mix) is applied every 10 to 14 days starting in early spring and extending through early summer, scab infection can be controlled. A better solution, because antifungal agents can injure the tree, is to plant apple varieties that are naturally resistant to scab, such as Liberty. Carefully research the varieties you plan to grow.

There are a number of other apple or pear diseases, such as fire blight, that require comprehensive management programs to produce good fruit. Antibiotics are combined with pruning of diseased tissue for treatment of fire blight once it becomes established.

The most prevalent pest of pomme fruits is the apple maggot, a little white worm. Luckily, the apple maggot is one of the few insects that can discern—and are attracted to—the color red. They can be effectively controlled by hanging red-painted balls coated with a sticky coating (such as Tangletrap). The balls should be hung just after flowering and remain through harvest, being renewed periodically to keep them sticky. Several are required for each tree.

The codling moth is another serious pest. This nondescript gray and brown moth lays eggs on the fruit. The first eggs hatch when the fruit is slightly less than one inch in diameter, and the small worm burrows into the fruit where it eats until it reaches full size then burrows back out, becomes a moth, and starts the cycle again. Codling moths are conventionally controlled by spraying carbaryl or permethrin at least once every 14 days following petal fall. These poisons can be avoided by aggressive organic measures including "trapping out" the male moths by using up to four pheromone traps per full-sized tree, encircling the tree trunks with flexible cardboard covered with a sticky coating to trap the larvae, and spraying frequently with the botanical insecticide ryania.

Stone fruits, like pomme fruits, require constant spraying to deal with a number of diseases and pests. Chief diseases include powdery mildew, leaf spot, peach leaf curl, crown gall, cytospora canker, black knot, and brown spot. Japanese beetles, fruit moths, aphids, borers, and spider mites round out the threats.

A regular spraying schedule is required for stone fruits. If raising the fruit organically, this includes fungicides such as Bordeaux mix, lime sulfur, and fixed copper and insect controls such as neem oil, horticultural oil, and organic insecticides used according to label directions. The spraying should start when buds swell in the spring and continue with the frequency specified on the product label until the fruit has been harvested. All dropped fruit and leaves should be raked up and removed from the area in the fall.

Black knot of the plum can't be controlled this way and instead requires that any sections of wood evidencing this distinctive infection be completely removed from the tree and destroyed by incineration.

Most nut trees never show signs of disease, and the regular spraying required for fruit trees is not needed in most cases. Major nut tree diseases include chestnut blight, pecan scab, walnut anthracnose, and walnut blight.

Chestnut blight was introduced into the United States before 1900 through the importation of various Asian chestnut species that carry the causative fungus but are resistant to it themselves. The American chestnut, native to Eastern North America, has no resistance to this fungus; within a generation this majestic tree, soaring up to 100 feet and measuring up to 10 feet across, was reduced to little more than a shrub that struggles a few years before succumbing to the threat. To put the impact of chestnut blight into perspective, it is estimated that in 1900, 25% of all the trees in the Appalachians were American chestnuts.

There are four ways of dealing with chestnut blight: prompt removal of infected branches, treatment of cankers in existing trees for five years with injections of a hypovirulent strain of the fungus, planting resistant Asian chestnut varieties, and planting American varieties that have incorporated disease-resistant genes through repetitive backcrossing and selection to maximize native DNA content while retaining resistance genes.[39]

Mini-farmers interested in growing and preserving American chestnuts should seek guidance (and seeds!) from the American Chestnut Cooperators' Foundation (www.accf-online.org). Farmers interested in resistant Asian stocks can find suitable varieties at local nurseries.

Pecan scab, evidenced by sunken black spots on leaves, twigs, and nuts, is more of a problem in the southern than northern states. At the scale of a mini-farm, it is most easily controlled through meticulous sanitation—the raking and disposal of leaves and detritus through burning. Severe infestations require multiple fungicide sprays yearly.[40]

Walnut anthracnose, a disease characterized by small dark spots on the leaves that can grow to merge together and defoliate entire trees in severe cases, affects black walnuts but not Persian varieties. Meticulous sanitation is normally all that is required on the scale of a mini-farm, but springtime fungicide spraying may be needed in severe cases.

Walnut blight is just the opposite in that it affects the Persian walnut varieties but not American black walnuts. Walnut blight looks like small, water-filled sunken spots on leaves, shoots, and/or nuts. The

---

[39] Anagnostakis, S. (2000) *Revitalization of the Majestic Chestnut: Chestnut Blight Disease*

[40] Doll, C., McDaniel, J., Meador, D., Randall, R., Shurtleff, M. (1986) *Nut Growing in Illinois, Circular 1102*

disease doesn't travel back into old wood, so the tree and crop can be saved by spraying fixed copper during flowering and fruit set.

Pest insects in nut trees can be controlled through keeping the area mowed and free of tall grasses that would harbor stinkbugs, meticulous sanitation to control shuckworms, and regular insecticide spraying to control hunkflies, weevils, and casebearers. For a handful of nut trees (unless the mini-farm is in close proximity to a large number of similar nut species), pests are unlikely to become a major problem, and it is likely that spraying will never be necessary.

# 7

# Raising Chickens for Eggs

**I wrote this** book for the purpose of learning about self-sufficiency through mini-farming, and self-sufficiency, in my opinion, has no political agendas attached to it. If, for personal, health, or religious reasons you are opposed to consuming animal food products, then skip this chapter and the next one. If you are a meat eater but are understandably squeamish about eating homegrown eggs or turning animals into meat, I nevertheless encourage you to continue reading simply for your own knowledge.

Nothing says "farm" like the sound of a rooster crowing in the morning, and nothing is more aggravating to neighbors than a rooster that seems to crow all day, every day. Still, small livestock have a place on the mini-farm because of the high-quality protein that they provide.

⊗ These chickens are so friendly they eat out of your hand.

If you currently purchase meat and eggs, know that homegrown meat and eggs can be raised at a very low cost that will save you money.

For the purposes of a mini-farm occupying half an acre or less, cows, goats, and similar livestock will place too high a demand on the natural resources of such a small space and will end up costing more than the value of the food they provide. In such small spaces, the greatest practical benefit can be derived from chickens, guineas, some species of ducks, and aquaculture. Rabbits are also a possibility, but remember that children (and adults!) can get attached to them easily. But chickens, overall, are the most cost-effective choice on a small lot.

# Overview

**Chickens are foragers** that will eat grass, weeds, insects, acorns, and many other things they happen to run across. They will virtually eliminate grasshoppers, slugs, and other pests in the yard, thus keeping them away from the garden. Many cover crops like alfalfa, vetch, and soybeans are delicacies for birds and since cover crops are recommended to be grown anyway, a small flock of 10 or 20 birds can be raised with minimal feed expenditures over the growing season.

Don't expect to get rich in the chicken and egg business because you would be competing at the wholesale level in a commodity market, so it's unlikely to be a direct money maker. But it *is* feasible to produce meat and eggs for yourself at costs that significantly undercut those of the supermarket while selling the odd dozen to friends and coworkers. On our own farm, the eggs we sell completely liquidate the cost of feed so that our own eggs are free, plus we get to keep the chickens valuable nitrogen-rich manure for our compost pile.

# Chickens

**A flock of** 12 laying chickens costs about $6.00 per week to feed during the winter months when they can't be fed by foraging. They will earn their keep by producing about two to four dozen eggs weekly (more during the summer, fewer during the winter). Obviously, the family can't eat that many eggs, so a little negotiation with friends or coworkers who appreciate farm-fresh eggs will net you $2 to $3 per dozen. (Egg cartons cost about $0.20 each from a number of manufacturers. For more information, just type "egg cartons" into an Internet search engine. We get ours at a local get-together known as a "chicken swap.") To put the cost of chicken feed into perspective, a flock of 12 chickens costs less to feed than a house cat.

At the supermarket, a chicken is just a chicken, but eggs run the gamut from cheap generic eggs costing less than a dollar a dozen to organic eggs costing more than five dollars a carton. From the standpoint of raising chickens, there are numerous breeds available, each of which has its strengths and weaknesses. Many chickens are bred specifically for meat yield, and others are bred mainly for laying eggs. There are also dual-purpose varieties that split the difference.

For a mini-farm, I would recommend a hardy egg-laying variety such as the Rhode Island Red, which has the benefit of being good at hatching its own eggs over the more cultured Leghorn (pronounced "legern") varieties. Another good choice would be a dual-purpose breed like the New Hampshire or Orpington. In my experience, the laying productivity of hens diminishes over time, so these birds can be transitioned into the freezer and replaced with younger hens. (Old layers transitioned into the freezer are tough and best used for soups, stews, and chicken pot pies, so label them accordingly.) If you choose to hatch eggs from your chickens to supplement your flock, new roosters of the chosen breed should be brought in every couple of years to reduce inbreeding.

You'll find that hens and roosters are fun to watch and provide endless amusement. When the farmer steps outside, plate in hand, to deliver meal leftovers to the chickens, they'll come running! Then, the chicken that managed to retrieve an especially attractive piece of food will be chased all over the place by other members of the flock. The roosters will be vigilant and defend the rest of the flock against attack but otherwise just strut around looking proud and important. Chickens definitely establish a "pecking order" amongst themselves, so new chickens should be separated from the rest of the flock until they are large enough to defend themselves.

⊗ With too few hens, roosters leave some bald spots.

You need only one rooster for every 20 or fewer hens. In fact, you need *no* roosters at all unless you are planning for the hens to raise babies. Too many roosters is a bad idea since they are equipped with spurs on their legs and will fight each other unless the flock is large enough to accommodate the number of roosters. Roosters are not usually dangerous to humans, but there have been cases of attacks against small children, so it's good to keep an eye on kids who are playing in the same yard with roosters. In addition, if your flock has fewer than 20 birds, the rooster will likely mount the chickens so often that they may develop bald spots.

I recommend the following breeds of general purpose chickens for a mini-farm: Rhode Island Red, New Hampshire, Wyandotte, Sussex, and Orpington. These breeds make good meat and eggs, will get broody and hatch their own eggs, and make good mothers. Especially important around kids or in suburbia, they have gentle dispositions. But don't be complacent, especially about roosters. If they feel that one of the hens is being endangered, they will attack, and once they do, breaking them of the habit is difficult.

# Caring for Baby Chicks

**All birds have** requirements in common with any other livestock. They need special care during infancy, food, water, shelter, and protection from predators.

Chickens can be started as eggs in a commercial or home-built incubator. Most often, they are purchased as day-old chicks. They can be obtained at the local feed and seed store in the spring or ordered from a reputable firm such as McMurray Hatchery (www.mcmurrayhatchery.com), Fairview Hatch-ery (www. fairviewhatchery.com), or Stromberg's (www.strombergschickens .com). After hatching or arrival, baby birds should be provided with a brooder, food, and water. For a mini-farm-scaled operation, a brooder need be nothing more than an area enclosed on the sides free of drafts, an adjustable-height heat lamp, and a thermometer. (These products are available at agricultural supply stores.) The floor of the brooder should be smooth (like flat cardboard or newspapers) for the first few days until the chicks figure out how to eat from the feeder, and then you can add some wood shavings. Make sure

⊗ Baby chicks in a brooder made from plywood.

to clean all the droppings and replace the litter daily. Feeding and watering devices for baby birds are readily available.

When the baby chicks are first introduced to the brooder, duck their beaks briefly in the water so they recognize it as a water source. Just before hatching, chicks suck up the last of the yolk so they are all set for up to 24 hours without food after hatching, but you want them to have food and water as soon as possible.

Incubators and brooding areas must be thoroughly cleaned and disinfected before populating them in order to keep a disease called coccidiosis controlled. Coccidiosis is caused by a parasite that is spread through bird droppings and is more dangerous to baby birds than to adults. It is easy to tell if a baby bird has contracted the parasite because blood will appear in the droppings. Feed for baby birds is often formulated with an additive for conferring immunity to the parasite; some small-scale poultry farmers report that the disease can be controlled by adding one tablespoon of cider vinegar per quart to the birds' drinking water for three days. Either way, the importance of cleanliness and disinfection in areas to be inhabited by baby birds can't be overemphasized.

Disinfection requires a thorough ordinary cleaning with soap and water to remove all organic matter followed by applying a suitable disinfectant for a sufficient period of time. A number of disinfectants are available including alcohols, phenolic compounds, quaternary ammonia disinfectants, and a large number of commercial products sold for that purpose. The most accessible suitable disinfectant is chlorine bleach diluted by adding 3/4 cup of bleach to one gallon of water. This requires a contact time of five minutes before being removed from the surface, then the area has to be well ventilated so it doesn't irritate the birds.

Baby chicks should be started on a type of feed called "starter crumbles" and kept on it for six to eight weeks or until fully feathered. Once fully feathered, they can go on layer rations and be put in the hen house. They don't usually start laying eggs until they are a little over 16 weeks old.

# Vaccinations

**You should check** with the agricultural extension agent in your local area for vaccination recommendations. Poultry are prone to certain diseases, such as Newcastle disease, that are easily protected against by vaccination but are incurable once contracted and can easily wipe out a flock.

I order vaccination supplies from an online veterinary supply company—Jeffers Livestock—and administer the vaccinations myself. Most vaccines come in a size suitable for vaccinating 1,000 birds, which is not particularly suitable for a backyard flock. I vaccinate my laying chickens for Newcastle disease and infectious bronchitis (IB).

Newcastle disease is a highly contagious viral illness of birds that has been recognized since the 1920s. It manifests in various forms, some of which cause as much as 90% mortality in a flock. Newcastle disease infects and is spread by all manner of birds, and it is endemic throughout Western Europe and North America. Most birds don't experience the levels of mortality and debility that manifest in domestic chickens, though. It is primarily spread by droppings. In plain English, this means that all that is needed for your flock to be wiped out is for a sparrow to poop into your chicken yard while flying over. (As a side note, the virus causes a mild conjunctivitis in humans and is particularly toxic to cancer cells in humans while leaving normal cells practically unharmed. Research into this is ongoing.)

So vaccinating your flock is a good idea. Meanwhile, while the Newcastle vaccine is available on its own, it can also be purchased as a combined vaccine for IB.

IB is caused by a highly contagious coronavirus that mutates rapidly. While the immediate mortality rate from IB tends to be low, it can permanently damage the kidneys and reproductive tracts of chickens, hurts shell pigmentation, and makes the eggs unappetizing. Thus, especially if you visit the backyard flocks of other poultry owners, vaccinating your flock for IB makes sense.

So, now that you've decided to vaccinate your flock, how do you go about doing it? First you have to get the vaccine—which I order from Jeffers Livestock. Trouble is, the teeny-weeny 7 ml (less than two teaspoons) vial contains enough dosage for 1,000 chickens. For those of us with a smaller flock of 20 birds or so, it isn't practical to use the watering directions. So how do you administer the vaccine?

The vaccine comes with directions. If you can't find them, you can get them from the company Web site.

Two methods are of interest. The first is to use an included plastic dropper and administer one (very small) drop of vaccine into either the nostril or the eye of each bird. My birds are pretty tame. They jump up onto my shoulders to keep me company and have no real issue with me picking them up or handling them. So in my case, this method works just fine. I set up a chair in the chicken yard and bring a couple of pieces of bread with me, and as each chicken takes a turn jumping up onto my lap, I gently hold its head still and beak closed and put a drop on one nostril. I then briefly close the other nostril with a finger until the drop gets sucked in, give the chicken a piece of bread, and send it on its way.

But not all chickens are so friendly and cooperative. When I was a kid, we had some chickens who thought they were kamikazes or something, and securing their cooperation in such an endeavor was unlikely. So we vaccinated them through their drinking water.

The question is how do you translate dosage instructions intended for 1,000 birds so they work for a small flock of 10–30 birds? Here's how I do it.

I rehydrate the vaccine in the vial using high-quality bottled water. I shake it thoroughly and then dump it into a 100 ml graduated cylinder. I add water to bring the total volume to 100 ml. Now I know that each milliliter has enough vaccine for 10 birds. I set that aside.

Then I turn my attention to the waterer. I take it apart and clean it thoroughly with hot soapy water, rinse it thoroughly, and then dry it with paper towels. My water at home isn't chlorinated. If you have chlorinated water, do the final rinse with bottled water.

Then, I put 1 gallon of bottled water, 1 teaspoon of powdered milk, and 1 ml of vaccine for every 10 birds into the waterer and stir it up. Then I make sure that for the next 24 hours it is the only source of water available for the birds. The next day, I clean out the waterer thoroughly and then fill it up with my normal watering solution plus a vitamin supplement. The vaccines are live virus vaccines, and they put some stress on the birds, so I give them the vitamins to help them deal with that.

Speaking of live viruses—I should mention that if you aren't careful while playing with this vaccine, you'll get a mild case of conjunctivitis—also known as "pink eye"—or maybe some coldlike symptoms. Nothing serious though.

While I use this method for the Newcastle vaccine, it will also work for other vaccines that are dosed for larger flocks.

# Antibiotics

**Sometimes vaccinating chickens** makes them sick, and they need medicine. Other times, they will get sick from germs you have brought home on your shoes from visiting someone else who has chickens or even from buying a couple of adult birds and introducing them to the flock—even if you keep them in a separated space for 10 days beforehand, which you should always do.

This is a tough situation. If you are raising birds organically and they need antibiotics and you use them, the chickens are no longer organic—so you may be stuck destroying the birds.

The most likely reason you would resort to antibiotics with chickens is respiratory illness. These sorts of illnesses aren't all bacterial—some are viral and unaffected by antibiotics. Nevertheless, I have found that most often the respiratory illnesses characterized by wheezing and nasal discharge or sneezing have all responded.

Antibiotics will find their way into the eggs of laying birds, so the eggs should be broken and added to the compost pile during treatment and for a week afterward. The two most common antibiotics used for chickens are variants of tetracycline and erythromycin, both of which are available mail order or right in the feed store without a prescription. A study of tetracycline residues in eggs found that on the second day after finishing treatment, any residues in the eggs

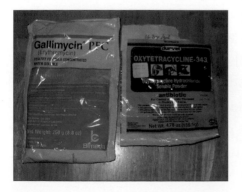

❯ Antibiotics commonly used for poultry.

were undetectably low.[41] So disposing of the eggs for seven days following treatment is fine. On the other hand, while the meat is safe to eat one day following discontinuance of erythromycin, I have no data indicating that the eggs are ever safe to eat again. So laying chickens treated with erythromycin to cure illness should be transitioned into being meat birds and replaced with new layers.

As with vaccines, antibiotics are usually packaged in sizes suitable for much larger flocks, but a bit of math will let you know how much to use. One thing you will definitely need, though, is an accurate scale weighing in grams. Digital scales used to be quite expensive but can now be found for less than $30.

# Food

**During the active** growing season, birds will provide about half of their own food by foraging if the farmer keeps the size of the flock suitable for the area being foraged, but during the winter and for the first weeks after hatching, they will need to be given commercial feed. (The amount of pasture required per bird depends on the type of vegetation being grown in the area. Start with 300 square feet per bird, and adjust from there.) You can also feed grain and vegetable leftovers—such as bread and pasta—to your chickens. Technically, you can feed them meat as well, but I would avoid the practice because too many diseases are being spread these days by feeding meat to livestock—things like mad cow disease that can spread to humans and is incurable. A small flock of birds will be much less expensive to feed than a house cat, and the feed is readily available at agricultural stores. A number of bird feeders are available commercially, or they can be built by the

---

[41] Donahue, D., Hairston, H. (1999) Oxytetracycline transfer into egg yolks and albumen, *Poultry Science* 78 pp. 343–345

farmer. Make sure that whatever you use for a feeder, it can be raised or lowered so that its lip is even with the backs of the birds. Building the feeder this way, and never filling it more than half full of feed will significantly reduce the amount of feed, that ends up on the floor since chickens have to raise their heads to swallow.

If birds are used for pest control, a fencing system should be created that allows the birds to forage in and around beds that are sown with cover crops but not in beds growing food crops A small flock of birds will devastate a garden in short order because they like to eat most things that humans eat. They make excellent manure that should be added to the compost pile if gathered. Otherwise, just leave it in the beds containing cover crops to naturally degrade and provide free fertilizer for the next growing season.

Commercial feed comes in many varieties. Both medicated and nonmedicated versions of mash, crumbles, and pellets are available. If you specify it is for laying hens, the clerk at the store will know exactly what you need. The medicated versions aren't typically necessary. You can also buy a mix of cracked corn and rye called "scratch feed." Scratch is about half the price of regular feed but is not, in and of itself, a complete ration—although chickens tend to prefer it over regular feed. All feeds are very attractive to rodents, easily rotted by water, and a lure for grain moths, so they should be kept in metal storage containers with tight-fitting lids.

❂ Containers for keeping feed safe from pests.

One winter, I kept a feeder with both scratch and regular feed available in the coop for the birds that were confined while the snow was deep. I also kept bales of alfalfa hay in the coop, covered with a tarp. Because the birds preferred the scratch to the complete ration, they became nutritionally deficient and sought to make up the difference by eating the hay. One of the hens developed an obstruction of her crop this way and had to be euthanized. So I have learned not to provide scratch while the chickens are confined, especially if an edible litter—like hay—is used.

What we do instead, when the chickens must be confined because of bad weather, is provide a daily bunch of greens such as lettuce or kale to supplement their feed. This helps give the yolks a nice color and keeps the chickens from getting bored.

# Housing

**All birds have** similar housing requirements though their habits are a bit different. A coop should be built for the birds with about three square feet of floor space per bird. Technically, as few as two square feet can be adequate for chickens, and ducks require only three square feet each, but the coop should be sized to account for temporary increases in flock size during the spring and summer. For a flock of 20 birds, which is the largest practical flock for a small lot, that means a 100-square-foot coop—a size that can be accommodated in a number of configurations such as 8 × 12, 10 × 10, and so forth. Enough floor space helps to reduce stress on the birds and prevents behavior problems. The most prevalent behavior problem resulting from inadequate living space is chickens pecking each other, which can lead to infections and other problems.

The subject of construction techniques required to build a chicken coop is beyond the scope of a book on farming. McMurray Hatchery (www.mcmurrayhatchery.com) has two suitable chicken house plans including a complete bill of materials for less than $15 each as of this writing. Judy Pangman has also written *Chicken Coops*, a comprehensive book

⊗ Some hen houses are an exercise in geometry, but they don't need to be.

⊗ Nearly completed chicken coop.

containing 45 illustrated plans for chicken coops to suit every circumstance and budget.

For our chicken coop, I used a product called Star Plates available from Stromberg's Chickens. It allows for building a floor in the shape of a pentagon and an extremely strong and secure shelter. It also, per square foot, works out to be less expensive than many other approaches plus allows for a natural draft when used with a small cupola.

No matter which way you'd like to build a coop, I'd like to convey a few aspects of coops that I believe to be important.

First, a coop needs to have a smooth floor, made out of plywood, for example, that is well coated with polyurethane or a similar substance that is impervious to moisture and easily cleaned or disinfected. The floor should be strewn with wood shavings, peat moss, or a similar clean absorbent material that is replaced anytime it becomes excessively damp or dirty in order to prevent infections. Some experts recommend against using hay, but that is precisely what we use without any difficulties as long as we don't store the hay bails in the coop.

Second, any windows should be made out of Plexiglas rather than real glass and preferably located high enough on a wall that the chickens can't get to it easily. That way they won't be tempted to fly into it and break their necks.

Third, even the smallest omnivores, like mice and rats, can cause serious problems in a bird coop, so it is important to construct the coop in a fashion that will exclude even the smallest predators. I learned this lesson the hard way back when I was 12 years old and a rat got into our chicken coop and managed to kill three adolescent birds. The easiest way to achieve this is to build the coop on pilings.

Finally, nests should be provided. These are most easily built onto the walls in such a way that the birds can get into them easily via the roosts and they are up away from the floor. Ducks, being more secretive, prefer a covered nesting box on the floor. Nests should be filled

⊗ Adequate and comfortable nesting boxes are important.

with straw, wood shavings, or peat and kept clean. The farmer should provide half as many nests as there are birds.

Because of the way the noses of birds are designed, birds cannot create suction with their beaks. As a result, they have to raise their heads to swallow. What this means in practical terms is that birds sling water all over the place and make the litter on the floor of the coop wet if the lip of a watering device is too low. If the lip of the watering device is even with the level of the backs of the birds, the mess created will be substantially reduced. It is more important with some birds than others, and particularly important with turkeys, to make sure plenty of water is available anytime they are given feed in order to avoid choking. Water provided should be clean and free of debris, and the container should be designed to keep birds from standing in it or roosting on it. If birds stand in or roost over the water source, they will certainly contaminate it with droppings.

Many books on poultry cover the lighting arrangements needed to maximize growth or egg laying. Light affects the hormonal balance in birds and therefore affects when a bird will molt (lose and replace its feathers), lay eggs, desire mating, and so forth. When birds molt, they temporarily stop laying eggs, which is a big deal on a commercial scale. Likewise, egg production naturally decreases as the amount of available light decreases. All of this can be affected by controlling the amount of light that birds receive and, to a lesser degree, the food supply.

This brings up a fundamental difference in the mind-set of a mini-farmer who is raising birds as compared to a large commercial enterprise. In a large commercial enterprise, the life span of a laying chicken is about 16 months because it has been pushed to its physical limits by that time and has outlived its usefulness in terms of the cost of food and water that it consumes compared to the wholesale value of eggs in a commodity market. Likewise, because it has laid eggs daily without respite since reaching adulthood, the minerals in its body have become depleted and the quality of the egg shells has declined. So by the time a chicken is 16 months old, it is consigned to the compost heap because it isn't even good for eating.

A mini-farmer can have a different outlook because the birds are multipurpose. The birds serve to consume pests and reduce the costs of gardening, consume leftovers, produce fertilizer, provide amusement with their antics, and lay eggs or provide meat for the table. The economic equation for the mini-farmer is strikingly different, so the treatment of the birds will likewise be different. If birds are allowed to molt when the seasons trigger molting and come in and out of egg production naturally because of seasonal light changes, they are subjected to considerably less stress, and their bodies are able to use dormant periods to recover lost minerals and nutrients. In this way, it is not at all unusual for nonspecialized bird breeds to live several years with moderate productivity.

One other thing to consider if you live further north is the need for heat in the coop. Where we live, temperatures below zero are not uncommon, and there can be days in a row with temperatures never budging out of the teens. In these conditions, their water can freeze, and they can suffer frostbite. The water is easily dealt with via a simple water fount heater available at agricultural supply stores. For general heating of the coop, mine is insulated using thermal reflective insulation, and I've installed a simple 400W flat-panel radiant heater behind the roosts so the chickens can stay warm at night.

⊗ A radiant heater behind the roosts keeps chickens warm in cold winter climates.

# Collecting and Cleaning Eggs

**Chickens usually lay** midmorning, but there's no predicting it completely. They're chickens, after all, and lay when they are good and ready. Ideally, you should collect the eggs immediately, but this is seldom practical—especially if, like me, you work a regular job. I've never had a problem with freshness simply collecting the eggs when I get home from work and putting them in the refrigerator immediately.

There are a couple of phenomena pertaining to eggs that may become an inconvenience: dirty and broken eggs. Every once in a while, chickens will lay an egg that has a thin shell and breaks while in the nest. Sometimes, they may lay an egg with no shell at all. When these break, they coat any other eggs in the nest with a slime that makes them unmarketable. Obviously, the proverbial ounce of prevention applies in that having enough nesting boxes will reduce the number of eggs coated with slime in any given box. However, chickens tend to "follow the leader" to an extent and have a decided tendency to lay eggs in a nesting box where another egg is already present. So even if you put up one nesting box for each bird, this problem wouldn't be solved completely.

Then, of course, there is the problem presented by the fact that eggs leave the body of a hen through the exact same orifice used for excrement. Meaning that sometimes eggs will have a bit of chicken manure on them. Not usually, but sometimes. In addition, chickens who have been running around outside in the mud on a rainy day will track mud back into the nest and make the eggs dirty.

For minor dirt and manure, just scraping it off with a thumbnail or using a sanding sponge is fine. But for slime and major dirt that won't come off easily, water washing is required.

Water washing can be extremely problematic and yield unsafe eggs if done improperly. When the egg comes out of the hen, it has a special coating that, as long as it is kept dry, protects the interior of the egg from being contaminated by anything on the shell. But once the shell becomes wet, the semipermeable membrane of the shell can be compromised, and a temperature differential can cause a partial vacuum inside the egg that sucks all of the bacteria on the shell inside—thus creating an egg that is unsafe.

Nevertheless, the techniques and technology for properly water washing an egg are very mature and well understood. Special egg-washing machines exist, but on the scale of a mini-farm, they are so expensive (about $6,000) they don't make sense economically. One alternative that I haven't tried yet is a product called "The Incredible Egg Washer" that sells for less than $120. But let me tell you about the safe and low-cost technique that I use for our small-scale operation.

First, clean your sink and work area thoroughly, and get a roll of paper towels so they are handy. Next, make a sanitizing solution from the hottest tap water by mixing two tablespoons of bleach with one gallon of water. You can multiply this by adding four tablespoons of bleach to two gallons of water, and so on. Put the sanitizer in a cleaned watering can and the eggs in a wire basket. Pour the sanitizing solution over the eggs very generously, making certain to wet all surfaces thoroughly. Wait a couple of minutes, and then use a paper towel that has been dipped in sanitizer to clean the egg. Use a fresh paper towel for each egg. Then, rinse them very thoroughly with sanitizing solution and then set them aside to dry on a wire

⊗ Farm-fresh eggs are easy to sell as they are qualitatively superior to even the best store-bought eggs.

rack. It's important to let them dry before putting them in egg cartons, because wet eggs tend to stick to egg carton materials.

# The Broody Hen

**Sooner or later,** you are going to run into a hen who is very interested in hatching some eggs. If that is part of your plan—great! She'll sit on any egg, so take some others from adjacent nests that were laid that day, and slide those under her too. If, as in my coop, the standard laying nests are up in the air, make her a new nest that is closer to the ground—6 to 12 inches. That way, once the chicks are hatched, they won't hurt themselves if they fall out of the nest.

Usually, though, when a hen goes broody, you don't want it to happen. The hen will sit on the eggs, keeping them at a high temperature, so that when you collect them a few hours later, they have runny whites and just aren't fresh anymore. Just collecting the eggs out from under her for a while won't work—she'll just keep setting forever. The solution to this problem is a "broody cage."

A broody cage is any cage fashioned with a wire bottom and containing no litter. I've used a small portable rabbit cage for the purpose. If you keep a broody hen in this for 36 to 48 hours, it will break her of the desire to sit on the eggs. It is extremely important that you provide adequate food and water in the cage or you will force her to go into molt.

# 8

# Raising Chickens for Meat

**A lot of** people are squeamish about killing animals of any sort for food. Still others have moral or religious objections to the practice. If you have moral or religious objections, please skip to the next chapter as there is plenty of other information elsewhere in this book to help you raise a healthy diet without meat. If you are merely squeamish, though, this chapter may put you at ease. Be forewarned, though, that this chapter contains graphic pictures of chicken slaughter.

## Selecting Chickens

**For sheer efficiency,** the easiest choice is to order day-old Cornish cross chicks from your local agricultural supply store. These are also known as "broilers." These are bred to

⊗ Broilers gathered around a waterer.

grow quickly with lower feed requirements and to pluck easily. These are a sort of hybrid franken-chicken and are simply voracious eating machines. In fact, they eat so much and gain so much weight so fast that they may start dropping dead or breaking their legs from sheer weight anytime after 12 weeks of age.

Another way to obtain chickens for meat is to let a couple of hens stay broody in the spring and raise a handful of chicks to broiler size by fall. Come fall, pick all the new roosters to be meat birds, plus any of the older hens that aren't laying, leaving yourself with a flock around the same size you started with in the spring—about 10 to 20. The meat birds get processed in the fall, vacuum sealed, and frozen. You should take newly hatched chicks and raise them in the brooder, and thenceforth keep them separate from your regular laying birds. Otherwise, your hens will figure out that you've killed them and get spooked, and your rooster will get aggressive.

# Housing for Meat Birds

**Unlike chicks of** other breeds, broilers can usually be removed from the brooder at about four weeks old because they are pretty well feathered, and it's during a warm time of the year. This is good, because otherwise they'd outgrow the brooder. Regular layingbirds raised for meat should be kept in the brooder for six weeks before going outside.

Meat birds are around for only three months of the year, at most, so permanent housing doesn't make as much sense for them as it does with laying hens. What a lot of small farmers use, and we use one too, is a device called a "chicken tractor." A chicken tractor is a portable enclosure that lets the chickens get fresh air and fresh grass. It is moved every day so the chickens don't end up lying around in their own excrement.

There are about a million ways to make a chicken tractor. Just search on the Internet, and you'll find hundreds of designs, many for free. Your choice of design should allow for about four square feet per bird. Many designs are completely enclosed to exclude predators and keep birds from escaping. So far, I've had no real predator problems, and the Cornish crosses that we grow are too heavy to fly, so our chicken tractor is on wheels and has sides made of only three feet of chicken wire.

# Feeding Meat Birds

**Meat birds should** receive a starter/grower from the day they arrive until the week before they are processed. The week before, they should be put on a leaner ration. For this you can use either a finishing feed

⊗ The easiest housing for meat birds is a chicken tractor.

or ordinary layer crumbles like you give your laying hens. As broilers, particularly, seem to have a nearly insatiable appetite, you should feed them by weight according to the directions on the bag.

Some breeds of meat birds will forage while in the chicken tractor, but the broiler crosses will mostly just lay around and eat feed. So you shouldn't count on forage providing a lot of their food.

# Slaughtering Birds

**As a kid,** my family raised chickens, and sometimes I got stuck with plucking them, which seemed to take forever and was less than pleasant. But then I got older and wiser and learned of better ways!

Food should be withdrawn from birds destined for slaughter 12 hours before the appointed time, though continuation of water is advisable. This precaution will make sure no food is in the upper digestive tract and thus reduce the possibility of contaminating the meat with digestive contents.

⊗ A killing cone. They don't need to be this elaborate.

Usually, you should not carry a bird by its feet due to the potential for spinal damage, but for purposes of slaughter it is acceptable if done gently. Catch the bird by its feet and immediately hold it upside down. Swing it a little on its way to the killing cone, and it should settle down. Provide support for its back while carrying if needed. Then insert it head down in the killing cone.

The proper way to slaughter a bird, except for farmers whose religions specify another method, is to cut off the bird's head while the bird is either hanging from its feet or inserted upside down in a funnel-type device called a "killing cone." Use a good, sharp, strong knife for this. Put a leather glove on your weak hand, and grab the bird's head, holding its beak closed. Then, take the knife and cut off the head in one smooth motion. Once the head has been removed, any squawks or twitches observed thereafter are a result of pattern-generating neurons in the spinal cord and *not* conscious volition. I checked with my local veterinarian on this, and he assured me that cutting off the chicken's head is entirely humane. When the head is cut off, the neck will flex all over the place, splattering blood everywhere. I put a piece of Plexiglass in front of the killing cone to avoid getting blood on me. The bird should bleed out in 65 seconds or less, but it doesn't hurt to leave it for a couple of minutes because you don't want to scald a bird if it still has a breathing reflex because it could inhale water while being scalded.

⊗ A proper knife makes slaughtering easier.

Hanging the bird upside down or using a killing cone is important for two reasons. First, it helps remove the greatest possible amount of blood from the bird's tissues, which presents a more appetizing appearance. Second, it helps keep the bird from struggling and hurting itself.[42] Blood collected from the bird can be added to the compost pile. If a killing cone isn't used, a noose can be used to hang the bird upside down by the feet.

A killing cone, mentioned previously, is a funnel-shaped device with a large hole on the top into which the bird is inserted head-first. The hole in the bottom is large enough that the bird's head and neck stick out, but nothing else. The entire device is usually about a foot long. Killing cones can be purchased via a number of poultry suppliers, just be sure to order the correct size for the birds being killed. They are simple enough that anyone can make one from sheet metal and rivets, and many people have improvised by cutting the top off of a small traffic cone.

Once the bird has been killed, it needs to be scalded and then plucked. In scalding, the bird is dipped and then moved around in hot water for 60 to 90 seconds to break down the proteins that hold the feathers in place. Commercial processors use rather elaborate multistage arrangements for this process, but a mini-farmer simply needs to have a bucket of water of the correct temperature ready. Most on-farm slaughtering processes for chickens and guineas use

---

[42] Mercia, L. (2000) *Storey's Guide to Raising Poultry*

what is called a *hard scald* that loosens the feathers and removes the outer layer of skin. For this, the water temperature should be between 138 and 148 degrees.[43] This temperature range is sufficiently important that it should be measured with a thermometer.

For a small operation, the easiest way to get the right temperature is to fill a five-gallon bucket half full of water and insert a thermometer. Slowly add boiling water from a large pot on the stove until the temperature of the water in the bucket is on the high side of the recommended range. Then, once the bird has been killed, grab it by the feet and hold it under the water for 60 to 90 seconds, sloshing it up

⊗ The first incarnation of the Markham Farm chicken plucker.

and down slightly. The timing on this has some room for flexibility, so you can just count. If more than one bird is being processed, keep an eye on the temperature and add boiling water whenever the thermometer drops close to the low side of the recommended temperature range. The water should be replaced every dozen chickens, any time it has been allowed to sit unused for a half hour or more, or any time the water has obviously been contaminated with feces. In the case of broilers, this is usually for every chicken.

---

[43] Fanatico, A. (2003) *Small Scale Poultry Processing*

The bird's entrails should now be removed in a process called evisceration.

1 Loosen the bird's crop, which is between the breast meat and the skin, by following the esophagus down to the crop and loosening it. As you'll note, I wear disposable gloves for processing.

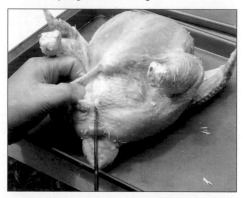

⊗ In this photo, the trachea is on the left and the esophagus is on the right.

2 A sharp knife is used to carefully (so as not to puncture any intestines and contaminate the meat) make an incision from the vent in the skin of the abdomen up to the breast bone. There will likely be a layer of fat there, which you can carefully pull apart by hand.

⊗ Opening the abdominal cavity.

3 The viscera are carefully removed by hand. With the breast facing up, just reach your hand into the body cavity as far as you can.

⊗ Reach your hand deeply into the cavity.

4 Gently grab a handful of viscera, and pull it completely out of the body cavity. Then scrape the lungs off the backbone. (They are bright pink.) Some people save the heart, liver, and gizzard. If you do, separate them from the rest of the viscera and refrigerate them immediately.

❂ You may need to remove a couple of handfuls of entrails.

❂ Carefully cut out the vent.

5 Cut out the vent, being careful not to contaminate the bird with the contents. Use a garden hose to wash out the body cavity afterward.

❂ Put the bird on its back and cut off the neck.

6 Turn the bird on its back and cut off the neck. A lot of folks use the neck for making chicken stock, so if you do, it should be refrigerated immediately.

7   Turn the bird right-side up and cut off the oil gland.

8   Now, give the chicken a thorough inside and out rinse with the garden hose and put the completed whole chicken in a tub of ice water. Make sure to keep an eye on the ice and keep it cold! I add a tablespoon of bleach (to kill germs) and a cup of salt (to pull residual blood out of the meat) to the water, but neither is strictly necessary. If you can keep the water ice cold for four hours before freezing the bird, it will be more tender than it would be if frozen immediately.

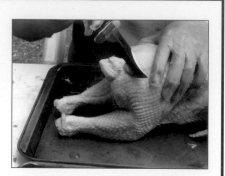

⊗ Don't forget to remove the oil gland.

⊗ Monitor the ice water to make sure it remains icy.

Once the bird has been scalded, the feathers are removed in a process known as plucking. It is easiest to hang the bird by its feet and use both hands to grab the feathers and pull them out. If the bird was killed and scalded correctly, this shouldn't take long, although it *is* messy. The feathers can be added to a compost pile and are an excellent source of nitrogen. A few small "pin feathers" will remain on the bird, and these can be removed by gently pressing with the back side of a butter knife. A few hairs will also remain, and these can be singed off by going very quickly over the carcass with a propane torch. If you process a lot of chickens, you might consider an automated plucker that is easily made at home. The most impressive homemade plucker is the Whizbang Chicken Plucker, designed by Herrick Kimball, and the plans are in his book titled *Anyone Can Build a Tub-Style Chicken Plucker*. I have designed a less expensive table-style chicken plucker and have included complete plans, parts list, and photos in the next chapter.

Bird blood, feathers, entrails, and other parts can be composted just like anything else, although many books on composting say to avoid it. Many authors counsel to avoid animal tissues in compost because they can be attractive to stray carnivores and rodents and because in a casual compost pile, sufficiently high temperatures to kill human pathogens may not be achieved. But if you make thermophilic compost, the only precautions needed are to make sure that any big parts of the bird are cut up and that the parts are buried in the middle of the pile with plenty of vegetable matter. In this way, the compost itself acts as a biofilter to stop any odors, and the high-carbon vegetable matter, combined with the high-nitrogen bird parts, will form seriously thermophilic compost in short order. Consequently, the nutrients that the birds took from the land are returned to the land in a safe and efficient manner.

# 9

# The Markham Farm Chicken Plucker

**If you are** processing only 1 or 2 chickens for meat, just plucking by hand is fine. But we usually process 10 to 15 chickens at a time, and under those conditions plucking becomes too time-consuming for efficiency. I had tried the cheap drill attachments with no luck, and building my own tub-style chicken plucker seemed awfully expensive—hundreds of dollars—to make economic sense. We needed something that could be built much less expensively and still do a good job; thus arose our own chicken plucker design that I'll be sharing with you.

## Construction

1   Use the two 7-1/2-inch pieces and two 12-inch pieces of 2 × 4 lumber to construct the drum holder as

# Parts List

| | | |
|---|---|---|
| 1 | 12" long 1/2" diameter steel shaft | Grainger Part # 5JW35 |
| 2 | ½" Pillow block bearings | Grainger Part # 2X897 |
| 2 | 4" sheaves for 1/2" diameter shaft | Grainger Part # 3X909 |
| 1 | 10" spoked sheave for 1/2" diameter shaft | Grainger Part # 3X934 |
| 1 | 4L V-belt, 1/2" × 54" | |
| 1 | 2" sheave to fit whatever motor you are using | |
| 1 | 1/4–1/2 hp motor; 1600–1800 RPM | |
| 1 | Piece of 4" diameter PVC pipe, cut 6.5" long | |
| 25 | Chicken Plucker fingers | Stromberg's Item # FIN |
| 2 | 7-1/2" pieces of 2 × 4 lumber | |
| 2 | 12" pieces of 2 × 4 lumber | |
| 1 | 24" pieces of 2 × 6 lumber | |
| 1 | 12" × 20" piece of flat wood 1-1/2" thick | |
| 4 | 1/4" × 2" lag bolts with 1/2" drive heads | |
| 4 | 1/4" flat washers | |
| 1 | 4-1/4" T-hinge with screws | |
| 2 | 4-1/2" lag bolts | |
| 12 | 2-1/2" deck screws | |
| 1 | 12" × 10" piece of 1/4" plywood | |
| Paint | | |

Additional hardware as needed to mount the motor to the piece of 2 × 6 board.

illustrated, using two deck screws for each union. The center of the second cross-piece is 3-1/4 inch from the connected end. Drill 3/16-inch holes at 1-1/8 inches and 4-3/8 inches from the free ends of the 12-inch pieces. When done, paint the piece and let it dry.

2 Cut off a piece of 4-inch PVC pipe that is 6-1/2 inches long, and then use a flexible ruler (like the kind you get in the sewing

section) to put four longitudinal lines evenly spaced every 3-1/2 inches around the circumference.

3 Mark two of the lines opposite each other at 1-1/4 inch, 2-9/16 inch, 3-7/8 inch, and 5-1/4 inch from one end. Mark the other pair of opposite lines at 1-15/16 inches, 3-1/4 inches and 4-9/16 inches from the same end. Then use a 3/4-inch spade bit to bore holes centered on each mark. After, pull plucker fingers until they sit in each hole. This will require some muscle!

4 Complete the drum by inserting the sheaves (with tightening screw facing outboard) into either end of the drum, running the shaft through both sheaves, aligning the outside edge of each sheave with the outside edge of the drum, and then tightening the sheaves to the shaft. Then, secure the sheaves to the drum with epoxy. For this sort of work, I prefer the putty type. Set aside while the epoxy cures.

5 Paint the large board and allow it to dry. Then, insert the steel loop. On the large board, the loop should be 1-1/2 inches from the rear

⊗ Unpainted drum holder.

⊗ Plucker drum marked longitudinally.

⊗ Plucker drum with fingers installed.

edge and 4-3/4 inches from the right edge. Use pilot holes to keep the steel loops from splitting the boards. Use screws to secure the rectangular end of the T-hinge on the big board with the hinge facing up, the back 8-1/4 inches from the back edge of the board, and the right 1-7/8 inches from the right edge of the board.

6    Paint the 2 × 6 board and allow it to dry. Insert the steel loop centered and 1-1/2-inch from the top edge and install mounting hardware for the motor as necessary to position the shaft 13-3/4 inches from the bottom and facing left.

7    Connect the 2 × 6 board to the large board using the T-hinge such that the right edge of the 2 × 6 board is 1-1/4 inches from the right edge of the large board, and then mount the motor to the 2 × 6 board.

8    Attach the drum holder you made in Step 1, holes facing up, to the front of the large board with the left side of the drum holder aligned with the left side of the large board and the rear edge of the drum holder 4-1/2-inch back from the front edge of the

⊗ Completed plucker drum.

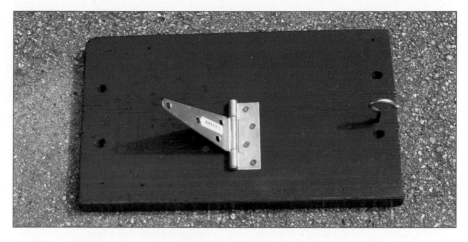

❷ The large board with hinge and hook installed.

large board. Use deck screws
drilled in from the bottom of
the large board into the long
boards of the drum holder.

9  Slide the shafts on either end of
the drum into the pillow block
bearings, mount the bearings
to the drum holder using the
1/4-inch lag bolts and wash-

❷ Recycled 2 × 6 board with hook and
hardware.

ers, and then loosen the Allen screws in the sheaves so that the
shaft is even with the end of the left-hand bearing and projecting
a few inches out of the right-hand bearing. Make sure the Allen
screws on both bearings are facing left and that the drum is centered and moves freely; then tighten down the Allen screws on the
bearings and sheaves. Finally, attach the large spoked sheave to the
right side of the shaft with the Allen screw facing to the right.

10  Place the entire machine on a stable flat surface with the drum portion
hanging off the edge. Run a V-belt between the sheave on the motor
and the sheave that rotates the drum. Adjust the sheaves on their

respective shafts until both are in the same plane. Then attach a bungee cord between the two steel loops to keep tension on the belt. Depending on your arrangement, you may need to use an alternative such as steel wire and a turnbuckle for tensioning.

⊗ The 2 × 6 board and the large board connected with the T-hinge.

11  Cut a slot suitable for allowing the shaft to pass through the 1/4-inch plywood, and then paint it and allow it to dry. Finally, attach it to the long right arm of the drum holder with short wood screws so that it prevents chicken parts from being caught in the spoked sheave.

⊗ The plucker drum and bearings mounted on the drum holder.

⊗ The drum holder attached to the large board.

⊗ Plucker with belt and tensioner installed.

⊗ Safety shield installed. Keep hands away from the belt and pulleys!

# About the Motor and Electrical Safety

**My first plucker** with this design was made using a motor I had picked up at a yard sale for $2, but the design illustrated here features a 1/4 horsepower farm-duty motor I purchased for $110. The motor should be wired according to the directions that came with it, paying close attention to make sure that it is turning clockwise (when viewed from the rear) and properly grounded. The clockwise turning means the chicken feathers will go down toward the ground rather than up into your face during operation.

Because chickens are wet from the scald while being plucked, there is a hazard with water being around electricity. Therefore, it is extremely important that you plug this device into a terminal strip that contains an integral ground-fault circuit interrupter (GFCI). These are not cheap, but they could save your life from an unexpected electrical shock. Don't skip this.

# 10

# Preserving the Harvest

**Since the purpose** of a mini-farm is to meet a substantial portion of your food needs, you should store your food so that it is available over the course of the year. The four methods of food preservation that I use and will be explaining in this chapter are canning, freezing, dehydrating, and root cellaring. These methods have all been practiced for decades in the United States and can be undertaken with confidence. Each method has its strengths and weaknesses, which is why they are all covered. Advanced techniques that I won't be explaining in this chapter include cheese making, wine making, and meat curing.

## Canning

**Perhaps the most** intimidating form of food preservation for the uninitiated is canning. Stories are everywhere about people dying from botulism because of improperly canned foods, so some people conclude that canning is an art like making fugu (the poisonous Japanese blowfish) in that the slightest mishap will render canned foods unfit. Fortunately, these impressions are not accurate. Modern canning methods are the result of decades of research and can be followed by anybody with a sixth-grade education. (Yes, I knew somebody personally with a sixth-grade education who canned safely.) Those few cases of poorly canned goods resulting in botulism poisoning in the modern era stem from people who do not follow the most basic directions on how to can.

Current standards for home canning come from research by the USDA that is continually updated. Most of the standards haven't changed for decades, because the research methods are quite thorough. The USDA researchers deliberately introduce viable heat-resistant bacteria spores into foods in home canning jars and then use temperature sensors inside the jars as they are canned. After canning, the cans are kept at the precise temperature necessary for best bacterial growth for several months and then opened in a sterile environment and tested for presence of the bacteria or any other spoilage.

The USDA standards published around World War I allowed for up to 2% spoilage, but the standards published since that time require 0% spoilage. This means that foods canned at home using current USDA guidelines are completely safe. Actually, the times and temperatures provided by the USDA also contain a safety factor. This means that if experimenters achieved 0% spoilage at 237 degrees for 11 minutes, the standards specify 240 degrees for 15 minutes. Times and temperatures are always rounded *up*, never down.

There are two methods of canning: boiling water bath and steam pressure. The choice of method depends on the level of acidity of the food being canned. This is because the length of time that spoilage organisms will survive at a given temperature is longer in foods that are *less* acidic. So less acidic foods get canned using the steam pressure method that produces a temperature of 240 degrees; more acidic foods get canned in a boiling water bath that produces temperatures of 212 degrees. The length of time specified for canning is based on how long it takes the heat to fully penetrate a particular food in a particular-sized jar. The standards are written for half-pint, pint, and quart jars. If a mixture (such as stew) is being canned, then the canning time and temperature for the entire mixture is based on that of the ingredient that requires the most time. By using the correct method, container, and processing time, you can be assured of the safety of your canned food.

## Home Canning Jars

Jars for home canning are available at Walmart and many hardware and grocery stores, although their availability is seasonal. These jars are heavy walled and specifically designed to withstand the rigors of temperature, pressure, and vacuum created by home canning. Forget the old-style (though attractive) jars with rubber gaskets and wire closures since they are no longer recommended by the USDA. Today's standards specify two-piece caps that include a reusable metal ring called a "band" and a flat nonreusable lid that has a sealing compound around its outer edge. The bands can be used until they have warped or rusted, but the lids must be thrown away once they have been used and bought new.

Home canning jars are expensive—about $7/dozen at the time of writing. So figure a bit over $0.50 apiece. However, their durability easily justifies their cost—home canning jars will last decades. By the time a jar has seen use for 20 seasons, its cost has dropped to $0.02. Once the jars and bands are purchased (new jars usually come with bands), you just need to buy new lids for each use—which are usually less than

$0.10 each. There are a handful of brands of home canning jars available, and on the basis of my own experience, I recommend Ball and Kerr, which are both manufactured in the United States by Jarden Corporation. I especially recommend Ball lids, because their underside is coated with a compound that keeps the food from coming into contact with the metal of the lid. This helps food stay fresher longer, and they cost the same as noncoated lids.

My stepmother often used glass jars from spaghetti sauce, mayonnaise, and similar products as long as the bands and lids fit and the rims were free from nicks or imperfections that would prevent a good seal. The good news is that she saved money. The bad news is that sometimes these jars would break and create a mess and lose the food. Most authorities counsel against using these one-trip glass jars because they aren't properly tempered, and their higher risk of breakage could cause injury and loss of valuable food. For these reasons, I recommend using jars specifically designed for home canning. If economy is a big consideration, then it is worthwhile to visit yard sales and flea markets where you can buy inexpensive, properly designed jars for home canning.

## Foods and Canning Methods

As I mentioned earlier, the type of canning method required depends on how acidic the food is. Acidic foods (with a pH of less than 4.6) need only a water bath canning method while less acidic foods (with a pH greater than 4.6) require steam pressure canning. Unfortunately, the combination of time and temperature in a pressure canner can render some foods less nutritious and other foods unappetizing. Broccoli is a good example in that it requires such an extensive period of pressure canning to be safe that the results aren't worth eating.

Broccoli is much better preserved through either freezing or pickling. The goal, then, is to use the method that preserves the maximum nutrition and palatability while maintaining a good margin of safety. So if I don't list a canning method for a vegetable (Table 19, page 198), it is because I have determined that it is better preserved using some other method.

An age-old method for canning foods that cannot be safely canned otherwise is to raise the acidity of the food by either fermenting it or adding vinegar. Sauerkraut is a great example because cabbage is not suitable for either canning or freezing in its fresh state, but if acidified through lactic acid fermentation (and thereby becoming sauerkraut), it can be canned in a boiling water bath while retaining its most important health benefits. (Technically, with great care, you can freeze grated cabbage, but your results may vary.) Pickles are made either by fermenting vegetables in a brine (which raises their acidity through the production of lactic acid) and/or by adding vinegar. These methods create a sufficiently acidic product so that only a brief period in a water bath canner is required.

Boiling water bath canning is suitable for all fruits, jams, jellies, preserves, and pickles. Tomatoes are right at the margin of pH 4.6, so they can be safely canned in a boiling water bath if a known amount of citric acid (or commercial bottled lemon juice) is added. The correct amount is one tablespoon of lemon juice or 1/4 teaspoon of citric acid per pint. Vinegar can be used instead, at the rate of two tablespoons per pint, but it can cause off-flavors. The only time I would recommend vinegar is in salsa. The acidity (or, rather, the *taste* of the acidity) can be offset by adding two tablespoons of sugar for every tablespoon of lemon juice, which won't interfere with the canning process. While few people choose to can figs (usually they are dehydrated instead), it is worth noting that they are right on the border line of acidity as well and should have lemon juice added in the same proportion as tomatoes if they are being canned. Everything else—vegetables, meats, seafood, and poultry—*must* be canned in a steam pressure canner.

Boiling water canners are pretty much maintenance free. Just wash them like any other pot, and you are done. Pressure canners, on the other hand, require some minimal maintenance. The the accuracy of the dial gage on top of the canner should be checked annually by your Cooperative Extension Service. If it is inaccurate, send it to the manufacturer for recalibration. When the canner is not in use, store it with the lid turned upside down on top of the body. Never immerse the lid or dial gage in water! Instead, clean them with a damp cloth and mild detergent if needed. Clean any vent holes with a pipe cleaner. The rubber seal should be removed and cleaned with a damp cloth after each use. Some manufacturers recommend that the gasket be given a light coat of vegetable oil, and some don't—so be certain to follow the manufacturer's directions. If you follow manufacturer's directions in using your pressure canner, it won't explode, as was sometimes the case years ago. Modern canners have a number of built-in safety features that our grandmothers' models lacked, and aside from deliberately defeating those safety mechanisms, an explosion is practically impossible.

Foods to be canned are packed into hot glass jars using either the fresh-pack or the hot-pack method. The methods are pretty much self-explanatory from their names: Fresh-packed foods are put into the jars fresh and then hot liquid, brine, or syrup is added, and hot-packed foods are put into jars after having been heated to boiling. In some cases, either method can be used. Once packed, the jar is filled with liquid (brine, broth, syrup, pickling juice, etc. depending on the recipe) up to within 1/4 to 1 inch from the top of the jar. This space is called headspace and is needed to accommodate the expansion of the food in the jar as it is heated and allow for a good vacuum seal.

## Using a Boiling Water Canner

Boiling water canners come with a wire rack that holds the jars so that they won't be sitting on the bottom of the canner or bumping into each other and breaking. Using a rack ensures that water of the same temperature surrounds the jars on all sides so that heating is even and therefore the best results are obtained.

Jars need to be sterilized for canning. My method is a little different from that in most books, but it works quite well, and I've never had a jar spoil.

1. Fill the canner halfway with the hottest water from the tap.
2. Put the jars you plan to use in the rack, without any lids.
3. Submerge the rack and jars in the canner, adding enough tap water to completely fill all the jars and stand 1-1/2 inches above the tops of the jars.
4. Put on the lid and bring water to a vigorous boil, then adjust the heat to obtain a steady rolling boil.
5. Meanwhile, put a smaller pot on the stove without water, uncovered, but apply no heat. Put the lids (but not the bands) in this pot, making sure that the sealing compound is facing up.
6. Remove the jars from the canner one at a time using a jar lifter, and empty the boiling water in them into the smaller pot until it is nearly full and set them aside on a dish towel. (Once the smaller pot is full, empty the water in the remaining jars into the sink.) Keep the lids in the standing boiling water at this point—additional heating of the lids is not required.
7. Lift up the rack in the canner so that it is supported by the sides of the canner.
8. Put the product into the jars (a special canning funnel is helpful for this), allowing for proper headspace, get the lids out of the

hot water in the smaller pot one at a time using tongs, and place them on the jars, then secure with a screw band tightened only finger-tight. (If you tighten it any more than that, the jar will break when you heat it in the canner.)

9. Put the filled jars in the wire rack, and submerge them in the water in the canner.

10. Turn up the heat on the burner a bit if needed to maintain a steady rolling boil. Start the timer once that boil has been achieved and put the lid on the canner.

11. Once the appropriate time has elapsed, remove the jars and place them on a dish towel at least 2 inches from each other on all sides and allow to sit undisturbed for at least 12 hours.

12. If additional product (more than one canner load) is being processed, pour the water back into the canner from the smaller pot, put clean jars in, and add any needed water to completely fill and submerge with 1-1/2 inches of water on top of the jars, then repeat the process starting at Step 4.

## Using a Pressure Canner

Each pressure canner is a little different, so read the manufacturer's directions and employ those in preference to mine if there is a contradiction. Pressure canners don't rely on completely submerging the jars. Instead, they rely on surrounding the jars with superheated steam at 240 degrees. They also come with a rack, but instead of being made of wire to hold jars securely in place like with a boiling water canner, it is a simple aluminum plate with holes in it. Put it in the canner so that the holes are facing up. When using a pressure canner, I don't sterilize the jars before use. Instead, I just make sure they are extremely clean, and I keep them in a large pot of near-boiling water at a simmer.

You can also wash them in a dishwasher and keep them hot with the dishwasher's heating element.

1. Put the rack in the canner and put three inches of very hot tap water into the bottom.
2. Put already-filled and lidded jars on the rack using a jar lifter, leaving some space between the jars.
3. Put the lid on the canner, but leave off the weighted gage, turn up the heat until steam starts coming out of the port where you would put the weighted gage, and let the steam exhaust for 10 minutes.
4. Put the weighted gage on the port and keep the heat adjusted for a steady rocking motion of the gage. Start timing from when the steady rocking motion starts.
5. Once the time is up, turn off the heat and let the canner sit until the dial gage reads zero or when no steam escapes when the weighted gage is nudged. Wait an additional 2 minutes just to be sure.
6. Remove the cover and then remove the jars with a jar lifter and put them on a towel, leaving 2 inches between them on all sides.
7. Leave the jars undisturbed for 24 hours.

## Fruits

Practically any fruit can be canned, and all except figs are sufficiently acidic that they can be canned without additives. (Figs require the addition of one teaspoon of lemon juice per pint.) Fruit should be in peak condition, free from obvious blemishes or rot, and well washed. To be sufficiently heated during the canning process, fruits that are larger than one inch should be cut up so that no single piece is larger than a one inch cube. Pits and stones of large-seeded fruit should be removed, and the fruit should be treated in an antioxidant solution, particularly once it has been cut to prevent discoloration. Antioxidant solutions can be bought commercially, or you can make your own by mixing 3/4 cup of bottled lemon juice with a gallon of water.

Fruits are usually canned in sugar syrups because the sugar helps the fruit keep its color, shape, and flavor, although the sugar isn't strictly necessary to prevent bacterial spoilage. If you prefer, can the fruits by using plain water rather than a syrup. I don't recommend the use of artificial sweeteners in syrup because saccharine turns bitter from canning and aspartame loses its sweetness. (If you have ever bought a diet soda and thought that it tasted a bit like dirt, that means that the product was stored in an area of high temperature and the artificial sweetener was damaged.) A "very light" syrup uses two tablespoons of sugar per cup of water, a "light" syrup uses four tablespoons per cup of water and a "medium" syrup uses seven tablespoons per cup of water.

To fresh-pack fruits, add them to the jars and then pour simmering syrup (or water) into the jar until it is filled up to within 1/4 inch of the rim. Put the lids and screw bands on the jars finger-tight, and completely submerge in a boiling water canner for the specified time for that particular fruit. Then remove the jars from the canner and leave them to cool for at least 12 hours. Hot-packed fruits are handled pretty much the same except that the fruit is mixed with the syrup and brought to a light boil, and then fruit and syrup are added to the jar together.

## Applesauce

Home-canned applesauce was a favorite of mine as a kid—I'd open up a couple of homemade biscuits on my plate, heap a generous quantity of applesauce on top, and dig in. Applesauce canned at home is simple, delicious, rich, and flavorful—nothing like the homogenized products available at the grocery store. Naturally, the same process used for applesauce can also be used for pears, quinces, and other fruits. Feel free to experiment! Here is my recipe and procedure for semichunky applesauce. Yield: 22–26 pints

### Semichunky Applesauce

- 1 bushel of at least two types of apples, one type being rather sweet
- a bag of white and/or brown sugar (the actual amount added depends on your taste and the apples selected)
- cinnamon to taste
- allspice to taste
- nutmeg to taste
- lemon if desired

### Procedure

- Wash 3/4 of the apples and remove stems, cut up into 1-inch chunks, including the core and peels, and put into a very large pot with about 1-inch of water in the bottom. (You can buy a simple contraption for a few bucks that cores and cuts apples into segments in just one motion—I recommend it highly!) Dip in an antioxidant solution once cut.
- Cook until all of the chunks are soft throughout. Start off on high heat and then lower to medium-high.
- Run the cooked apples through a strainer to remove the skins and seeds and put them back in the pot. (You can do this hot if you are careful.) I use a Villaware V200 food strainer because I could get it for less than $50 and it came with the right screen for my two favorite foods—applesauce and spaghetti sauce.

There are a number of strainers on the market—including the classic Squeezo strainer—that will also work fine.

- Peel and core the remaining apples, cut up into small chunks, and add them to the pot as well. (I have a "Back to Basics" Peel-Away apple peeler that peels, cores, and slices quickly in a single operation. It costs less than $20 at a cooking store.)
- Continue cooking on medium-high until the newly added chunks are soft.
- Add sugar, lemon, and spices to taste. You will probably need less than 1/4 cup of sugar per pint if you used some sweet apples.
- Reduce heat to a simmer to keep the sauce hot while canning.
- Pour the sauce into freshly washed pint or quart canning jars, leaving 1/2 inch of headspace.
- Put on the lids and bands finger-tight.
- Completely submerge jars in boiling water in a boiling water canner for 15 minutes for pints or 20 minutes for quarts.
- Allow the jars to cool in a draft-free place for at least 12 hours before removing the bands, labeling, and storing in a cool dry place for up to two years.
- Enjoy!

## *Jellies*

Jellies are made from fruit juice and sugar, and use heat and sugar for their preservation. The distinctive consistency of jelly comes from an interaction between the acids in the fruit, the pectin it contains, the sugar, and heat. Many fruits contain enough natural acid and pectin to make jelly without having to add anything but sugar. These include sour apples, crab apples, sour cane fruits, cranberries, gooseberries, grapes, and currants. Some fruits are slightly deficient in acid, pectin, or both and will require a small amount of added lemon juice, pectin, or both.

These include ripe apples, ripe blackberries, wine grapes, cherries, and elderberries. Finally, some fruits simply won't make jelly without adding a significant quantity of lemon juice and/or pectin. These include strawberries, apricots, plums, pears, blueberries, and raspberries.

Because sugar plays an important role in the preservation of jellies, the amount called for in a recipe shouldn't be reduced. It also plays an important role in making the product gel, so using too little sugar can result in a syrup instead of a jelly.

The juice used to make jelly can be extracted in a number of ways. If you use a juice machine, use it only for fruits that would require added pectin anyway, such as berries, plums, and pears. This is because a juice machine won't properly extract the pectin from high-pectin fruits. The traditional way of extracting the juice is to clean and cut up the whole fruit (it is important to leave the peels on because pectin is concentrated near the peel) and put it in a flat-bottom pot on the stove with added water. For soft fruits, use just enough water to prevent scorching, but with hard fruits like pears you might need as much as a cup of water per pound of fruit. The fruit is cooked over medium heat until soft and then poured through a jelly bag. If you want a crystal-clear product (which I don't personally care about but many folks find aesthetically important), it is important not to squeeze the jelly bag but instead let the juice come through naturally and slowly. You should get about one cup of juice per pound of fruit. Jelly bags in various sizes can be purchased from cooking stores and over the Internet. If you use a juice machine, you should still strain the resulting juice through a jelly bag. If you can't find jelly bags, you can use a double-layer of cheesecloth lining a colander instead.

Once the juice has been extracted, it is combined with sugar and other ingredients (e.g., lemon juice and/or pectin depending on the recipe) and boiled on the stove until it reaches a temperature of 220 degrees as measured with a candy thermometer. The boiling point of pure water is 212 degrees, but that boiling point is raised when other substances such as sugar are added to the water. As water evaporates and the proportion of sugar in the water increases, the boiling point will slowly increase. If you live in the mountains, subtract 2 degrees for every 1,000 feet you live above sea level. So if you live at 3,000 feet, subtract 6 degrees—so boil the mixture only until it reaches 214 degrees. This is because the higher you are above sea level, the more easily water will evaporate because of lower air pressure.

Once the required temperature has been reached, fill sterilized jars with the hot mixture up to 1/4 inch from the top, put the two-piece caps on the jars finger-tight, and process in a boiling water canner for five minutes for half-pint or pint size. There are all sorts of jelly recipes on the Internet, but here are two of my favorites.

**Strawberry Rhubarb Jelly**
- 3 pints of strawberries
- 1-1/2 lbs of rhubarb stalks
- 6 cups of sugar
- 3/4 cup of liquid pectin

Pulverize and then liquefy the strawberries and rhubarb in a blender. Using either a jelly bag or two layers of cheesecloth, gently squeeze out 3-1/2 cups of juice and put it in a saucepan, mixing with the sugar, and then bring to a rolling boil. Add the pectin and allow to boil vigorously for *one minute only,* remove from heat, and immediately pour into hot sterile jars, leaving 1/4 inch of headspace. Process five minutes in a boiling water canner. Yield: 5 half-pints.

**Apple Jelly**
- 5 lbs apples
- 5 whole cloves

- 1/2 tsp cinnamon
- 8 cups water
- 8 cups sugar

Wash the apples and cut them in quarters, and put them in a covered casserole pan with the eight cups of water and spices. Put in the oven at 225 degrees overnight. In the morning, strain through cheesecloth or a jelly bag and collect the liquid. Add it to the cooking pot one cup at a time, simultaneously adding one cup of sugar for every cup of liquid. Heat to a rolling boil, stirring constantly, and check with a candy thermometer until it is boiling at 220 degrees. Immediately pour into hot sterilized pint or half-pint jars, tighten the lids finger-tight, and process for five minutes in a boiling water canner. Yield: 8 half-pints.

✶

The same techniques covered in the recipes above can be used successfully with other fruits. For fruits high in natural pectin and acid, use the second recipe as a guide, and use the first recipe as a guide for fruits lacking pectin. For fruits that lack both pectin and acidity, use the first recipe as a guide but add 1-1/2 tsp of lemon juice per cup of liquid. Jams are made the same way except the entire fruit is pulverized and used, rather than just the juice.

## Brined Pickles and Kraut

Pickling preserves food by raising its level of acidity. It is used for foods that are not naturally acidic enough to be safely canned using a boiling water method. The two methods most widely used are lactic acid fermentation in brine, and infusing with vinegar.

Brine fermentation is most often used with cucumbers to make kosher-style dill pickles, but it is also used to make sauerkraut. Many other vegetables—like collard greens—can also be processed this way, but since I've never tried it myself, I can't guarantee the results will be tasty! There are three very important aspects of doing brine fermentation. First, keep everything clean. Second, use only plain salt with no additives whatsoever, or all sorts of cloudiness and discolorations will result. (Regular salt contains anticaking agents that will make the brine cloudy as well as iodine that will inhibit proper fermentation. Use canning salt!) Finally, pay close attention to the correct procedure, or your pickles will be soft and possibly even slimy.

Brine fermentation can take several weeks. It is also temperature sensitive and works best at temperatures ranging from 55 to 75 degrees. Before starting brined pickles, make sure you have both the time and the space to leave the containers undisturbed for a while. You should only use glass, nonchipped enamel, or food-grade plastic containers for fermentation. Under no circumstances should you consider using a metallic container because the product will become contaminated and possibly even poisonous. Don't use old-fashioned wooden barrels because sterilizing them is practically impossible. Start off with well-cleaned containers and well-washed produce.

### Brined Dill Pickles
- 5 lbs of 3- to 4-inch pickling cucumbers
- 3 heaping Tbsp whole pickling spice
- 8 heads of fresh dill (1/3 of a bunch)
- 3/4 cup white (distilled) vinegar
- 1/2 cup pickling salt
- 5 pints (10 cups) of clean pure water

The proportions of salt, vinegar, and water in this recipe are not approximations—measure them exactly! You can double or quadruple the recipe if you keep the proportions the same for a larger batch of pickles. Put half of the pickling spices and a light layer of dill in the bottom of a clean food-grade plastic pail or pickling crock. Put in the cucumbers. Mix the remaining dill and spices with the salt, vinegar, and water and pour over the cucumbers. If the amount of liquid isn't enough to come about two inches above the cucumbers, make more liquid from water, salt, and vinegar according to the same proportions. Take a clean plate and place it on top of the cucumbers so they are held completely under the brine. The plate may need to be weighted down with a second plate. Cover the container loosely with plastic wrap covered with a clean towel held on with a couple of bungee cords tied together around the container like a big rubber band. Try to keep at room temperature—certainly no warmer than 72 degrees and no cooler than 60 degrees.

Uncover and check the pickles for scum once a day. Use a clean spoon to scoop off any scum, then put the towel back on. This should be the only time the pickles are uncovered. After three weeks, check the pickles by removing one from the container, cutting it lengthwise, and tasting it. If it is translucent and tastes like a good dill pickle, you are ready to can the pickles. If not, wait another week and try again.

Once the pickles are ready, remove them from the brine and pack into cleaned and cooled glass jars with a couple of heads of dill added to each jar. Take the brine, pour it into a large saucepan, and bring it to a boil, then pour it over the pickles in the jars, leaving 1/4-inch head-space. If you run out of brine, make additional brine from 4 pints of water, 1/4 cup of salt and 2 cups of vinegar raised to boiling. (Again, proportions are exact rather than approximate—use measuring cups!)

Put the lids on finger-tight, and process 10 minutes for pints or 15 minutes for quarts in a boiling water canner. Yield: 10 pints.

### Sauerkraut
- Cabbage
- Canning/pickling salt

Any sort of cabbage can be used for this recipe, but larger heads tend to be sweeter. Remove any damaged outer leaves, quarter the heads, and remove the hard cores, then weigh the cabbage on a kitchen scale. Weighing the cabbage is important because the weight determines the amount of salt to use—3 Tbsp of salt per 5 pounds of cabbage. Shred the cabbage into slices of about 1/8 inch thickness, and using clean hands thoroughly mix the cabbage with the salt. Put the mixture into a five-gallon food-grade plastic container a little at a time and use a clean potato masher to mash the mixture until enough juice has been squeezed out of the cabbage that at least one or two inches of juice are above the cabbage by the time all the cabbage has been added.

Fill and seal a noncolored food-grade plastic bag with a mixture of 6 Tbsp salt and one gallon of water, and put this on the cabbage to weigh it down and keep it completely submerged, then cover the top of the container with plastic wrap. Keep the container at room temperature, and in four weeks, your sauerkraut will be ready. Just like with the brined pickles above, check daily for scum and remove any that you find. Once the kraut is ready, pour it in a large pot (or a portion of it at a time depending on the relative size of your pot) and heat while stirring to 190 degrees as indicated by a candy thermometer. Do NOT let it boil. Pack into clean canning jars and add brine to leave 1/4 inch of headspace, and process in a boiling water canner for 15 minutes for pints or 20 minutes for quarts. Yield: depends on how much cabbage you use.

## Quick Process Pickles

Quick process pickles rely on vinegar for their acidity rather than fermentation, so they are faster and easier to make. (And you needn't worry about scum!) The vinegar used to make pickles lends its own character to the pickles, so be cautious about using flavored vinegars such as red wine, cider, or balsamic vinegar unless specifically required in a recipe. When the type of vinegar isn't mentioned in a recipe, use white distilled vinegar. The preservation process relies on a certain specific amount of acid, so always use vinegar that is 5% acidity.

**Bread and Butter Pickles**
- 4 lbs cucumbers, washed but not peeled
- 3 thinly sliced medium onions
- 1/3 cup of canning salt
- 4 cups distilled vinegar
- 3 cups sugar
- 2 Tbsp mustard seed
- 1 Tbsp + 1 tsp celery seed
- 1-1/2 tsp turmeric
- 2 tsp whole black pepper

Slice the cucumbers 1/4-inch thick and the onions as thinly as practical. Combine all of the ingredients except the cucumbers and onions in a large sauce pot and bring to a simmer (not a boil!). Add the cucumber and onion slices, and bring to a very light boil before turning down the heat to low. Pack the slices into jars and then fill with pickling liquid to 1/4 inch headspace, and put the lids on the jars finger-tight.

For the most crisp pickles, pasteurize by placing the jars in water deep enough to be at least 1 inch over the top of the jar lids that is kept at 180–185 degrees (check with a candy thermometer) for 30 minutes. Alternately, you can process in boiling water for 10 minutes for either pints or quarts. Allow to sit six weeks before using for the development of full flavor. Yield: 4 pints.

# Vegetables

Vegetables (other than tomatoes) are not acidic enough to be canned using the boiling water method. Instead, they must be processed in a pressure canner for a fairly long period of time. The process is essentially the same for all vegetables, the only difference being in the processing time. For larger vegetables, cut into pieces so that there is at least one dimension less than 1/2-inch thick, bring pieces to a boil in water (to which 1/2 tsp of salt per quart can optionally be added), pour hot into clean jars allowing the right amount of head space, put on the caps finger-tight, and process for the time specified in Table 19. You might consider using a little sliver (1/2-inch × 1-inch) of kombu kelp instead of salt. Kelp enhances the flavor of canned vegetables because of the natural glutamaic acid that it contains.

Generally, the pressure canning methods employed with vegetables destroy a good portion of the vitamin C, so I recommend freezing instead. Regardless, the macronutrient and mineral values of vegetables remain intact after canning, so it is worthwhile if you don't have a freezer or reliable electric service.

# Meat

Meat is usually better vacuum sealed and frozen, but where the electrical supply is unreliable or too expensive, canning meat is a viable alternative. Because canning times and temperatures for meats are significant, most vitamins that can be destroyed by heat, especially vitamin C, are destroyed in the process. On the other hand, both the protein and mineral value is unaffected, so as long as you have plenty of vegetables in your diet, canned meat isn't a problem.

While the USDA says that putting raw meat into jars and then processing it is safe, it is my opinion that the flavor suffers. So I recommend that all meats first be soaked for an hour in a brine made with 1 Tbsp salt to a gallon of water and then at least lightly browned in a little vegetable oil until rare and then packing into the jars. Once the meat is packed into the jars, the jars should be filled with boiling water, meat broth, or tomato juice to leave the amount of headspace described in Table 19. Most people prefer 1/2 tsp of salt added per pint, but this is optional. Put on the lids finger-tight, and process for the appropriate length of time. You can season meats before canning them, but avoid sage because the prolonged high temperatures can cause bitterness. Also, any meat broth you use *shouldn't contain flour, corn starch, or any other thickening agent* because under pressure canning conditions, thickening agents congeal and make it impossible to get all of the air properly evacuated from the cans, and the risk of spoilage is increased.

## Soups, Stews, and Other Mixtures

When canning anything that is a mixture of more than one ingredient, the time and head-space requirements from Table 19 that are the longest and largest for any of the ingredients apply. So if, for example, a mixture of carrots and peas were being canned, the processing time and headspace requirements for peas would be used since those are the greatest. The same warning about thickening agents regarding meats applies to stews as well.

### Buffalo Stew
- 4 lbs buffalo stew meat cut into 1-inch cubes
- 12 medium red potatoes cut into 1/2 inch cubes
- 5 medium yellow onions, diced
- 2 lbs of carrots sliced 1/4-inch thick
- 2 stalks celery
- 1 Tbsp cooking oil

- 1 tsp salt
- 1/2 tsp ground black pepper
- 1 tsp thyme
- 1 clove garlic
- 3 quarts water

Get the three quarts of water boiling in a large saucepan and brown the stew meat in oil in the bottom of another large saucepan. Add all of the spices and vegetables to the meat, stir thoroughly, cover, and allow to cook down for five minutes. Then pour in the three quarts of boiling water slowly and carefully, and bring everything to a boil. Put into jars leaving 1 inch of headspace, and process in a pressure canner for 75 minutes for pints or 90 minutes for quarts. Yield: 9 pints.

# Freezing

**Like canning, freezing** has its pros and cons. In its favor is that it is easier and quicker to freeze vegetables and meats than it is to pressure can them, and the resulting product is usually closer to fresh in terms of quality. Some things, like broccoli, are just plain inedible when canned but perfectly fine when frozen. The downside is that when freezing an appreciable amount of food, a large freezer is required—which isn't cheap. Figure at least $300 for a new one at current market price. Also a consideration is the ongoing ever-increasing cost of electricity. And, if you are in an area prone to long electrical outages, you could lose the entire contents of your freezer if you don't maintain a backup power supply of some sort. So you'll have to weigh the advantages and disadvantages. We have a reliable electric supply and not a lot of spare time at my house, so we do a lot of freezing.

I used to freeze in regular freezer bags from the grocery store or wrap things in freezer paper. No more! Now, the only method I use, and the only method I recommend, is vacuum sealing. Vacuum sealing consistently yields a superior product that keeps up to five times longer, so it is what I'll describe.

## Getting a Sealer

I got my first vacuum sealer at a Boy Scouts yard sale, complete with instructions and a bunch of bags, for $3. Evidently, people often purchase sealers thinking they will be handy and use them once or twice, and then they end up in the yard sale bin. It may not be practical to wait around for a sealer to show up at a yard sale while harvest season comes and goes—but it never hurts to look.

There is another big reason why these sealers end up in the yard sale bin: the price of bags. The name-brand bags at the store that carry the same name as the sealer you buy will cost over $0.50 each. You don't have to do a lot of math to see that spending that much on just the bag to store a product (like broccoli) that you could buy frozen at the store for $0.99 isn't a winning proposition. I'll give you some solutions to that problem in the next section.

There are two suitable sealers on the market in various configurations available at department stores—the Seal-a-Meal and the FoodSaver. I've found both to be adequate, though you will find the FoodSaver a bit more expensive. I prefer the Seal-a-Meal since its design allows it to work better with a wide variety of bags. These are light-duty home-use units. They work fine for the amount of freezing that I do for the carbohydrates and vegetables for a family of three because we tend to freeze in relatively small batches of 10 or fewer packages at a time. Heavy-duty commercial units are available— but you should hold off on these until you see if the less expensive home-use units will meet your needs. Certainly they will work fine as you ramp up for the first couple of years.

## Bags

As mentioned earlier, the name-brand bags for sealers are expensive—sometimes even more than $0.50 apiece. Luckily, you can get around this problem a number of ways. First, keep an eye out for the sealers and bags at yard sales. Second, use plastic rolls instead of premade bags because by cutting them to size for what you are freezing, you will use a lot less and save money. Finally, you can buy bags and rolls from brands other than those made by the manufacturer of your sealer. Two sources come to mind. First, a number of manufacturers make less expensive bags and/or rolls including Black and Decker, FoodFresh Vacstrip, and Magic Vac. These usually cost less than half of what the other bags do. Second, check the Internet. There are eBay stores dedicated strictly to vacuum sealers that offer good deals and also Web sites dedicated entirely to getting good prices on bags, such as vacuum-sealer-bags.com. With these resources in hand, you will see the superior properties of vacuum sealing become financially viable.

❂ Weighing produce for consistent portions helps with menu planning.

## The Freezing Process

Freezing is a six-part process that requires harvesting, blanching, cooling, drying, sealing, and freezing. First, since no form of food preservation can actually improve the quality of food, harvest as close to freezing time as possible, and thoroughly clean the produce. Hose it off with the garden hose outside first, then put it in a big bucket to soak that contains two tablespoons of salt per gallon of water to draw out any insects. Then cut it up as needed, rinse out the salt, and weigh it into portions using a kitchen scale. For vegetables, figure 4 ounces per person. So for a family of four, you'll want your bagged portions to be about 16 ounces, or 12 ounces for a family of three.

◆ This steam blancher is just one of many steamers available.

◆ Cooling down the produce in ice water after blanching.

Next comes blanching. Blanching serves to inhibit the enzymes that destroy the quality of food in storage. There are two common methods—placing the produce in boiling water for a period of time, or steaming it for a slightly longer period of time. Both methods work, but I recommend steaming because it preserves more of the vitamin content of the

*Table 18:* **Blanching Times**

| Produce | Water Blanch | Steam Blanch |
|---|---|---|
| Artichoke, globe | 7–10 min | Not recommended |
| Artichoke, Jerusalem (chunks) | 5 min | 7 min |
| Asparagus spears | 3 min | 4 min |
| Beans, lima, butter, edamame | 3 min | 5 min |
| Beans, string | 4 min | 6 min |
| Beet roots, sliced 1/4" | 12 min | Not recommended |
| Broccoli | 4 min | 4 min |
| Brussels sprouts | 4 min | 6 min |
| Cabbage, shredded | 2 min | 3 min |
| Carrots | 3 min | 5 min |
| Corn (on the cob) | 10 min | Not recommended |
| Corn (whole kernel) | 5 min | 7 min |
| Greens of all sorts | 3 min | 5 min |
| Parsnips, sliced | 2 min | 3 min |
| Peas, shelled of all sorts | 2 min | 3 min |
| Peppers | 3 min | 4 min |
| Potatoes, sliced/cubed | 5 min | 7 min |
| Turnips, diced | 3 min | 4 min |

food. The blanching time varies depending on what is being frozen (see Table 18).

When the allotted blanching time has passed, the produce should be dumped into a bucket of ice water so that it is cooled down immediately. (I slip a metal colander into the bucket first so that it holds the produce and makes it easy to retrieve.)

Leave the produce in the ice water for the same amount of time as it was being blanched, then take it out and put it between a couple of superclean, dry, and fluffy towels to pat dry. You have to do this

⊗ Drying the produce with freshly cleaned towels before bagging.

For some vegetables, particularly potatoes, and Jerusalem artichokes, discoloration can be a problem. This is easily solved by adding one tablespoon of citric acid or two tablespoons of lemon juice per gallon of water to the ice water being used to cool the vegetables after blanching.

Meats and fruits aren't handled the same way as vegetables. Usually, meats are frozen raw, though I find that they freeze better if first soaked in a light brine (one tablespoon salt/gallon) to draw out any blood and then patted dry. The reason for drawing out the blood is so it doesn't

when vacuum sealing otherwise the large water content gets in the way of making a good seal.

Once the produce has been dried, it is placed into bags and sealed. After the bags have been sealed, put them into the freezer in various locations so that they will freeze more quickly. Come back and rearrange them in 24 hours.

⊗ Sealing with a vacuum sealer preserves freshness longer.

interfere with vacuum sealing. Another way to accomplish the same thing (which I do with ground meats) is put the meat in a regular zipper bag and put it in the freezer overnight, then remove it from the zipper bag and immediately seal it in a vacuum bag—the frozen juices then won't interfere with sealing. With wild game such as squirrel or deer, I recommend soaking for an hour in a light brine, as that removes some of the "gaminess" from the meat.

Fruit is best frozen in a sugar syrup like used when canning. Once the sugar is dissolved in the water, you can add 1/4 teaspoon of vitamin C or 2 teaspoons of lemon juice per pint of syrup to prevent darkening. Slice or dice the fruit and put it in a can or freeze jar or suitable plastic container and then cover the fruit with syrup, leaving one inch of headspace to allow for expansion in the freezer.

# Dehydrating

**Drying food is** one of the oldest methods of food preservation. By removing most of the moisture from foods, enzymatic action and microbial growth are retarded, and the food will keep for a long time. Food loses more nutritional value from drying than from freezing, and dehydrated foods will seldom reconstitute with water to look like appetizing fresh produce. But even at that, dehydrated products make a conveniently stored, tasty, and healthy addition to soups, stews, and sauces. When my daughter was little, I used to powder mixed dehydrated vegetables in a blender and stir that powder into her spaghetti sauce so she'd get a mix of vegetables without knowing it. She also loves dehydrated apple rings as a snack, and other dehydrated fruits make a great addition to oatmeal in the morning.

Just like vacuum sealers, dehydrators run the gamut from inexpensive units available at department stores costing less than $50 all the way to commercial-sized behemoths. I recommend starting with a small model that includes a fan and thermostat since that will be easy and trouble free. You can always switch to a more expensive commercial or even homemade unit later. (Dehydrators lend themselves easily to homemade solutions, and literally dozens of free designs—including solar designs—are available on the Internet just by doing a Web search that includes the terms "homemade" and "dehydrator.") You can use a dehydrator for fruits, vegetables, and meats, though the process for the three is somewhat different.

Vegetables destined for the dehydrator need to be cut in slices no more than 1/4 inch thick and blanched just as though they were going to be frozen. This helps them dehydrate better and keep longer. Fruits should also be sliced no more than 1/4-inch thick and then dipped in a solution containing one tablespoon lemon juice per quart of water before being put in the dehydrator. Fruit shouldn't be blanched. Every dehydrator is different in terms of its drying characteristics, so use the drying times and temperatures recommended in the literature that comes with your particular model.

Meats, especially ground meat and poultry, are problematic because dehydrating is not the same thing as cooking, and the temperature seldom gets high enough to ensure pathogen destruction. This becomes an issue because bacterial contamination of these meats is common, so failure to thoroughly cook them can result in serious illness or even death. There are some jerky mixes available at department stores that are specifically formulated to deal with potential contamination of ground meats through the use of nitrites. If you choose to use one of these mixes, follow the directions precisely! Outside of this exception, I don't recommend making jerky or dried meat from either ground meats or poultry. Other meats—like beef steak/roast, venison, buffalo, and so forth—are perfectly fine.

Most jerky recipes are for raw meat. In recent years, a number of universities have done studies and concluded that the practice can no longer be considered safe and that meat for jerky should be precooked in a boiling marinade. With the foregoing in mind, then, here is my general-purpose jerky recipe.

### Brett's General-Purpose Jerky

- Start with prefrozen and partially thawed beef, buffalo, moose, venison, and so on. Trim away any visible fat and slice meat into uniform 1/4-inch-thick slices across the grain.
- Create marinade in a saucepan by combining 2-1/4 cups of water, 3/4 cup teriyaki soy sauce, 1/2 tsp of liquid smoke, and a dash of Tabasco sauce. Raise to a gentle rolling boil.
- Putting only a few strips of meat in at a time, boil a few strips in the marinade until uniformly gray then remove from the marinade with tongs and place on the drying rack of the dehydrator. Repeat this process until all of the meat strips have been used.
- Dry according to manufacturer's directions, or at a temperature of 140 to 150 degrees for six or more hours.
- Test to see if the jerky is done by taking a piece off the dehydrator, letting it cool to room temperature, then bending it. If it cracks but doesn't break, it is done.

# Root Cellaring

**Root cellaring is** one of the best methods of preserving certain foods, including onions, cabbage, potatoes, carrots, parsnips, and apples, among others. The key to success at cold storage is establishing conditions conducive to long storage life, and these conditions include darkness, certain temperatures, and particular ranges of humidity.

Many things can be preserved via root cellaring for some small period of time ranging from days to a couple of weeks, while others can be preserved for times ranging from several weeks to several months. Invariably, food that can be stored only for a short time is better preserved via some other method. This includes all brassicas except late cabbage, asparagus, beans, sweet corn, cucumbers, summer squash, lettuce, tomatoes, eggplant, spinach, melons, and peas.

Other foods, though, can be preserved in a root cellar for extended periods assuming proper temperatures and humidity are maintained. Unfortunately, these aren't the same for all crops, but thankfully we don't have to be too fine-grained in our specification because, in general, crops that do well in a root cellar fall into broad categories.

Everything but onions and garlic will do well with humidity ranging from 85% to 95%. Onions and garlic require humidity ranging from 50% to 75%. All fruits store best at temperatures as close to 32 degrees F as possible, and almost all vegetables as well, except for late potatoes, which do best at 35 degrees F to 40 degrees F.

So, in general, cold storage requires an environment that is humid, dark, and close to 32 degrees F without going under. The real question becomes how to create and maintain such an environment in homes that were not designed with root cellars.

If you have a cellar of any sort, a portion of it can be turned into a root cellar simply be walling off a corner, insulating the walls thoroughly, providing some sturdy shelves up off the floor, and installing some ventilation that will allow cool air to enter near the floor (PVC pipe is good for this) and warm air to exit near the ceiling. You'll want a thermometer so you can keep an eye on the temperature and shut off or limit ventilation if it starts to sink too low. (This may or may not be a problem depending on where you live.) If humidity is insufficient, you can add a humidifier.

Most produce should be placed in open-weave baskets and kept up off the floor and shouldn't be piled deeply as the pressure from the weight of produce on the lower layers could cause premature rotting. Fruits should be stored only one layer deep and, if possible, individually wrapped in tissue and not touching other fruit. Carrots and parsnips should have the tops snapped off and then be buried in dampened clean sand in a box sitting on the floor.

If you don't have a basement, you could bury a drum in the ground or build an external root cellar. For more details on how to build root cellars, check out the book *Root Cellaring* by Mike and Nancy Bubel.

*Table 19:* **Canning Times and Methods**

| Food | Packing Method | Head-space | Canning Method | Time for Pints | Time for Quarts |
|------|----------------|------------|----------------|----------------|-----------------|
| Apples (sliced) | Hot packed | 1/2" | Boiling water | 20 min | 25 min |
| Applesauce | Hot packed | 1/2" | Boiling water | 15 min | 20 min |
| Asparagus | Hot packed | 1" | Pressure (10 lbs) | 30 min | 40 min |

| Food | Packing Method | Head-space | Canning Method | Time for Pints | Time for Quarts |
|---|---|---|---|---|---|
| Beans (dry) | Hot packed | 1" | Pressure (10 lbs) | 75 min | 90 min |
| Beans (shelled lima) | Hot packed | 1" | Pressure (10 lbs) | 40 min | 50 min |
| Beans (snap) | Hot packed | 1" | Pressure (10 lbs) | 20 min | 25 min |
| Beef, lamb, pork, venison, and bear (strips, cubes, ground, or chopped) | Hot packed | 1" | Pressure (10 lbs) | 75 min | 90 min |
| Beets (sliced) | Hot packed | 1" | Pressure (10 lbs) | 30 min | 35 min |
| Berries (all types) | Either | 1/2" | Boiling water | 10 min | 15 min |
| Carrots (sliced) | Hot packed | 1" | Pressure (10 lbs) | 25 min | 30 min |
| Cherries | Fresh packed | 1/2" | Boiling water | 20 min | 25 min |
| Cherries | Hot packed | 1/2" | Boiling water | 10 min | 15 min |
| Corn | Hot packed | 1" | Pressure (10 lbs) | 55 min | 85 min |
| Fish | Fresh packed | 1" | Pressure (10 lbs) | 100 min | Don't use quarts |

| Food | Packing Method | Head-space | Canning Method | Time for Pints | Time for Quarts |
|---|---|---|---|---|---|
| Fruit purees | Hot packed | 1/4" | Boiling water | 15 min | 20 min |
| Greens, spinach, chard, kale, collards | Hot packed | 1" | Pressure (10 lbs) | 70 min | 90 min |
| Jams and jellies | Hot packed | 1/4" | Boiling water | 5 min | Don't use quarts |
| Meat stock (any nonseafood meat with seasoning) | Hot packed | 1" | Pressure (10 lbs) | 20 min | 25 min |
| Peaches, pears, plums, and nectarines | Fresh packed | 1/2" | Boiling water | 25 min | 30 min |
| Peaches, pears, plums, and nectarines | Hot packed | 1/2" | Boiling water | 20 min | 25 min |
| Peas (shelled) | Hot packed | 1" | Pressure (10 lbs) | 40 min | 40 min |
| Peppers (hot/sweet) | Hot packed | 1" | Pressure (10 lbs) | 35 min | Don't use quarts |
| Pickles (fermented) | Fresh packed | 1/2" | Boiling water | 10 min | 15 min |

| Food | Packing Method | Head-space | Canning Method | Time for Pints | Time for Quarts |
|---|---|---|---|---|---|
| Pickles (quick process) | Hot or fresh | 1/4" | Boiling water | 10 min | 15 min |
| Potatoes (1/2" cubes) | Hot packed | 1" | Pressure (10 lbs) | 35 min | 40 min |
| Poultry, rabbit, or squirrel with bones | Hot packed | 1-1/2" | Pressure (10 lbs) | 65 min | 75 min |
| Poultry, rabbit, or squirrel without bones | Hot packed | 1-1/2" | Pressure (10 lbs) | 75 min | 90 min |
| Pumpkins and squash (pureed) | Hot packed | 1" | Pressure (10 lbs) | 55 min | 90 min |
| Rhubarb | Hot packed | 1/2" | Boiling water | 10 min | 10 min |
| Sweet potatoes (cubed) | Hot packed | 1" | Pressure (10 lbs) | 65 min | 90 min |
| Tomatoes (acidified) | Fresh packed | 1/4" | Boiling water | 40 min | 50 min |
| Tomatoes (acidified) | Hot packed | 1/4" | Boiling water | 35 min | 45 min |

# 11

# Planting Guides and Seeders

**Ah! The joy** of planting! Your beds are prepared and ready to accept the seeds that will bring forth an abundant harvest, and the anticipation feels almost electric as you breathe in the smell of soil mingled with the scents of spring. You rush out the door eagerly with packets of seeds in one hand and a map of where everything will go in the other.

About an hour later, after you have painstakingly punched about 200 precisely spaced holes in the soil at two-inch intervals, your back is aching, your knees are dirty and the mosquitoes have come out in force. All you have done is poke holes and you still haven't even planted a seed, but when it comes to that the seeds are so tiny you can barely pick them out of your hand. You know placing the seeds in the holes will take forever.

Intensive agricultural techniques that involve close plant spacings are certainly space efficient, but as you slap another blood sucker off your forearm, you start wondering if it is worth it. The produce aisle at the supermarket is starting to look appealing.

❷ Leveling

Let's face it—as much as we may enjoy the fruits of our labor, on some days the details of mini-farming are sheer drudgery, and the initial planting of tiny and closely spaced seeds such as mustard and carrot is enough to make you think twice. Whenever I try to handle seeds that small, my fingers feel about six feet thick and as clumsy as an ox. It's frustrating. And how on earth am I supposed to precisely space all of the holes for those seeds? After poking a couple of hundred holes, I want to space them further apart just to make the task end more quickly, and nature doesn't reward shortcuts.

❷ Tamping

❷ Making Holes

After thinking about these problems a bit, I developed a couple of solutions to making a lot of precisely spaced holes in your seedbed in a hurry, and have some methods for placing these seeds. This will help remove the drudgery and bring back the eager anticipation!

# All-Purpose Fixed Planting Guide

**Almost all seeds** or transplants are spaced at multiples of two or three inches. That is to say plants are spaced at two, three, four, six, eight, nine, twelve or eighteen inches. This means that with rare exceptions, **spacing** can be accommodated using fixed measurements of two or three inches.

An easy way to accomplish this is to take a piece of board, mark off two-inch intervals, and drill a long deck screw into each mark, leaving about an inch and a half protruding.

This board can be used to level the soil in a bed. It can also be used to tamp down the soil for a firm seed bed. Once the soil is leveled and tamped down, you can use the board to make hundreds of perfectly spaced seed holes in a hurry. To use it, lay it along the flattened soil in your bed, press the heads of the screws into the soil and wiggle it a bit. Now you have evenly spaced holes every two inches. If your seeds are spaced at four inches, just plant in every other hole. If they are spaced at six inches, then skip two holes after each one that is planted and so forth. So this board will work for spacings that are a multiple of two inches.

On the other edge of the board you can mark spacing at three inches, and this will work for spacings of three, six, nine, twelve inches and so forth. Using these two edges you can easily poke hundreds of perfectly spaced holes for seeds or transplants in just a minute.

Even better, the boards can also be used to make evenly spaced furrows for mesclun mix as well as evening out the soil in beds after mixing in soil amendments. After evening out the soil, you can use the flat side of the boards to pack down the soil a bit to make a picture-perfect seed bed prior to using the edge of the board to make the holes.

For this purpose, I would advise using 2"x4" stock between three and four feet long. Anything else will likely be either too fragile or too unwieldy. Once you have made the board, if you paint it with an exterior latex paint to protect it from the elements it will last for many years with just a touch-up of paint now and then.

# Adjustable Planting Guide

**The adjustable planting** guide is the Rolls Royce approach to this problem. It is more flexible but can easily cost as much as $50, plus is more difficult to make. Nevertheless, I made one and I have to admit is works really well and that the larger head leaves a better hole for seeds. The materials that I have used in this case are just one way of accomplishing this task. Once you see how it works, you can do the same thing using other materials.

## *Materials:*

1   6' length of ½" aluminum "U" channel
24   ⁵⁄₁₆" 18 thread bolts, stainless
48   ⁵⁄₁₆" 18 thread nuts, stainless

## *Tools:*

Hack saw
Drill or drill press
²¹⁄₆₄ drill bit
Combination square
Measuring tape
Metal scribe or sharp nail
Nail
Hammer

## *Procedure:*

Cut the aluminum U channel to a 4' length, saving the 2' piece for other projects.

Mark a center line along the exact center of the length of the channel using the combination square and a metal scribe or a fine-point magic marker. Using the measuring tape, use

the scribe to mark one inch intervals along the center line. Use the hammer and a nail to make a slight indentation at each intersection between the one inch interval and center line.

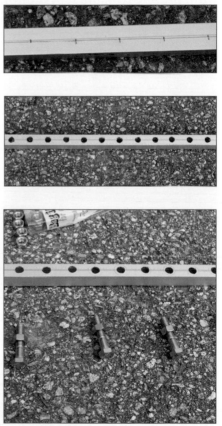

Drill a ²¹⁄₆₄ inch hole using the drill or drill press at each indentation.

To use the adjustable planting guide, put a nut onto the bolt, leaving an inch of the thread protruding.

Put another nut into the U channel above the hole into which the bolt will be inserted. (The U channel fits the nut perfectly so no wrenches are needed.)

Screw the bolt into the nut through the hole in the U channel. Do this for whatever distance is needed. Adjust the bolts and nuts for proper depth and a snug fit.

To use the planting guide, place the properly spaced bolt heads on leveled earth and press to leave an indentation of the required depth. Then, lift and place the guide a suitable distance from the first row and repeat until done.

# Putting Seeds in the Holes

**Larger seeds, such** as beans, peas, corn and so forth are easily handled and placed in the holes. But smaller seeds such as carrots, onions and lettuce can be challenging. It can be frustrating trying to pick up those seeds and place them in the beds one at a time. Usually, I use my daughter with her small fingers for such chores, but when she isn't around other options are required.

Some seed producers have come up with pelletized seed to help with this. Carrot and lettuce seeds are surrounded by a coating that makes it easy to handle by hand or in automated seeders. The coating dissolves once the seeds are watered. This is a pretty good solution but so far it has unfortunately only been applied to a few vegetables. Luckily, there are some other solutions, though they all require some practice to master.

Seed spoons are tiny spoons formed in bright yellow plastic. You hold the seed in the cup of your hand, and use the other hand to manipulate the spoon. If you pick the right size (it comes with four sizes), every time you push the spoon into the mass of seeds in your hand, you will pull it back out with exactly one seed. Then you can easily put it where you wish. These cost less than a packet of seeds and work well.

Another option is a "Dial Seed Sower." This device holds seeds in a reservoir and you regulate the rate at which seeds leave the reservoir to slide down a slick slide by changing the seed size on the dial and lightly shak-

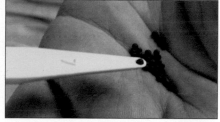

⊗ Seed spoon

ing the device. Once you get practiced at it, you can put exactly one seed of practically any size exactly where you want it.

Yet another option is a plunger-style hand seeder called the Mini-SeedMaster that looks like an oversized syringe. This takes a limited amount of seed into its canal at any given point in time and when held at a 45 degree angle it delivers seed from the reservoir to the soil with a depression of the plunger. I have found this works well with seeds like spinach and turnips, but not as well with the even smaller seeds such as carrot. Still, it allows planting a lot of chard in a hurry.

All of the foregoing devices are inexpensive in that they cost $10 or less. Considering that developing a bit of skill with them would easily repay their cost in time, they are a decent investment. At nearly $25, a vacuum hand seeder is a bit more expensive. This device uses a vacuum bulb with tips sized for the seeds you are planting. It allows you to pick up one seed at a time and deposit the seed where you'd like it. It requires a bit of manual dexterity, but once you get the hang of it you'll start using it for seeding your indoor transplants as well. It's a real time-saver.

## Dial Seed Sower

## Mini SeedMaster

A vacuum handseeder

# 12

# Easy Trellising

**Maximizing your productivity** per unit area depends on making the best possible use of the space available. For many crops, including pole beans, indeterminate tomatoes, cucumbers, peas and vining squash, this means using a trellis. The problem with trellising on a mini-farm is that because of crop rotation, you might need a trellis for a particular bed one year but not for the next three. Because of this, portability and easy setup/take-down are important factors.

In a prior book, I discussed using electrical conduit cut into designated lengths for this task. And that certainly works well, except that the conduit can be difficult to cut, tends to rust where it contacts the ground, and requires a screwdriver for assembly. That system is good and if you are already using it, that's great! If you aren't already using electrical conduit, or just need to expand your trellising, you might consider the PVC pipe method I describe here.

PVC pipe is UV-stabilized so it handles the elements well. It doesn't rust, and the pipe fits tightly into the fittings without need for tools. Assembly and disassembly are as easy as using Tinker Toys™, only the parts are larger. In comparing PVC pipe to galvanized electrical conduit, the conduit bears weight better but the PVC is considerably less expensive. Comparing the two, even though PVC pipe would need support in more places, it is still less expensive.

To start with this system, buy ten pieces of 10'-long ¾" schedule 40 PVC pipe. The first six pieces are cut into two pieces, one six feet long and the other four feet long. This gives you twelve uprights total: six that are six feet tall and six that are four feet tall. The remaining four pieces of pipe are each cut into two pieces 46-¾" long and one piece 22-¾" long. This will give you eight long cross-pieces and four short cross-pieces. You

⊗ Re-bar hammered into the ground

will also need a collection of fittings. You will need elbows for connecting the cross-pieces to the uprights at the ends of the bed, tees for connecting cross-pieces together and allowing for additional supports and side outlet elbows for running trellises around corners. You can get started with six of each. You can expand this system as needed by getting more PVC pipe and fittings, and cutting the PVC to the specified lengths.

Just as with the system based on electrical conduit, the pipe slides down over 18" pieces of rebar you have hammered straight into the ground at the ends of the bed and at four-foot intervals.

Four-foot intervals are required for most plants because PVC isn't as strong as electrical conduit. But if you decide to grow something extremely heavy, you can use the shorter cross-pieces and put more vertical supports using tees.

Place deck screws along the trellised side of the bed spaced every six or twelve inches as needed, and use these to anchor string or wire running between the bed and the cross-piece.

⊗ Deck screws along the trellised side of the bed.

# 13

# Overview of Winemaking

**Anyone who has** seen a wine critic on television can be a bit intimidated by the prospect of trying to make a wine that is even drinkable, much less enjoyable. Fortunately, Frederic Brochet conducted two studies using 57 wine experts at the University of Bordeaux in 2001 that will forever put the wine experts into perspective.[44]

In the first study, the experts were given two glasses of wine to describe, one being a white wine and the other a red wine. Unknown to the experts, both glasses were a white wine but the wine in one of the glasses had been dyed red. Not even one of the 57 experts at the University of Bordeaux could distinguish that the red wine was really white,

---

[44] Downey, R. (2002), Wine Snob Scandal, *Seattle Weekly*, Feb. 20, 2002

and they even went on to describe the fake red wine as having characteristics associated with red wines such as "tannic notes."

In the second study, a cheap wine was put into bottles denoting both a cheap and an expensive wine. Same wine, different bottles. The experts described the wine in the expensive bottles as "woody, complex, and round" while describing the exact same wine in the cheap bottles as "short, light, and faulty."

What this means is that you need not be intimidated by wine snobbery. All you need to do is make a sound product using good ingredients and proper methods, and as long as you put it in a nice bottle with a nice label and serve it in a nice glass it will be fully appreciated. Perception of the details really matters in the impression, so even if you performed your primary fermentation in a plastic bucket, don't you dare serve it in a plastic cup!

Winemaking is among the oldest methods of food preservation. In wine the levels of sugar in the original juice are reduced to make the juice unattractive to organisms that require sugar for growth, and the sugar is replaced with alcohol that makes the juice an inhospitable environment for most spoilage organisms. Meanwhile, many of the beneficial nutrients in the original juice are preserved, including vitamins and antioxidants. The yeast used to convert the sugar to alcohol also imparts a number of B vitamins to the mix.

Later, wine became an end in itself for which fruits were grown, and an entire culture and mythology have grown up around grapes, winemaking, and wine. What started as a method of preserving the essential nutrients of grapes and compensating for dangerous water supplies in an era when aseptic packaging and refrigeration did not exist has now grown into a multi-billion dollar global industry, and there are bottles of wine that can only be had for a cost exceeding that of a new car.

The term wine, in the purest sense of the term, applies only to the results of fermenting the juice of European vitis vinifera grapes. These are a species that is distinct from the grapes indigenous to North America, and only vitis vinifera grapes—and no other grape or fruit—have the right levels of sugar, tannin, acidity, and nutrients to produce wine without adding anything. Grapes grown in particular regions lend their unique flavors to wines named after them, such as Champagne; and wines produced by some wineries have even become status symbols, such as those produced by Château Lafite Rothschild.

Here, however, I am using the term "wine" to refer to country wines. That is, wines made from any fruit available and to which sugars, tannins, organic acids, spices, and other ingredients have been added to not only compensate for the areas in which the ingredients fall short of vitis vinifera grapes, but also to create their own experience of taste and smell.

Country wines are in no way inferior, and in fact being free of the constraints of traditional winemaking leaves you open to experiment broadly and create delightfully unique wines that are forever beyond the reach of traditional wineries. Home winemaking of up to 200 gallons annually is legal in the United States so long as you don't try to sell it. (If you try to sell it you will run afoul of the infamous "revenuers" who always get their culprit in the end.)

Americans drink nearly two gallons of wine per capita annually, meaning the consumption for a standard household is just shy of eight gallons. That's 40 bottles of wine. If you figure $12/bottle, that's nearly $500 per year. At that rate, and using fruit you either get inexpensively in season or free in your back yard, you will quickly recoup your investment in materials and supplies. In addition, homemade wines make excellent personal gifts; every year I give bottles to friends and business associates for holiday presents. The wine is always appreciated.

The technique of making wine is conceptually straightforward. The juice (and sometimes solids) of a fruit are purified of stray microbes and supplemented with sugar, acid, and other nutrients to make a must, inoculated with an appropriate strain of yeast, and fermented.

The fermentation takes place in two distinct phases. The first phase, known as the primary fermentation, is very fast and lasts only a couple of weeks. The wine is then siphoned (a process called racking) into a new vessel and fitted with an airlock where it may continue its secondary fermentation for several months with a racking again after the first couple of months or any time substantial sediment has formed.

I'll explain the specifics of the equipment throughout this chapter, along with some of the nuances. For now, I want to convey that if you normally consume wine or would give wine as a gift, making your own quality wines is inexpensive, fun, and easier than most would believe.

There are places where you will be tempted to skimp or make do on the list of ingredients and equipment I am about to present, but let me encourage you to get everything on the list. Because the techniques I describe rely on natural ingredients whose constituents will vary, all of the testing equipment is necessary. The other equipment and ingredients are necessary to maintain sanitary conditions or make a quality wine. If you don't live near a store for wine hobbyists, there are a number of excellent sources on the Internet that can be located via a web search. To save on shipping, I'd recommend getting as much from one store as possible.

# *Winemaking Equipment*
# Primary Fermenter

**The primary fermenter** is a large plastic bucket made of food-grade plastic. It is sized at least 20% larger than the largest batch of wine you plan to make in order to keep the constituents of the vigorous primary fermentation from spilling out of the fermenter and making a mess you will not soon forget. The bucket should be equipped with a lid and gasket, and also have provisions for fitting an airlock. These are available in various sizes from beer and wine hobby suppliers. I'd recommend a two-gallon and a six-gallon bucket. Even though it is possible to get these buckets for free from restaurants, I would advise against it as most were used to hold something that was previously been pickled using vinegar. You don't want vinegar organisms in your wine.

In general, the primary fermentation evolves carbon dioxide so rapidly that an airlock isn't strictly necessary. Furthermore, the first stages of fermentation require oxygen until the yeast cells multiply enough to reach a critical mass before the start of fermentation. Just plugging the hole in the lid with a clean cotton ball that allows air movement but blocks dirt, dust, and insects will suffice. (Replace the cotton ball if it becomes saturated with must.) Even so, I usually use an airlock after the first week.

It is possible for the smells and tastes of plastic to become infused into wine. This is not a concern for the primary fermentation because the wine is only in contact with the container for a couple of weeks. Also, you will have used a container of food grade plastic selected for its low diffusion which you cleaned thoroughly prior to use.

# Secondary Fermenter

**Because the wine** stays in contact with the secondary fermenter for months or even years, this is best made of glass. You can also use specially made oak casks for long secondary fermentation, but these are very expensive and need special care and maintenance. So for now, I would skip the oak casks.

The glass vessels come in various sizes from one gallon up to five gallons. The smaller one-gallon vessels are just one-gallon jugs, and the larger three- or five-gallon vessels are glass carboys used on water coolers.

You will also see some plastic carboys available in winemaking magazines and from various suppliers. These are advertised as being

⊗ One- and five-gallon primary and secondary fermenters.

made in a way that makes them impervious to the diffusion of the plastic into the wine, and they offer the advantage of being much lighter than glass so the shipping costs are lower. Nevertheless, plastic is harder to clean than glass, so I would not recommend these if glass can be obtained instead.

You will also need to get a special brush for cleaning your jug or carboy because the opening is too small for even the smallest hands and a regular bottle brush is too short and isn't bent for cleaning around the edges.

The fermentation that takes place in the secondary fermenter is long and slow. As the carbon dioxide is evolved more slowly, it is possible for air to be drawn into the vessel, especially if temperatures change. During secondary fermentation, you want to prevent oxygen from coming into contact with the wine, because oxygen adversely affects the quality of the wine by changing the character of some of the evolved organic compounds.

By fitting the hole in the fermenter with a stopper and an airlock, you will allow a protective blanket of carbon dioxide to cover the surface of your wine. You will need rubber stoppers with one hole in them that are sized correctly for your secondary fermenter. The airlock is prepared, put into the hole in the stopper, and then the stopper is placed in the hole at the top of the fermenter.

Because you will be racking your wine from one secondary fermenter into another, you need two secondary fermentation vessels.

One thing that people often overlook is a carrying handle. If you are making wine in batches larger than a gallon, those carboys are extremely heavy and difficult to handle. The handle that you order can be installed on a carboy and then removed to be used on another, so you only need one. They cost about $10 at the time of this writing and are well worth it as they make the task of handling carboys a great deal easier.

# Airlocks

**Airlocks are devices** installed on a fermenter that allow gas to escape, but do not allow air to leak back in. They come in a variety of configurations, but all are filled with water or a solution of potassium metabisulfite. The airlock is filled to the level specified on the device, inserted in a one-hole rubber stopper and then attached to the fermenter. You should have at least two of these. The style you choose doesn't usually matter, but if your wine will experience swings in temperature, avoid the type illustrated on the left because the liquid in it could be sucked back into the fermenter.

# Racking Tube

**A racking tube** is a long two-part tube that is inserted into the wine and pumped to start a siphoning action in order to transfer the wine from one container into another. It has a knob at the bottom that directs the flow of fluid in such a way as to minimize the amount of sediment transferred in the process. You will also need five feet of plastic tubing to go with it. A stop-cock, which is a plastic clip that can be used to stop the flow temporarily, will come in handy when using the racking tube to transfer wine into final wine bottles for corking.

Racking tubes come in two sizes; one that is smaller and will fit into a gallon jug and one that is larger and will not. Get the smaller one initially as it will work for both gallon jugs and five-gallon carboys.

Always clean your racking tube and plastic tubing before and after use, and run a gallon of sulphite solution through it to sterilize the components. Otherwise, it will accumulate debris attractive to fruit flies that carry vinegar bacteria and you will unwittingly start manufacturing vinegar instead of wine. The tubing is inexpensive and it is best to replace it after several uses.

# Corker

**Corkers are used** to insert corks into wine bottles. As you've discovered if you have ever tried to put a cork back into a wine bottle, corks are slightly larger than the holes they are intended to fit. A corker compresses the cork enough for it to slip inside the bottle. Corkers come in many sizes and styles, but I would recommend a metal two-armed lever model which, although somewhat more expensive than the plastic models, does a better job and will serve you well for your lifetime.

Corks need to be soaked before insertion. You don't want to inadvertently transfer a spoilage organism on the corks, so I recommend boiling the corks for 20 minutes and then allowing them to set in the boiled water for another 10 minutes before corking. This will make the corks pliable without contaminating them.

⊗ Vinyl tubing and racking tubes sized for five-and one-gallon fermenters

❂ I've had the corker on the left for eight years. The one on the right is just a toy.

Another problem you may encounter is the cork backing out of the bottle after it was inserted. This is caused by the fact that the cork fits so tightly that the air in the bottle is compressed as it is inserted. The compressed air forces the cork back out of the bottle. You can solve this problem with a bent sterilized paper clip. Straighten the paper clip except for a hook that you leave for it to hang on the edge of the bottle's mouth. Insert the straight part into the bottle mouth and leave it hooked in the edge. Insert the cork as usual. The paper clip has allowed room for compressed gases to escape. Pull the paper clip out and you are done.

# Wine Thief

**A wine thief** is a long tube with a special valve on the end that allows you to remove wine from a container very easily. Clean and sanitize it before and after use. It is generally recommend that wine removed not be returned to the container to avoid contamination. However, unless you have added an adulterant to the wine (such as sodium hydroxide for testing acidity), as long as the wine thief and any equipment used are cleaned and sanitized, I have never had a problem from putting the wine back into the same container.

The biggest reason why you would want to "steal" wine in this fashion is so it can be tested for specific gravity and acidity. I cover these tests and the required equipment extensively in the next chapters.

# Nylon Straining Bags

**These are fine-meshed** nylon bags with zippered closures used to hold fruit for crushing in a fashion that allows you to remove the solids later with minimal mess. The bags can be cleaned, sterilized, and re-used many times. These come in very handy when making wines from crushed blueberries, cherries, and similar fruits. They come in various sizes in order to accommodate different sized batches of fruits and wine.

# Wine Bottles

**You will need** wine bottles. Usually, light-colored wines are bottled in clear bottles and dark-colored wine in green or brown bottles. This is predominantly a social convention, though the darker glass serves the purpose of protecting the coloring matter in the wine from being bleached out by ultraviolet light and sunshine. Your wine should be stored well away from sunshine anyway.

Either way, you will certainly want to use real wine bottles that require a cork. Real wine bottles usually have a concave section at the bottom that allows for solid sediments to remain separate from the wine and have a top made to facilitate a perfect seal with a cork.

There is debate among experts over the use of plastic, screw-top caps, or genuine cork, and whether this has an effect on the long-term taste and quality of wine. In my opinion corks are best simply because they are easiest. Corks are inexpensive in quantity, easily inserted for a perfect seal using simple equipment, and will literally last forever if a bottle is stored on its side to keep it wet. Unlike the experts, I can't tell the difference between a wine stored in a corked bottle as opposed to one using a screw closure, but I recommend corking because it is easier and cheaper in the long run. Also, it just looks better, and the presentation of your wine is as important as any of its other qualities in terms of the reception it receives.

If you decide to make a sparkling wine, you will need to get bottles specifically for that purpose because ordinary wine bottles aren't rated for that pressure. You will also need special plastic corks and wire closures that will hold the corks in place on the bottle.

Wine bottles come in 375 ml and 750 ml sizes. You will need five of the 750 ml bottles or ten of the 375 ml bottles for each gallon of wine that you are bottling.

# Consolidated Equipment List

**The following list** will make it easy to get everything you will need for the foreseeable future in one shopping trip. I priced this out with a well-known Internet beer and wine hobby shop for $228.60 plus $63.22 for shipping. At that price for shipping, if you can find the gear locally it is worth the trip. You could also save some money by only getting the equipment needed to make one-gallon batches, and the equipment would only cost $134.75 plus $25.95 for shipping. These costs also don't take into account that it is often easy to get wine bottles for free. I get mine from a co-worker who works part-time at a bar. He brings me a few dozen empty bottles and I give him a couple bottles of wine yearly.

| | |
|---|---|
| 1 | Five or six gallon plastic fermenter with sealing plastic lid and grommet |
| 1 | Two gallon plastic fermenter with sealing plastic lid and grommet |
| 2 | Five gallon secondary fermenters, preferably glass |
| 2 | One gallon secondary fermenters, glass jugs |
| 1 | Cleaning brush for carboys |

| | |
|---|---|
| 1 | Carboy handle |
| 2 | #6.5 universal rubber stoppers with one hole |
| 2 | One-gallon secondary fermenters, glass |
| 2 | #6 rubber stoppers with one hole |
| 4 | Airlocks |
| 1 | Racking tube, sized to fit the one-gallon secondary fermenters, but will work with both |
| 5ft | ⅜" plastic tubing |
| 1 | Hose clamp, ⅜" |
| 1 | Wine thief |
| 2 | Nylon straining bags |
| 1 | Two-handed corker |
| 36 | Wine bottles |
| 50 | Corks |

❷ Airlocks, wine thief, racking tube, stoppers, corkers and other gear. These will give many years of faithful service if given proper care.

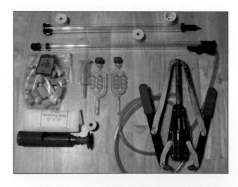

In addition to equipment, making country wines requires a variety of innocuous but nevertheless important additives. All fruits other than European grapes will require additional sugar in the form of either sugar or honey. Most fruits will lack sufficient acid, though without dilution a few may have too much. Likewise, most won't have sufficient tannin to give a properly wine-like mouth-feel. Of course, yeast will need to be added, and the fruits don't have enough nutrients on their own to sustain a healthy fermentation to completion, so nutrients will need to be added for the yeast.

# Citric, Malic, and Tartaric Acids

**Though most fruits** contain more than one of these acids, citric acid is usually associated with citrus fruits, malic acid with apples, and tartaric acid with grapes. You can buy these mixed together as a so-called "acid blend," but they are inexpensive and I recommend buying them separately. This way, you can use the right acid for the fruit you are using or the character you want your wine to have and you aren't locked in to the formula of a given manufacturer. If you are using a recipe that requires "acid blend" you can make it yourself by thoroughly mixing an equal quantity of each of the three acids together.

The acidity of your must should be checked prior to the beginning of fermentation. Most often, acid will need to be added.

# Grape Tannin

**Tannins are responsible** for the astringent taste of a wine. They are present in the skin and seeds of grapes, and so wines that result from conducting the primary fermentation with the skins and seeds will tend to have more tannin and have more astringency. White wines derived from pressed juice are therefore less astringent than red wines derived from fermenting with the skins.

Ingredients other than grapes can have more or less tannin content, and that content will vary based upon the amount of time whole fruit is left in the primary fermenter as well.

# Pectic Enzyme

**Pectic enzyme is** needed to break down the pectins in fruits so they won't leave a cloudy haze in the wine. Grapes have enough pectic enzyme naturally, but all other fruits you are likely to use will need some help.

# Fermentation Inhibitor

**It can be** difficult to judge when fermentation is completed. Early in winemaking it is also common for the home wine maker to be a bit impatient (and justifiably so!) for the finished product. The unfortunate side effect of bottling a bit too early is a wine bottle with a popped cork (and corresponding mess) or even a shattered bottle. Sometimes you can get lucky and just end up with a barely perceptible sentiment and a lightly sparkling wine. In wine judgings, this is considered a defect in a still wine, but for home use it is a delightful thing. Still, if you want to make sparkling wines it is better to make them on purpose rather than accidentally, because their accidental manufacture is attended by some risk.

Potassium sorbate, a semi-synthetic preservative that inhibits fermentation, is added to wines as a stabilizer to prevent further fermentation. It is used in two instances. First, to absolutely guarantee an end of fermentation in wines that are bottled young. Second, to stop fermentation in wines that are intentionally sweet and the only thing inhibiting the yeast is the high alcohol content.

The positive is that potassium sorbate works well, is generally accepted as safe, and will give you good insurance against exploding bottles. It is seldom noticeable at all when used for young wines and white wines. The downside is that it can develop off-smells in some wines over a period of years. So if you are making a wine that you plan to keep for many years, rather than using potassium sorbate I would recommend bulk aging it for at least a year in a secondary fermenter to assure the end of fermentation prior to bottling.

Another method of ending fermentation is to add supplemental alcohol to the wine in the form of brandy (which is distilled from wine). This process is called fortification. Raising the alcohol level in the wine above the alcohol tolerance of the yeast (usually 20%) assures its dormancy. Fortification is used in the manufacture of port wines. Port wines are typically sweet and dark, though some dry and white ports exist. These sweet wines were stabilized for shipping purposes by racking them into a secondary fermenter that already contained enough brandy (about ¼ of the volume of the wine) to raise the alcohol level to 18% to 20%. This brought about a quick end to fermentation while retaining as much as 10% residual sugar. The stability of port wines can allow them to keep for decades.

# Yeast Energizer

**Yeast energizer supplies** crucial nutrients for yeast that allow it to reproduce and do a good job of converting sugar to alcohol. Any wine made from anything but vitis vinifera grapes will need this. Yeast energizer usually contains food grade ammonium phosphate, magnesium sulfate, yeast hulls to supply lipids, and the entire vitamin B complex, of which thiamine (vitamin $B_1$) is the most important.

# Sulfite

**Sulfite is used** to retard spoilage organisms and wild yeasts and as an antioxidant. Though it is possible to make sulfite-free wine, its use increases the likelihood of success for beginners, particularly when they are using real fruits instead of pasteurized bottled juices. Sulfite is even permitted in wines labeled as USDA Organic.

You should get two forms of sulfite. The first is potassium metabisulfite in the form of Campden tablets. Campden tablets are sized with the idea in mind of accurate dosing of wine and musts to purify must prior to initiating fermentation and help clear and preserve the wine later. The second is powdered potassium metabisulfite. In powdered form it is used to make sterilizing solutions for sterilizing equipment.

# Yeast

**Home winemaking has** been popular so long across so many countries that there are literally hundreds of varieties of yeast available. Because covering them all would be a prodigious task, I want to cover some common yeasts that will be most generally useful for practically anything you'd like to try to turn into wine. Later, you can branch out and try the other excellent varieties of yeast that are available.

## Red Star Pasteur Champagne

This is an excellent all-around yeast for making dry wines. It produces glycerol as well as alcohol, and this gives wines a nice mouth-feel. I particularly like using this yeast in wines containing apple, pear, and flower ingredients because it produces fresh aromas that match these ingredients. It works well at lower temperatures, even as low as 55 degrees, and tolerates up to 16% alcohol.

## Red Star Montrachet Yeast

If you don't have much control of the ambient temperature of your must, this yeast is a good choice. It can work at temperatures ranging from 55 to 95 (though it does less well at the extremes than it does in the middle of that range), and produces less acetaldehyde than most yeasts. The aromas are nice, and with an alcohol tolerance of 15%, this yeast is well-adapted to making sweet port-style wines. I like using it to make blueberry and cherry wines.

## Lalvin D-47

If you'd like to make a dry white wine starting from apples or pears, this is an excellent choice. Its temperature range is narrow—only 58 to 68—but that makes it perfect for fermentations that proceed in the house during the winter when homes are usually maintained precisely in that range. The sediment formed by D-47 is compact, which makes racking easier.

## Lalvin ICV-D254

With an alcohol tolerance of 18%, ICV-D254 will ferment any practical must to dryness. This yeast ferments quickly, so you'll want to keep the temperature under 80 degrees to avoid foaming. You might want to keep the temperature even lower to preserve volatile flavor components because ICV-D254 creates a very complex and fruity flavor profile that really enhances the fruit character of a wine. This would be a good choice for blueberry wine.

## Wyeast 4632 Dry Mead Yeast

Meads, also known as honey wines, are enjoying a resurgence in popularity. Many yeasts will work to make mead, but this yeast in particular creates flavor notes that have resulted in many award-winning meads. The temperature range is 55 to 75, but you'll want to stay as close to 65 as you can to maximize flavor production. Wyeast 4632 has an alcohol tolerance of 18% and will result in a very dry mead.

# Consolidated Ingredient List

**The following ingredient** list will allow you to make many successful gallons of wine. As your experience expands, you may wish to adopt different materials and techniques; but most home wine makers find that this list is more than sufficient for their needs. In compiling this list, I went to two well-known online retailers of winemaking supplies, and in both cases the total cost was under $40. You can save $7 by omitting the Wyeast #4632 from the list.

| | |
|---|---|
| 4 oz | Citric acid |
| 4 oz | Malic acid |
| 4 oz | Tartaric acid |
| 2 oz | Liquid tannin |
| ½ oz | Pectic enzyme liquid |
| 2 oz | Yeast energizer |
| 1 oz | Potassium sorbate |
| 100 | Campden tablets |
| 4 oz | Powdered potassium metabisulfite |
| 2 pkt | Red Star Pasteur Champagne yeast |
| 2 pkt | Red Star Montrachet yeast |
| 2 pkt | Lalvin D-47 yeast |
| 2 pkt | Lalvin ICV-D254 yeast |
| 1 pkt | Wyeast #4632 Dry Mead yeast |

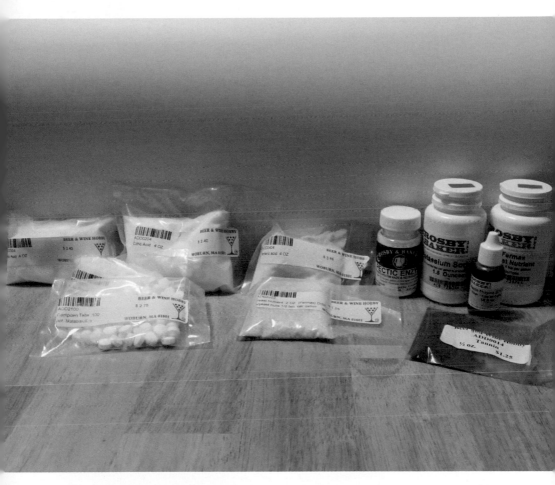

⊗ Important additives and adjuncts used for making wine. These are inexpensive and last a long time.

# 14

# The Science of Wine

**At its core,** the theory of making wine (also beer and bread) is nothing more than the conversion of sugar into ethyl alcohol and carbon dioxide by the enzymes in yeast:

glucose $\rightarrow$ ethyl alcohol + carbon dioxide + energy

$$C_6H_{12}O_6 \rightarrow 2(CH_3CH_2OH) + 2(CO_2) + Energy$$

Using the foregoing formula based upon the molecular weights[45] of the compounds, 180 grams of glucose will be converted into 92 grams of ethyl alcohol and 88 grams of carbon dioxide. This means that the yield of alcohol, by weight, in a

---

[45] The molecular weight of a compound is computed by adding the atomic weights from the periodic table of each constituent atom. The atomic weights of carbon, hydrogen and oxygen respectively are 12.0107, 1.00794 and 15.9994. So the molecular weight of glucose would be 6*12.0107 + 12*1.00794 + 6*15.9994. For ease of discussion I have rounded the results to the nearest gram.

perfect fermentation is 92/180 or 51%, and that nearly half of the weight of the sugar is lost in the form of carbon dioxide gas.

The density of glucose is 1.54 g/cm$^3$, so the volume occupied by 180 grams of glucose is 180/1.54 or 116.88 cm$^3$. The density of ethyl alcohol is .789 g/cm$^3$, and the volume occupied by 92 grams of ethyl alcohol is 92/.789 or 116.6 cm$^3$.

In other words, even though nearly half of the mass of sugar is lost in the form of carbon dioxide gas, the volume of the solution stays so nearly the same as to be indiscernible without resorting to very precise measurements.

Furthermore, the percentage of alcohol in beverages is not measured by mass, but rather by volume. This means that the volume occupied by alcohol in a completely fermented solution will be nearly identical to the volume of sugar that was in the solution. So if you know how much sugar is in a solution before fermentation starts, you know how much alcohol could be produced in a completed fermentation.

As we discussed a bit in the last chapter, what happens over the process of making wine is a lot more complex than a simple conversion of sugar into alcohol, so I'd like to expand on that some more.

# Sugar

**Unless you are** using vitis vinifera grapes, all of your wine musts will contain less sugar than is needed to make a self-preserving wine. The sugar content of common fruits (other than wine grapes) is insufficient. In order for a wine to be self-preserving without need for pasteurization or the addition of preservatives, it needs an alcohol content of at least 9%. In practice, because you may add water between rackings in order to fill air space, you'll want enough sugar to yield an alcohol content of 10% or higher.

# Measuring Sugar Levels

**Many winemaking books** and pamphlets are full of recipes that specify a certain fixed amount of sugar for a given fruit. Such recipes rely upon the false assumption that the sugar content of a given fruit is the same no matter how close to ripeness it was when harvested, how long it has been stored, or even the variety of the fruit in question.

The key to getting the sugar right is using a hydrometer. The hydrometer was discussed briefly in the previous chapter. As stated, it looks a lot like a thermometer with a big bulb on the end. It measures the amount of dissolved solids in a solution by how far it sinks. There is a long stem and a scale, and the specific gravity is read where the liquid touches the glass. This is important because the surface tension of the liquid will give a false reading anywhere else, so be sure to read the value where the liquid is touching the glass.

I use a wine thief that doubles as a hydrometer jar. So I clean and sanitize the wine thief and hydrometer, and then give the hydrometer a spin as I put it into the liquid. Giving the hydrometer a spin is necessary because otherwise air bubbles could cling to it and give it false buoyancy that would give inaccurate readings.

❷ Using the weight method of determining specific gravity.

Once you have your reading, you will need to correct it to compensate for the temperature of the must, because hydrometers are calibrated for 60 degrees. If the temperature is between 40 and 50 degrees, subtract 0.002 from the reading. If the temperature is between 50 and 55 degrees, subtract 0.001. If the temperature is between 65 and 75, add 0.001, and if the temperature is between 75 and 80, add 0.002. If the temperature is over 80, let it cool before measuring.

There is another method that I have never seen mentioned in books on winemaking, but I believe is superior even though it requires the use of math. The method is as follows:

Buy a jug of distilled water at the supermarket. Leave it at room temperature next to your primary fermenter so that it is at the same temperature (by doing this, you won't need to make temperature corrections later). Use a scale accurate to within 0.01g to weigh an empty and dry 10ml graduated cylinder.[46] Then fill the cylinder with 10 ml of the distilled water and record that weight. Finally, empty the cylinder, and using a large sterilized syringe, fill the graduated cylinder to the 10ml mark with wine must and record that weight. When measuring volume, put your eye at a level with the markings on the cylinder and fill until the lowest part of the liquid is perfectly aligned with the 10 ml mark.

We now have three numbers. A is the weight of the empty cylinder, B is the weight of the cylinder filled with distilled water, and C is the weight of the cylinder filled with wine must. The equation for the specific gravity is: $SG = (C-A)/(B-A)$. For example, my graduated cylinder weighs 37.65g. When filled with distilled water it weighs 47.64g, and when filled with a light sugar syrup it weights 48.57g. $SG = (48.57-37.65)/(47.64-37.65)$ or 1.093. Because both the distilled water and the must were weighed at the same temperature, temperature corrections aren't needed. Even better, the amount of must used for testing was truly tiny—less than an ounce. Discard the sample in the sink after testing.

---

[46] I use the American Weigh AWS-100 scale. Complete with calibration weights it costs less than $20. Graduated cylinders are likewise ubiquitously available online for less than $10. Get a glass one rather than plastic. Large syringes are available from livestock stores and online for less than $3. You don't need the needle.

# Adjusting Sugar Levels

**As I mentioned** earlier, in order for a wine to be self-preserving, it should have at least 9% alcohol. The following table gives you the potential alcohol based upon specific gravity, and how much sugar is present in a gallon of must to give you that much alcohol if it is completely fermented by the yeast.

Because water may be added to the wine at some rackings—thereby diluting the alcohol—you should also aim for a starting specific gravity that exceeds 1.080, corresponding to 10.6% alcohol. Also, even though a particular strain of yeast might have a theoretical alcohol tolerance exceeding 20%, such yeasts will not thrive in musts containing enough sugar to make that much alcohol. Higher levels of alcohol like that are achieved by fortification or by adding small amounts of sterile sugar syrup as existing sugars in the must are depleted. In order to avoid a fermentation failing due to excessive sugar levels, you should limit the initial specific gravity of your musts to no greater than 1.100, which corresponds to 13.6% alcohol. So, aim for a starting gravity between 1.080 and 1.100. In practice, I use 1.090 for almost all of my wines.

Almost all of your musts made from pressed or juiced fruits will contain insufficient levels of sugar to reach the minimum necessary alcohol content. Even though I am about to cover the math in more depth, the following shortcut equation will work fine:

Ounces of Sugar = (Desired S.G. - Measured S.G) x 360

If you decide to add honey rather than sugar, then multiply the amount of sugar needed by 1.3 to make up for the moisture content of honey. Ideally, you would use a scale for measuring sugar to be added; but if you don't have one, you can use measuring cups and allow for seven ounces of granulated sugar per cup.

| Specific Gravity | Potential Alcohol | Ounces Sugar Per Gallon Must |
|:---:|:---:|:---:|
| 1.000 | 0.0 | 0 |
| 1.004 | 0.6 | 1.4 |
| 1.008 | 1.1 | 2.8 |
| 1.012 | 1.7 | 4.3 |
| 1.016 | 2.2 | 5.7 |
| 1.019 | 2.6 | 6.8 |
| 1.023 | 3.2 | 8.2 |
| 1.027 | 3.7 | 9.6 |
| 1.031 | 4.3 | 11.0 |
| 1.035 | 4.8 | 12.4 |
| 1.039 | 5.4 | 13.9 |
| 1.043 | 5.9 | 15.3 |
| 1.047 | 6.5 | 16.7 |
| 1.050 | 6.9 | 17.8 |
| 1.054 | 7.4 | 19.2 |
| 1.058 | 8.0 | 20.6 |
| 1.062 | 8.6 | 22.0 |
| 1.066 | 9.1 | 23.5 |
| 1.070 | 9.7 | 24.9 |
| 1.074 | 10.2 | 26.3 |
| 1.078 | 10.8 | 27.7 |
| 1.081 | 11.2 | 28.8 |
| 1.085 | 11.7 | 30.2 |
| 1.089 | 12.3 | 31.6 |
| 1.093 | 12.8 | 33.1 |

*Specific Gravity Table*

For example, if you are making cyser from juiced apples and the measured S.G. of your must is 1.040 but you want a starting S.G. of 1.090, you first determine how much sugar is needed:

$$(1.090—1.040) \times 360 = 18 \text{ ounces}$$

Because you will be using honey instead of sugar, you'll multiply that by 1.3 to compensate for the moisture content of the honey: 18 x 1.3 = 23.4 ounces.

Sometimes, you might want to start with a high-quality bottled juice to make wine. You can tell how much sugar is in the juice just by reading the label, and it usually amounts to anywhere from 30g to 50g per 8 fl. oz. serving. Your first task in that case is to do unit conversion. Let me illustrate with an example.

I might have some 100% black cherry juice that I would like to turn into wine. It has 50g of sugar per eight-ounce glass. How many ounces of sugar does it have per gallon? A gallon is 128 ounces, so there are 16 eight-ounce glasses per gallon. So the total amount of sugar in a gallon of the juice is the amount in 16 eight-ounce glasses, or 16 x 50g = 800g. You convert grams to ounces by dividing by 28.35, so 800 g / 28.35 grams per ounce = 28.2 ounces of sugar per gallon. Looking at our table of specific gravities, we can see it already has plenty of sugar.

I may also have some organic concord grape juice that contains 40g of sugar per eight ounce glass. Doing the same math, (16 glasses x 40g)/28.35 = 22.6 ounces of sugar per gallon. That corresponds to only 8% alcohol, which is too low for a self-preserving wine. I want to bring it up to 12.3%, but to account for the increased volume from adding the sugar, I'll use the sugar quantity corresponding to 12.8% alcohol. So I need to add 33.1—22.6 = 10.5 ounces of sugar.

Sometimes using honey instead of cane sugar can give wine a really nice background flavor. When using honey as a substitute for sugar, just multiply the number of ounces needed by 1.3 to compensate for

| Fruit | S.G. Range | Fruit | S.G. Range |
|---|---|---|---|
| Apples | 1.040—1.060 | Blackberries | 1.020—1.035 |
| Blueberries | 1.045—1.055 | Currants | 1.042—1.060 |
| Cherries (sweet) | 1.045—1.075 | Cherries (tart) | 1.040—1.070 |
| Cranberries | 1.015—1.020 | Grapefruit | 1.028—1.041 |
| Lemon | 1.025—1.050 | Peach | 1.030—1.040 |
| Pear | 1.040—1.045 | Pineapple | 1.045—1.060 |
| Plum | 1.045—1.055 | Black Raspberry | 1.030—1.050 |
| Strawberry | 1.020—1.040 | Watermelon | 1.030—1.040 |

*Specific Gravity Ranges of Common Fruits*

the honey's water content. Many cookbooks advocate oiling the containers used for handling honey. Do not do this, as you'll end up with a persistent oily layer in your wine. Instead, heat the honey by placing the jar and any handling tools in simmering water. That will make it easier to use without adding oil to your must.

To give you some idea of how much sugar would need to be added to the juices of various fruits, I have included a table listing some fruits and the range of specific gravities I obtained when testing different varieties. Keep in mind that this is just a guideline. Don't substitute use of this table for testing the specific gravity yourself because the particular fruits you use will be of different varieties, grown in other places, and harvested at different times.

# Tannins

**Tannins are complex** polyphenols[47] produced by plants. In foods, they are bitter and astringent, and it is theorized that they serve to

---

[47] Phenol is a benzene ring compound with an -OH group on one of the carbons, making it an alcohol. Polyphenols are compounds composed of multiple phenol groups bonded together. The molecular weights of tannins range from 500 to more than 3000.

deter herbivores, though it is likely that they serve other purposes as well. Chemically, they can be divided into several categories, but they all have in common the characteristic that they are able to bind to proteins and precipitate them out of solutions.

Tannins are more present in the skins, seeds, and woody portions of plants. Hence, when red wine is made by fermenting the seeds and skins of the grapes, tannin is dissolved into the wine. The solubility of tannin is affected by the pH of the solution. Tannins are more soluble in neutral solutions than in acidic ones, and they are more soluble in alcohol than in water. So when a fermentation first starts, very little color and tannin is extracted but once some alcohol is produced, the extraction proceeds more rapidly. In addition, tannins are imparted to wines through aging processes that utilize oak barrels or the addition of oak cubes to the fermenter.

The ability of tannins to precipitate proteins has important implications for the aging of wines and beers. Precipitation refers to the dissolved tannins combining with dissolved proteins to form a compound that can't be dissolved. This compound, once formed, slowly sinks to the bottom of the vessel. When this happens, the astringent or bitter flavors imparted by the tannin are lessened and the haziness imparted by the protein is diminished.

Tannins are also chelators. That is, they combine with the ions (positively charged atoms) of metals in order to make them non-reactive. A major effect of tannins is that they combine with iron in such a way as to make it biologically useless to living things. Pathogenic bacteria love iron. They love iron so much that they invade the human body to get it.[48] One of the reasons why red wines keep so much better than others is because the tannins have tied up the iron, making the environment unattractive for pathogenic bacteria. Tannins also

---

[48] Ewald, Paul (2002), *Plague Time: The New Germ Theory of Disease*

chelate magnesium, copper, and other metals, but do so without making the metals unavailable. This alters the taste by altering the nature of the compounds.

Ingredients other than grapes can have more or less tannin content, and that content will vary based upon the amount of time the whole fruit is left in the primary fermenter as well.

Unfortunately, because tannins encompass such a vast array of compounds, assessing the tannin content of a must is a devilishly complex exercise in experimental chemistry. If you are curious, please see *New Tannin Assay for Winemakers* by Moris L. Silber and John K. Fellman for the most accurate method using protein dye markers or the older (and more controversial) precipitation technique published by Hagerman and Butler in the *Journal of Agricultural Food Chemistry* in 1978.

Some fruits already have so much tannin that they should be diluted in order to make a drinkable wine, whereas others will require the addition of tannin to help pull proteins out of solution. I have included a table of common fruits that shows how much relative tannin they have, divided into low (less than 3 grams per liter), medium (3–4 grams per liter) and high (more than 4 grams per liter). If a juice is in the "low" category, add ⅜ teaspoon of grape tannin per gallon. If a juice is in the "medium" category, add ¼ teaspoon per gallon. If it is in the "high" category, you will likely need to dilute the juice with water or a juice with lower tannin content to avoid making a wine that is too astringent to be enjoyable. If you have to dilute the juice anyway because of its acidity (later in this chapter), consider the diluted juice to be one category lower for purposes of tannin content.

Your fruits will certainly differ to some degree from those I used for testing and my testing method used my own home lab rather than a professional lab, so I recommend that you mix up your must and add half the tannins specified, and then take a clean spoon and actually taste the must. If it isn't giving you any "pucker effect" go ahead and

| Low Tannin | Medium Tannin | High Tannin |
|---|---|---|
| Apples, Bananas, Cranberries, Lemons | Blueberries, Blackberries, Cherries (sweet), Currants, Gooseberries, Grapes, Grapefruit, Passionfruit, Plums, Raspberries, Strawberries | Apricots, Blueberries, Cherries (sour), Guava, Kiwi, Mango, Oranges, Peaches, Papaya, Pears |

*Relative Tannin Content of Common Wine Ingredients*

add the rest of the tannin specified. A must that starts out tasty will likely turn into a tasty wine!

If you have a finished wine that for some reason has excessive tannin, keep in mind that some wines are at their best after being stored for several years, during which time the tannins slowly polymerize, combine with proteins or otherwise become less astringent. If that doesn't work, or you need to use a wine early, you can precipitate out the tannins using a combination of gelatin and kieselsol.

To use gelatin, use your scale to measure out one gram of fining gelatin (from a winemaking store), and mix that with two tablespoons of cold water in a clean coffee cup. Separately, put seven tablespoons of water in a glass measuring cup, and heat on high in the microwave for one minute. Add the hot water to the dissolved gelatin in the coffee cup, mixing thoroughly. Allow this to cool down to a temperature of 80 degrees, and then gently stir in two tablespoons per gallon of wine or the whole amount for five gallons. Leave it for two to five days before adding the kieselsol.

Whenever you use gelatin, it will impart some haze to the wine. This can be removed with kieselsol, a soluble silica gel. Soluble silica gel has an ionic charge that will attract uncombined gelatin and gelatin-tannin complexes. This will precipitate quickly. Use one ml per gallon of wine. Stir it in gently. Wait at least five days but not more than ten before racking the wine to leave the precipitated tannins behind. (Racking is explained in the next chapter.)

# Acids in Wine

**The acidity of** wines is important because the organic acids help establish an environment favorable to yeast. They also combine over time

| Fruit | Average Acidity in grams/liter | Primary Acids |
|---|---|---|
| Apple | 6.5 | Malic, citric, lactic |
| Banana | 3 | Citric, malic, tartaric |
| Blackberry | 13 | Malic, citric, isocitric |
| Blueberry | 13 | Citric, malic |
| Cantaloupe | 2.5 | Citric, malic |
| Cherry (sweet) | 11 | Malic, citric, isocitric |
| Cranberry | 30 | Citric, malic, quinic |
| Grapefruit | 20 | Citric |
| Grape | 6 | Tartaric, malic |
| Guava | 12 | Citric, malic, lactic |
| Lemon | 40 | Citric |
| Mango | 3 | Citric, tartaric |
| Orange | 15 | Citric, malic |
| Papaya | 0.5 | Citric, malic, ketoglutaric |
| Passion Fruit | 25 | Citric, malic |
| Peach | 8 | Malic, citric |
| Pear | 4 | Malic, citric |
| Pineapple | 10 | Citric, malic |
| Plum | 6 | Malic, quinic |
| Raspberries | 14 | Malic, citric, isocitric |
| Strawberries | 10 | Citric, malic |
| Watermelon | 2 | Citric, malic |

*Acidity of Common Wine Ingredients*

with alcohols to enhance flavor and smell, and they assist sulfite in sanitizing the must. Most importantly,they convey a taste of their own that balances the wine.

Depending upon the fruit you use, your wine must will already contain a combination of organic acids. Every fruit has some amount of citric acid, as citric acid is crucial to metabolism, but often a different acid is predominant and the combination of acids is unique for every fruit. Each fruit also has a different overall level of acidity. Some fruits are so acidic (> 9 grams per liter) they cannot be used exclusively to make a wine must, and their juice must be diluted with either water or the juice of a less acidic fruit. The following table lists common fruits, their acidity as tested by titration and the primary organic acids in each fruit in decreasing order of relative quantity.

# Measuring Acidity

**Thankfully, unlike tannins,** which are hard to measure, the overall acid content of wine musts is easy to determine. Wine musts contain a variety of acids, but it isn't possible for a home winemaker to separate these out and measure them independently. Because each of the primary organic acids has a different molecular weight (150.9 for tartaric, 134.1 for malic and 192.1 for citric), but a mole of each is neutralized by two moles of sodium hydroxide, what winemakers have standardized upon is interpreting the results of the tests as though the acid being neutralized were tartaric. Likewise, wine makers don't usually like to think in terms of moles, so the results are converted via a multiplier into the more familiar "parts per thousand." So acid measurements of wine must are provided in terms of TA (titrateable acidity) as tartaric in PPT (parts per thousand). This is the same thing as grams per liter, abbreviated as g/L.

The method of measuring the acid content is called titration, and it takes advantage of the fact that acids and bases neutralize each other. You might have observed this phenomenon as a kid by mixing baking soda with vinegar. The combination generated carbon dioxide gas initially, but after a while settled down and did nothing once either component was fully neutralized. We won't be using baking soda because we don't want to generate gas. Instead, we'll use a standardized solution of sodium hydroxide—otherwise known as lye.

The widely available acid test kits have a problem. That is, they rely upon the color change of an indicator (phenolphthalein) which turns pink when enough sodium hydroxide has been added. But if you are dealing with a pink, blue, or purple sample, ascertaining when it has changed color is really difficult. I recommend using an inexpensive pH meter[49] instead.

By using either an indicator that changes color when the solution has been neutralized or a pH meter, you can tell when enough base has been added to neutralize the acid. Because you know the concentration of the base you are using, the amount of acid in your test sample can be easily calculated. The calculation is as follows:

(Normality of Base) × (Volume of Base) = (Normality of Unknown) × (Volume of Unknown)

Because the calculations are just the arithmetic of converting molarity to grams per liter, I have designed the procedure below to take that into account, and use just a one-time multiplication.

## Supplies

150 ml beaker
1 glass stirring rod
110 ml syringe
1 cup distilled water
1 container of 0.1N sodium hydroxide solution

---

[49] I use the Milwaukee pH600. It costs about $20 from various vendors.

## *Procedure*

Wear safety glasses.

Use the clean syringe to measure 5 ml of wine must and transfer it into the beaker.

Clean the syringe and then rinse with the distilled water.

Fill the syringe to the 10ml mark with sodium hydroxide solution

Add the sodium hydroxide to the beaker 0.1 ml at a time. After each addition, stir the contents of the beaker and test the pH with the meter.

Repeat the previous step until the pH meter reads 8.3 or higher. Then stop.

Make note of the reading on the syringe.

The TA (tartaric) in PPT (or g/L) of your must is equal to 1.5 × (10— reading on syringe).

Clean, rinse, dry, and store your equipment.

# Adjusting Acidity

**Acids affect flavors** and indirectly create new flavors in a maturing wine. When making wine, the acidity of a must needs to be adjusted so that it is high enough, but not so high as to make an unpleasant flavor. Though your sense of taste is the final arbiter, there are some ranges of acidity that have been established by wine makers over time that can serve as a general guideline:

Dry White Wine: 7.0-9.0g/L

Sweet White Wine: 8.0-10.0g/L

Dry Red Wine: 6.0-8.0g/L

Sweet Red Wine: 7.0-9.0g/L

Dry Fruit Wines and Meads: 5.0-6.5g/L

Sweet Fruit Wines and Meads: 6.5-9.0g/L

Sherries: 5.0-6.5g/L

Many country wines are blended. For example, you might make a blueberry wine that contains a fair amount of red grape concentrate. So consider the full nature and character of your wine in assessing which category of acidity is appropriate. In the case of a dry blueberry wine containing red grape concentrate, I'd be aiming for about 7.0g/L.

If you find your wine is too acidic, no more than 2g/L too much, you can reduce the acidity by adding potassium carbonate. Potassium carbonate has a molecular mass of 138.2, and tartaric acid has a molecular mass of 150.9. There are 3.79 liters in a gallon, and potassium carbonate removes one molecule of acid for every molecule of potassium carbonate added, so for every PPT reduction in acidity required, add 3.5 grams of potassium carbonate per gallon.

For example, if I have five and a half gallons of wine must as described above, it has an acidity of 8.2g/L and I want an acidity of 7.0g/L, the amount of potassium carbonate I would need to add is:

(5.5 gallons) × 3.5 grams (8.2g/L−7.0g/L) = 23.1 grams. Measure it with your scale for best accuracy.

For reductions greater than 2.0g/L, I do not recommend adding potassium carbonate as it can impart undesired salty tastes. Instead, I recommend blending. You can blend with water or other juices with lower acidity. In general, you don't want to blend with too much water as that will reduce the flavor and increase the amount of sugar you'll need to add. Keep in mind that whatever fruit juices you use for blending shouldn't overpower the primary ingredient. This will require a bit of algebra.

Pretend I want to make blueberry wine. To that end, I have juiced some blueberries, and tested the acidity of the must at an excessively sour 11g/L. I want 7g/L. I am making 5.5 gallons of must.

There are 3.79 liters in a gallon. If my desired acidity is 7g/L, then the total amount of acid in 5.5 gallons of must will be 7g/L × 3.79L/gallon × 5.5 gallons = 145.9 grams. My blueberry must contains 11g/L of acidity, which works out to 11g/L × 3.79L/gallon = 41.7 grams per gallon.

If I wanted to dilute the juice with water alone, it would be easy to determine how much blueberry must I could use by dividing the total amount of desired acid in 5.5 gallons of must (145.9 grams) by the number of grams of acid in a gallon of my blueberry must (41.7 grams). So 145.9 grams / 41.7 grams per gallon = 3.5 gallons. So to make 5.5 gallons of must with the proper level of acidity, I would use 3.5 gallons of blueberry must and make up the remaining two gallons with water. Because blueberries are very strongly flavored, this would likely work fine as long as we added tannin and sugar as needed.

Of course, we wouldn't have to use water. We could use watermelon juice instead! If we have one gallon of watermelon juice has an acidity of 3g/L, how much blueberry juice and water would we need to use?

The total acidity available from the watermelon juice is 3.79L/gallon × 3g/L × 1 gallon = 11.4 grams. The must requires a total of 145.9 grams, so the amount of acidity remaining is 145.9 grams−11.4 grams = 134.5 grams. If we divide that by the number of grams of acid per gallon of blueberry juice (41.7 grams) we get 134.5 grams / 41.7 grams per gallon = 3.22 gallons. That's close enough to three gallons plus a quart, so now our recipe is 3.25 gallons of blueberry juice, one gallon of watermelon juice, and the remaining (5.5 gallons−3.25 gallons−1 gallon) 1.25 gallons made up with water. As you can see, the math for blending to get the right acid levels isn't very difficult.

Usually, however, excessive acid is not the problem. The problem is more likely to be insufficient acid. This is especially the case with low or medium acid fruits that are fully ripened, and with fruits whose quantities need to be kept low due to high tannins such as cherries.

If I were making a cherry wine, because cherry is high in tannin, I would likely use half cherry juice and half red or white grape juice in my must. Because the result would be a red wine, I'd want the acidity to be at around 7.0g/L. In all likelihood, though, when I measured, I'd find the acidity closer to 5.5g/L.

To increase the acidity, you add acid directly to the must and stir it in. Winemaking shops make citric, tartaric and malic acids available, as well as an acid blend composed of equal parts of all three. The only place I can see acid blend being used is in meads (honey wine) that have no fruit component. Otherwise, what I recommend is the use of acids based upon the nature of the fruit.

Earlier in this chapter is a table that lists, in order of influence on taste, the primary organic acids present in a variety of fruits. For some fruits, the primary acid is malic, for others it is citric or tartaric. When correcting the acidity of a must whose primary character is that of a particular fruit, you should use the two most important acids for that fruit in a 2:1 ratio.

For example, if I am making an apple wine, the primary acids are first malic and then citric acid. When I add acidity to the must, I will add a blend of acids composed of two parts malic acid and one part citric acid.

Determining how much acid to add is straightforward. If I want my must to have 6.5g/L acidity and it only has 5.0g/L of acidity, then I need to add 6.5g/L−5.0g/L = 1.5g/L of acid. Converting that to gallons simply requires multiplying the result by the number of liters in a gallon, which is 3.79. So to increase the acidity of 5.5 gallons of must from 5.0g/L to 6.5g/L I would need to add 1.5g/L X 3.79 L/gallon X  5.5 gallons = 31.3 grams of acid. In even numbers, then, I would add 20 grams of malic acid and 10 grams of citric acid.

There is a school of thought that citric acid should never be used in wine musts. The reason is because citric acid can promote acetification (i.e. the process of turning wine to vinegar) or can contribute to the development of diacetyl (buttery) flavors. Both statements are true. However, if you are scrupulous in your sanitation, acetification is not likely to happen and some wines could benefit from any diacetyl developed. That having been said, if you are concerned about this, you can substitute tartaric acid for citric acid, and by doing this you will increase the grape flavors in your wine.

# Pectins

**Pectins are long** chains of carbohydrates composed of various sugars that form the cell walls of the fruits used to make wine. Pectins are responsible for turning the juices of some fruits into jelly. European grapes contain enough pectic enzyme—an enzyme that destroys pectin—to destroy that pectin so you end up with a clear fluid wine rather than a semi-solid gelatinous mass. Other fruits don't usually have enough of this enzyme naturally, which makes them excellent for making jelly but suboptimal for wine.

Pectic enzyme purchased from the winemaking store is used in small amounts to supplement the natural pectic enzymes in the must. Over time, this degrades the pectin and thereby either makes its sugars available for fermentation or precipitates the leavings into the bottom of the fermenter so they are left behind at the next racking. Therefore, pectic enzyme helps to produce clear wines.

You may recall that one reason most fruits and vegetables are blanched before freezing or dehydrating is that the high temperature of blanching inactivates the enzymes that cause the produce to degrade over time. The same will occur with pectic enzyme, so pectic enzyme should only be added to a must with a temperature under 80 degrees and the must cannot be reheated thereafter.

When making wines with no added sulfites or when making wines in which honey is the primary ingredient, it is common to heat the must in order to assure its sterility. Anytime heated ingredients are added to the must, the temperature of the must should be allowed to drop adequately before pectic enzyme is added. The container of pectic enzyme has instructions printed on the label for how much to add

| *Enzyme According to Directions* | *Double Pectic Enzyme* |
|---|---|
| Blackberries, Blueberries, Cherries, Nectarines, Peaches, Plums, Raspberries, Watermelon | Apples, Pears, Strawberries |

*Pectic Enzyme Requirements of Various Fruits*

to your must, but this is a general direction. Some fruits require the standard amount, but some require double. The following table will let you see at a glance.

# Yeast Nutrient, Yeast Energizer, Thiamine, and Lipid Supply

**During the reproductive** phase of yeast in the must, the sheer volume of yeast that is created from a tiny packet is impressive. There will literally be millions of yeast cells per milliliter of must. All of this cellular budding and division requires core building blocks for protein and the other parts of a yeast cell. As with many important factors, though these are usually present in European grapes to a sufficient degree, they are lacking in practically all other primary ingredients for winemaking.

A wine can be made successfully in some cases without the addition of nutritional building blocks for the yeast, but adding those building blocks will go a long way toward stacking the deck in favor of a successful outcome.

You will see wine supply stores selling many supplements for yeast with names such as yeast nutrient and yeast energizer. There is no universal standard, and so the precise ingredients will vary with the supplier. In general, they will contain purified sources of nitrogen and phosphorus at a minimum, though many will also contain a variety of

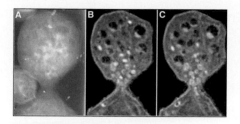

⊗ Yeast cell division requires proper nutrition.

B-vitamins. Yeast nutrient usually contains only food grade ammonium phosphate, whereas yeast energizer will contain this along with magnesium sulfate, killed yeast, and the entire vitamin B complex; of which thiamine (vitamin $B_1$) is the most important. Sometimes you may see urea as an ingredient. If you do, don't worry. This is purified food-grade urea that supplies nitrogen for building proteins and it is perfectly safe.

I would recommend using yeast energizer in preference to yeast nutrient. But if you use yeast nutrient instead, at least add a 100% RDA thiamine tablet and a pinch of Epsom salt in addition for each gallon of must.

The cell walls of yeast also require lipids (fats), and such fats are in short supply in some wine musts—especially meads made predominantly from honey with little or no fruit. In such cases, you can use yeast hulls as an additive or a specialized additive that contains essential fatty acids such as FermaidK or Ghostex.

# Sulfite

**Some people who** get headaches from drinking wine believe themselves to be sensitive to sulfites. Usually, however, they get headaches from red wine but not from white wine, both of which contain sulfites. So sulfites are not the issue.[50] This headache is called Red Wine Headache, and experts disagree widely on its true cause. Less than 1% of people are truly sensitive to sulfites which are found ubiquitously in lunch meats, dried

---

[50] K. MacNeil, (2001) *The Wine Bible*

fruits, and even white grape juice from the supermarket. Obviously, if you are truly sensitive to sulfites you should avoid them at all costs.

Sulfite is used so pervasively in winemaking and considered so essential that its use is even permitted in wines labeled as USDA Organic. Though it is possible to make wines without the use of sulfites and I have successfully done so, the odds of success for a beginner are greatly enhanced by using sulfites, especially if you are using fresh or frozen fruits in the must.

Sulfite is used in winemaking as a sanitizer to kill or inhibit wild yeasts and bacteria so you end up making wine instead of vinegar. It is also used to help clear wines during racking to arrest fermentation and to help prevent oxidation and consequent degradation of flavor.

Sulfite comes in many forms, but for our purposes two forms are important. The first is potassium metabisulfite in the form of Campden tablets. Campden tablets are sized with the idea in mind of accurate dosing of wine and musts to purify must prior to initiating fermentation and help clear and preserve the wine later. To use Campden tablets, do not just plunk them into the wine or must. Instead, use a cleaned and sanitized wine thief to remove four to eight ounces of must or wine, and put it into a sanitized glass. Thoroughly crush the requisite number of tablets, and add the powder to the must or wine. Stir to dissolve. Once the tablets are dissolved, add the must or wine back to the original container. For the initial sanitizing of a must, use two tablets per gallon of must. For protecting wine from spoilage and oxidation, add one tablet per gallon before racking.

The second is powdered potassium metabisulfite. In powdered form it is used to make sterilizing solutions for sterilizing equipment.

Make a gallon jug (a clean empty plastic water jug is fine) of sanitizing solution. To make the sanitizing solution, dissolve a measuring teaspoon of potassium metabisulfite powder in a gallon of water. You can use this solution repeatedly, and pour it back in the bottle after each use to rinse a fermenter or a racking tube until it loses its potency or becomes obviously dirty. If you keep the container tightly sealed when not in use, it will stay effective for a very long time. You can tell if it is potent by sniffing the solution. If the scent just barely tickles your nose, it needs to be replaced.

There are other sanitizers available and when you have become more experienced and confident, you can branch out and start experimenting. But sulfites are the easiest to use not only for the beginner, but also for the most prestigious of professional wineries.

# Testing Sulfite Levels

**It is very** rare that you would need to test the sulfite levels in wine. Simply following the directions in this book will assure adequate but not excessive levels of sulfite for most purposes. However, there are instances where you'll want to know how much sulfite is in the wine. For example, if you plan to follow your secondary fermentation with a malolactic fermentation in order to reduce perceived acidity, most malolactic cultures will be inhibited by sulfite levels greater than 20 ppm. So if you have been dosing regularly with sulfite between rackings, when you rack into a container to initiate malolactic fermentation, you should test the sulfite levels in your must, and reduce them if they are too high.

You can purchase sulfite test kits from wine equipment suppliers. These test kits use what is called the "Ripper" method and they work quite well with wines that are not strongly colored. With strongly colored wines, they give a reading that is too high because the compounds that impart color to the wine combine with some of the test ingredients making them inert. You can "guesstimate" the error by subtracting 10ppm from the results of the test, or you can do a more elaborate test on your own. I've detailed that test in the advanced techniques chapter.

To reduce sulfite levels, stir 3% hydrogen peroxide solution from the pharmacy into your wine and wait an hour. The amount you need is equal to 1 ml for every ppm reduction per gallon of wine. So if I have 5 gallons of must with a sulfite level of 33 ppm and I want to reduce the sulfite level to 15 ppm before adding a malolactic culture, I need a reduction of 33ppm−15 ppm or 18 ppm. The amount of 3% hydrogen peroxide solution to add is calculated like this:

(Gallons of wine) × (ppm reduction desired) = ml of 3% hydrogen peroxide solution to add

So 5 gallons × 18ppm = 90ml of 3% hydrogen peroxide solution.

# Yeast

**Yeast is the** star of the show. Wild yeast naturally colonizes the surfaces of fruits, so sometimes crushed fruit, left to its own devices and protected from other organisms, will ferment all by itself. In fact, this is the case in certain famous wine regions where the wild yeasts inhabiting the area have co-evolved with the wine grapes. Though most wine yeasts are of the species *Saccharomyces cerevisiae*, there are hundreds if not thousands of variations of this species, some with dramatically different properties. The genome of wine yeast has over twelve million base pairs, making for substantial possibilities for variation.

In practice, wine makers do not rely on wild yeasts because the unpredictability can often result in serious failures or faults in the finished product. Instead, wine makers usually purify the musts of wild yeasts and bacteria by adding sulfite. Once the sulfite has been added, the must is stirred thoroughly and then allowed to sit for a day before a cultured wine yeast of known character is added.

Adding yeast to the must is known as pitching the yeast, though in reality little real pitching occurs because one- and five-gallon batches are relatively small. In batches of this size, the packet of yeast is just sprinkled as evenly as possible on top of the must in the primary fermenter. Do not stir. If you stir, it will take the yeast far longer to multiply enough to become active. You want the yeast to become active as quickly as possible because it is added after the sulfite has dissipated, so long lag times expose your must to a risk of spoilage by delaying the onset of production of alcohol.

Because yeast needs oxygen in its initial replication stage before fermentation begins, you should aerate the must by stirring it vigorously before pitching the yeast. Some wine makers put a sanitized fish tank aerator connected to an air pump into the must for an hour or so before pitching the yeast, but I have found a good vigorous stirring (carefully so as to avoid sticky messes) to be sufficient.

Yeast comes powdered in packets, in liquid in vials, and in many other forms. As you become a more advanced wine maker, you might decide to use liquid yeasts. The liquid yeasts require amplification, which I have covered in the chapters on beer. But your initial use should be

of powdered dry yeast in individual foil packets. These are very well-characterized and foolproof. Just open the packet and sprinkle on top of the must—and it works. Don't be fooled by the simplicity of use or the fact these yeasts are inexpensive. Dry wine yeasts are a very high quality product and I have used them successfully for years. If you skimp and use bread or beer yeast to make your wine, don't complain if your wine tastes like bread or is syrupy-sweet because the alcohol tolerance was too low.

# 15

# Ingredients and Techniques

**Theoretically, you could** make "wine" or at least a liquid containing alcohol, from just sugar, water, yeast and some nutrients. But the whole point of wine is to preserve the nutritional content of the starting fruits or vegetables, so we'll look at it from that point of view. Any fruit or vegetable can be used to make wine. Other than wine grapes, all fruits will require some amount of supplemental sugar. The juice of some fruits will require considerable dilution due to their high degree of acidity or astringency, and some will produce wines so tasty you'll wonder why you can't find them commercially. Others, like asparagus, will be downright unpalatable in some cases and suitable only for making marinades.

# Fruits

**Wine grapes are** the perfect fruit for making wine. All you need to do is crush them and they make the perfect amount of juice with the perfect levels of acidity and sugar. Every other fruit is imperfect in some way. While fruits other than grapes are imperfect, they can be made perfect through proper adjuncts and technique.

With air transportation for produce so prevalent, there are more fruits available in our local markets than I could ever list, and quite a few I haven't tried because they are so expensive, such as starfruit and guava. In general, the higher the quality of the fruit, the higher the potential quality of your finished product. You will never make great wine from bad fruit—no amount of technique will improve its quality. But if you start with the highest quality fruit, there is at least the potential for creating great wine through solid technique.

You can use fruit in nearly any form to make wine: fresh fruits, dehydrated fruits, canned fruits, and frozen fruits. Fresh fruits and frozen fruits give the best results, and in many cases frozen fruits are superior to fresh because the process of freezing breaks down the cell walls to release more juice and flavor. Canned fruits often have a distinctly "cooked" taste that can detract from a wine, making it taste flat. They are best used for no more than half of the fruit in a wine. Wine-making shops sell specially canned fruits that come out better in wines than the canned fruit at the supermarket, but even these should constitute no more than half of the fruit by weight.

Dehydrated fruits retain their sugar, but have been subjected to oxidation and the loss of some of their more volatile flavor components. Usually, they are used in the form of raisins for purposes of adding some grape components to a wine so that it has a more vinous quality; dehydrated fruits in general, such as prunes and apples, are good for adding sherry-like taste qualities. Dehydrated banana is good for adding body to a wine such as watermelon wine that would otherwise be very thin. Very often, dehydrated fruits are sulfited to preserve their color. This is not a problem when they are added to a primary fermenter. In general, one cup of minced dried fruit will impart three ounces of sugar to the must, but this rule of thumb

⊗ Always use unwaxed fruit. Waxed fruits will create a mess rather than wine.

is no substitute for measuring with a hydrometer. Do keep in mind that making wine out of a dried fruit can concentrate the effects of that fruit, as I found to my chagrin with some prune wine I made.

Fruits, you will discover, are pretty expensive in the quantities you'd use for making wine. For example, you'll need twenty pounds of blueberries to make five gallons of blueberry wine. If you buy frozen organic blueberries at the supermarket for $3.69/lb, that means $73.80 just in fruit. Since you get twenty five bottles of wine from five gallons, that works out to just under $3/bottle, which is still a decent deal. Even so, it quickly becomes clear that your best bet is to either grow fruit yourself, go to a pick-it-yourself place or buy it in bulk from a farm stand. I pick the blueberries for my wine at Mrs. Smith's Blueberries nearby, and it's a lot more affordable. (You can also make wine in one-gallon batches so your initial outlay isn't so much. This is a good idea when experimenting!)

Fresh fruits for country wines are primarily processed using only one technique. In this technique, the fruit is placed in a clean nylon straining bag in the bottom of the primary fermenter, crushed with cleaned/sanitized hands, with the difference in volume being made up by adding water. The water helps to extract the dissolved sugars and flavor compounds, and as fermentation begins, the alcohol created helps to extract the color. This technique is best suited to softer fruits that are easily crushed by hand, though it is used for practically all fruits for the overwhelming preponderance of country wines.[51]

As an alternative, especially for harder fruits such as apples, I recommend using a high quality juice machine such as the Juiceman™ or Champion™. With these machines, the expressed juice goes into one container and

❷ Organic fruit juices can make a valuable adjunct to homemade wine

the pulp goes into another. For darker fruits from which you want to extract color, such as cherries or blueberries, scoop the pulp from the pulp container into a nylon straining bag that you put in the bottom of the primary fermenter. (Note: Exclude the pits from stone fruits as they contain a cyanogenic glycoside that is poisonous.)

# Juices

**I have made** very good wines from high-quality bottled juices. For example, two quarts of apple plus two quarts of black cherry with the sugar and acid levels adjusted and a hint of vanilla added will make a gallon of really great wine.

Bottled juice that hasn't been treated with an additive that suppresses fermentation (such as potassium sorbate) can also be used to

---

[51] If you are using purchased fruits, please make sure they are un-waxed. The wax that purveyors use to make fruits look pretty will turn your intended wine into a useless mess.

make wine. Keep in mind that something like the generic apple juice you can buy cheaply by the gallon is hardly more than sugar water and doesn't make very good wine. But there is a big difference between brands, and sometimes you can make a really excellent wine out of a blended Juicy Juice™.

Bottled juices and juice blends from the natural food section of the grocery store are often 100% juice from the described fruit. These have been specifically formulated to retain the distinctive flavor of the fruit, and can be easily used as an addition to wines. You might want to be sparing in their use though, as they often cost as much as $10/quart.

Grape juice concentrates can help add "vinous" quality to a country wine, making its mouth-feel resemble that of traditional wines. These are special concentrates purchased from winemaking stores that have had the water removed under vacuum, and have been preserved with sulfites rather than through heat; therefore, they preserve a distinctive grape character. At roughly $16/quart (they make a gallon of must when water is added) they are expensive, but they make good additions as part of a must. They come in white and red varieties.

# Vegetables

**Vegetables are used** for wine either by boiling them in water and including the water in the must, or by juicing the vegetables with a juice machine. Many vegetables, no matter how they are handled, will impart a haze to wines, but this effect is more pronounced when using boiled vegetables. This is because boiling tends to set the pectins while denaturing the natural enzymes in the vegetable that would otherwise break down the pectins over time. There's no reason why you couldn't try bottled vegetable juices so long as they haven't been treated with a fermentation inhibitor, but the results can be pretty iffy when using brands that include added salt. Salt is added to vegetable juice to balance natural sugars for a tasty beverage. But when you use salted vegetable juice in wine, the sugar is converted to alcohol during fermentation but the salt remains. The results can be good for making marinade but decidedly not good for drinking. On the flip side, there's nothing wrong with having a variety of self-preserved marinades ready and waiting!

Speaking of marinades, both wines and vinegars are commonly used for this purpose, and both are self-preserving. You can make very good marinades by fermenting mixtures that include onions, herbs, celery, parsley, and similar ingredients. With their high alcohol content, they will keep for decades.

If you aren't making marinades but you are instead looking to make drinkable wines, both carrots and tomatoes can be excellent candidates for a wine. Carrots also blend quite well with apple. But don't let the fact that I've never made okra wine deter you if you want to give it a try.

# Herbs and Spices

**Though spices are** not added to wines very much today, in past times spices were quite expensive so heavily spiced wines were an indicator of wealth and status. Unlike the traditional wine makers of France, as a home wine maker you don't have to contend with the traditional rules for making wine. One bonus is that you can add anything you'd like. You can add mulling spices to an apple wine, a hint of vanilla and cinnamon to a blueberry wine, and just a touch of rosemary to a carrot wine. The only rule is to make something that you and your friends will enjoy drinking, so if spices can enhance a wine to your tastes, then there's no reason not to use them. However, just as with food, it can be easy to over-do spice. Better too little than too much.

When adding spices, use whole rather than powdered ingredients. For one thing, powdered spices tend to have lost some of their volatile flavor components and will give inferior results. For another, they often form a haze in wines that is harmless but unsightly.

The technique for use is straightforward. Put the chosen spices in a spice bag, and lightly boil the bag in a quart of sugar water for ten to fifteen minutes, then discard the bag. Allow the spiced sugar water to cool to room temperature before adding to the must.

| Spice | Goes best with | Amount to use |
|-------|----------------|---------------|
| Peppercorns | Used to add warmth to most wines | 5–10 whole peppercorns per gallon |
| Cassia Buds | Apple, blueberry, cherry, and most fruit wines | 10–30 buds per gallon |
| Cinnamon | Fruit wines | 1 stick per gallon |
| Cloves | Fruit, vegetable, and grain wines | 3–6 cloves per gallon |
| Allspice | Fruit, vegetable, and grain wines | 4–10 berries per gallon |
| Nutmeg | Fruit and vegetable wines | No more than ½ meg per gallon |
| Ginger | Best in lightly flavored wines such as apple and carrot | 2–8 ounces, grated |
| Star Anise | Fruit wines | 1 star per gallon |
| Vanilla | Fruit wines | 1 vanilla bean or less per gallon |

# Sources of Sugar

**Because yeast contains** enzymes that turn many forms of sugar into a sort more easily used, any common source of sugar will have the same result in terms of alcohol production. You can use granulated cane sugar, dextrose, glucose, fructose, honey, molasses, brown sugar, maple syrup, high-fructose corn syrup, dried fruits, concentrated fruit juices, and more.

Though the source doesn't matter in terms of creating alcohol, it can make a big difference in terms of taste—for example, many of the chemical compounds that make honey or brown sugar have a distinctive taste and aroma which will be preserved in wines that include them. For this reason, I would recommend against using brown sugar or molasses.

Glucose, dextrose, fructose, and sucrose (cane sugar) are all treated identically by yeast. If the sugar isn't in a form the yeast can use, the yeast employs an enzyme called invertase to change it into a usable form. Nothing is gained by using the more expensive fructose from a health food store over an inexpensive bag of granulated sugar from the grocery store. None of these contribute flavor to the wine, and simply serve as a source of sweetness or alcohol. They are a good choice for wines in which you want the tastes and aromas of the primary fruit to dominate their character.

Bottled juices and juice concentrates can also be used as a source of sugar, especially given that sugar is their primary solid constituent.

Containing a wide array of minerals, amino acids, and vitamins, honey is a tasty addition to many wines. A number of cultural traditions (including the honeymoon) have grown up around honey wines. Strictly speaking, a wine made from honey alone is called mead. Wine that combines honey with apples is called cyser, whereas wine made from honey and any other (non-grape) fruit is called melomel. Wine made from honey with added herbs is called metheg-lin, and wine made from honey and grapes is pyment.

When making mead variants, the source and quality of the honey you use makes a difference in the taste of the finished product. The generic blended honeys in the supermarket are fine when the honey is primarily used as a source of sugar. If you are making mead, however, blended honey is useless because it has been pasteurized and homog-enized until it is nothing but sugar. If the tastes and aromas of the honey will be important to the end product, use a single-source honey from a bee keeper. The nectar that the bees collect positively affects the mineral content and flavor of mead. Clover, alfalfa, orange blossom, wildflower, and mesquite are just a few of the types of honey available; in general, darker honeys impart stronger flavors. You can get single-source and wild honeys from a local bee keeper, order them over the Internet or, if you are ambitious, start keeping bees yourself[52] and cre-ate your own honey.

# Cleanliness and Sanitation

**Before I get** into the details of making wine, I want to delve a bit into cleanliness and sanitation, as these are crucial for a successful outcome. You don't need a laboratory clean room or a level 3 hazmat facility to make wine. You can make wine in your kitchen or any room in your home. But you need to be attentive to detail. Everything that touches your must, wine, or wine-in-progress must be clean and sanitized.

"Clean" simply means "free of visible dirt or contamination." Dish soap and water are adequate cleansers. Wine bottles, fermentation ves-sels, wine thief, plastic tubing, and hydrometer along with all utensils

---

[52] In my opinion, I don't have enough experience to write a book on beekeeping, however I have found Kim Flottum's *The Backyard Beekeeper* to be very good. If you are interested in keeping bees for honey, I highly recommend it.

that touch your wine need to be cleaned. Sometimes, all that is needed is to add some soapy water and shake. Other times, as with carboys, you may need to use a special brush. For subsequent sanitation procedures to work, the surfaces must first be clean. Once they have been cleaned, they should be thoroughly rinsed.

To sanitize the equipment, all surfaces that will touch the must or wine should be rinsed or wiped down with a sanitizing sulfite solution. Don't rinse afterwards. For bottles, vessels, and carboys you can add a portion of the sulfite solution and swish it around thoroughly so that it contacts all surfaces, and then pour it back into your container of solution. For other utensils, soak paper towels in sanitizing solution and use those towels to wipe them down immediately before use.

Your hand siphon and tubing might look to pose a problem at first, but there is an easy technique for keeping them clean. For this technique, you need two clean plastic gallon jugs that were previously used for water. Put one with soapy water on your counter and the empty one on the floor. Now, use your siphon to pump the soapy water all the way up into the tube and through the tubing into the empty container on the floor. Then, switch the containers and repeat the process until the equipment is clean. Empty out the containers and rinse them thoroughly. Next, put the bottle of sanitizing solution on the counter, and siphon that into the empty container on the floor. Make sure to wipe down the outside of the equipment and tubing as well, as these may contact the wine.

# Making the Wine Must

**As noted previously,** your wine must doesn't have to be made from a single source. You can use apples mixed with pears, carrots mixed with apples, juiced table grapes combined with bottled cherry juice, or whatever strikes your fancy. As long as you use good sanitation

## General Recipes for Making Wine from Common Fruits and Flowers

| | Pounds | Fruit Preparation | Adjuncts | Pectic Enzyme | Tannin | Yeast Variety | Notes |
|---|---|---|---|---|---|---|---|
| *Apple* | 10 lbs | Juice machine | ½ lb raisins in straining bag | Double specified on container | ¼ tsp | Red Star Pasteur Champagne | *Use the juice but not the pulp* |
| *Blackberry* | 4 lbs | Crushed in straining bag | ½ lb raisins in straining bag | As specified | None | Red Star Montrachet | |
| *Blueberry* | 8 lbs | 4 lbs juiced, 4 lbs crushed in straining bag | ½ tsp vanilla and one stick cinnamon in bag | As specified | None | Lalvin ICV-D$_{254}$ | |
| *Cherry, Sweet* | 4 lbs | Juice machine, add pulp to straining bag | 1 quart bottled cherry juice | As specified | None | Red Star Montrachet | *Exclude the pits* |

## General Recipes for Making Wine from Common Fruits and Flowers

| | Pounds | Fruit Preparation | Adjuncts | Pectic Enzyme | Tannin | Yeast Variety | Notes |
|---|---|---|---|---|---|---|---|
| **Dandelion** | 5 cups flower heads | Put the flower petals (only!) in straining bag | 1 lb raisins in straining bag | None | ¼ tsp | Lalvin D$_{47}$ | *Ferment at under 70 degrees* |
| **Nectarine** | 3 lbs | Pitted and juiced in machine | ½ lb raisins in straining bag | As specified | ¼ tsp | Red Star Pasteur Champagne | |
| **Peach** | 3 lbs | Pitted and juiced in machine | None | As specified | ¼ tsp | Lalvin D$_{47}$ | |
| **Pear** | 10 lbs | Juice machine | ½ lb raisins in straining bag | Double specified on container | ¼ tsp | Red Star Pasteur Champagne | *Add one stick cinnamon to straining bag* |
| **Plum** | 5 lbs | Pitted and crushed in straining bag | 1 lb raisins in straining bag | As specified | None | Red Star Montrachet | |

## General Recipes for Making Wine from Common Fruits and Flowers

| | Pounds | Fruit Preparation | Adjuncts | Pectic Enzyme | Tannin | Yeast Variety | Notes |
|---|---|---|---|---|---|---|---|
| *Raspberry* | 4 lbs | Crushed in straining bag | None | As specified | None | Red Star Montrachet | |
| *Rhubarb* | 4 lbs | Crushed in straining bag | 1 lb strawberry in straining bag | As specified | ¼ tsp | Red Star Pasteur Champagne | |
| *Strawberry* | 4 lbs | Crushed in straining bag | ½ lb raisins in straining bag | Double specified on container | ¼ tsp | Lalvin ICV-D$_{254}$ | *Comes out straw-colored rather than red* |
| *Watermelon* | 10 lbs | Juice machine | 1 lb raisins in straining bag | As specified | ¼ tsp | Lalvin D$_{47}$ | *Peel the outer skin off, and juice the rind and fruit* |

and technique, the results will be at least as good as most wines you can buy.

Some fruits are either highly acidic or highly tannic to such an extent that you wouldn't want to use their extracted juice exclusively to make wine because the results would be too sour or bitter. In those cases, only a portion of the must is made from that fruit, and the rest is made up from water or other juices.

What follows is a recipe table that indicates how many pounds of a given fruit to use in making a gallon of wine from that fruit, how much tannin to add to that wine per gallon, and any other adjuncts that I'd recommend. Any deficit in juice to make a gallon is made up with water.

# The Primary Fermentation: Step-by-Step

1. **Start with fruit** juice obtained as described earlier in this chapter.
2. If needed, add enough water to the fruit juice to equal the amount of wine you wish to make. (It is helpful to add previously-measured amounts of water to your primary fermenter in advance and use a magic marker to mark gallons and quarts on the outside of the vessel for easy reference.) I use bottled water because my well water is sub-optimal, but if you have good water where you live, tap water is fine. Don't worry about whether or not your water is chlorinated, because the Campden tablets we'll be adding later serve to remove chlorine from the water.
3. Use your hydrometer to measure the specific gravity (SG) of the must. You are aiming for an SG of between 1.085 and 1.110, but in all likelihood your must measures much lower. Add the required

amount of sugar or honey to your must. This will slightly increase the volume of your must, but that's fine.

4. Use your acid testing kit to test the acidity of your must. If needed, add acid. Try to use the specific acid (or acid blend) that will best enhance the character of the fruit. For example, malic acid will enhance apples and pears whereas citric acid will enhance watermelons and tartaric acid will enhance grapes. If you are in doubt, use an acid blend made up of equal parts of the three acids.

5. Add one teaspoon of yeast energizer for each gallon of must.

6. Add pectic enzyme as directed on the container, or double the amount if the recipe table specifies doing so.

7. Add tannin as appropriate for the fruit being used. (This is described in the accompanying recipe table.)

8. Crush and add one Campden tablet dissolved in a bit of juice per gallon of must. Vigorously stir the must.

9. Cover your primary fermenter, and plug the hole with a bit of cotton ball to keep foreign objects out. Wait 24 hours.

10. Vigorously stir the must to oxygenate. Once movement ceases, sprinkle yeast from the packet over the surface of the must. Do not stir.

11. Place the cover on the fermenter, and plug the hole loosely with a bit of cotton ball.

12. Allow to sit for a week. During this time, you should smell the fermentation. Also, it may foam heavily and come out through the hole in the lid. If it does, clean up on the outside and insert a new cotton ball. After the week, replace the cotton ball with an air lock filled with sanitizing solution.

13. Allow to sit for another week or two, until the air lock only "bloops" once every few seconds. This marks the end of the primary fermentation phase. Once the primary fermentation phase

has ended, rack as soon as possible. If it sets for more than a couple of days, the dregs at the bottom (known as lees) will impart bad flavors to your wine.

# Your First Racking: Step-by-Step

1.  **A day before** you plan to rack, move your primary fermenter to a table or counter top. (By doing this a day in advance, you give any sludge stirred up by movement a chance to settle.) Put a wedge, book, block of wood, or something else from 1" to 2" high underneath the fermenter on the edge that is away from you. This will allow you to sacrifice the smallest amount of wine possible with the lees.

2.  Clean and sanitize your racking tube, tubing, and your secondary fermenter and get your rubber stopper and fresh air lock ready. Put your secondary fermenter on the floor in front of the primary fermenter, and then carefully remove the lid from the primary fermenter, creating as little disturbance as possible. Put a bit of the wine in a sanitized glass, and dissolve one crushed Campden tablet per gallon, then add it back to the wine.

❂ Racking requires a bit of coordination but with practice it comes easily.

3.  Put the plastic tubing from your racking setup in the secondary fermenter and the racking tube in the primary fermenter. Keeping the racking tube well above the

sediment, pump it gently to get it started. It may take a couple of tries. Gently lower the racking tube as the liquid level diminishes. Watch the liquid in the tube very carefully. The second it starts sucking sediment, raise the racking tube up to break the suction.

4. Place the rubber stopper with an air lock filled with sanitizing solution in the secondary fermenter. Using a carboy handle if necessary, move the secondary fermenter to a location out of sunlight where even temperatures are maintained.

5. Immediately clean and sanitize your primary fermenter, racking tube, and tubing and stow them away. If you don't clean them immediately they will likely be ruined.

# The Secondary Fermentation: Step-by-Step

1. **Wait. And wait.** Then wait some more. Patience, I have been told, is a virtue. After your first racking from the primary to secondary fermenter, the yeast will lag for a couple of days while it tries to catch up. Allow the secondary fermenter to sit unmolested until: the wine starts to become clear, you have more than a dusting of sediment at the bottom of the container, or the air lock only operates once every couple of minutes. This will likely take about a month. Because the secondary fermenter sits for so long, don't forget to check the airlock periodically and top up the sanitizing solution in it so it doesn't evaporate and leave your wine vulnerable.

2. The day before racking, sit the secondary fermenter up on a table or counter, and tilt it using a book or other wedge, as before.

3. Boil some water in a pot on the stove and allow it to cool to room temperature while covered. Clean and sanitize another fermentation vessel as well as the racking tube and tubing. Place the

sanitized vessel on the floor in front of the secondary fermenter, put the plastic tubing in the vessel, and put the racking tube in the secondary fermenter. Operate the racking tube and transfer the wine from the old vessel to the new. Add one Campden tablet dissolved in wine for each gallon of wine.

4.  Likely, there is an air space between the wine and the top of the new vessel. This will expose too much surface area of the wine to oxygen and potential infections. Pour in the sterilized water until the wine is just up to the neck.

5.  Clean the rubber stopper and airlock, sanitize them, re-fill the airlock with sanitizing solution, and install them on the new secondary fermenter. Put the secondary fermenter in a location without sunlight and with even temperature.

6.  Thoroughly clean and sanitize the empty secondary fermenter, the racking tube and the tubing.

⊗ The secondary fermentation in this vessel is almost complete.

7.  Now it is a waiting game. Over weeks and months your wine will ultimately cease to ferment, and the haze within the wine will settle onto the bottom of the container. Keep an eye on the wine. Anytime a substantial sediment develops, rack the wine again and top up with sterilized water. Make sure the airlock doesn't go dry and permit foreign organisms to enter. Depending on ingredients, you may not have to rack again or you could have to rack one to three more times.

8. Once the wine has gone at least three months without requiring racking and is crystal clear, it is ready for bottling. You can allow it to age in the fermenter as long as you'd like—even several years.

# Bottling Your Wine

1. **Gather, clean, and sanitize** the wine bottles that will be accepting the wine. You will need five bottles per gallon of wine. Boil an equal number of corks for 15 minutes, and then allow them to sit in a covered pot. Clean and sanitize your corker.
2. Rack the wine, but do not add water to top off on this final racking. Add one Campden tablet per gallon by crushing the tablet and dissolving in a bit of wine and then adding that wine into the new vessel.
3. If you want to add potassium sorbate to prevent re-fermentation, dissolve that also in the wine and add back into the new vessel. Use ¼ tsp per gallon of wine.
4. Place the secondary fermenter holding the wine on a table or counter top, tilting as before.
5. Arrange the bottles on a towel on the floor in front of the fermenter and install the plastic hose clamp on the plastic tubing so you can turn off the flow of wine when switching from bottle to bottle.
6. Put the plastic tubing in a bottle and the racking tube in the wine, pump the racking tube and start the flow of wine, pulling the tube higher in the bottle as the level of the wine increases. Stop the flow of wine when it is about half an inch into the bottom of the neck of the wine bottle. Put the tube in the next bottle and repeat the process until you run out of wine or there are no more bottles to fill.
7. One at a time, place the bottles on a solid floor, and use your corker to install one of the sterilized corks. Only work with one bottle at a time. As each bottle is corked, set it out of the way.

Repeat until all of the bottles are corked.

8. Clean and sanitize your fermenting vessels, racking tube, and plastic tubing.

9. Now you can make and apply wine labels if you wish.

10. Enjoy at your leisure or give as a gift.

⊗ Bottled blueberry wine. Magnificent!

# Creating Your Own Recipes

**Most wine books** are full of recipes. I'm sure they are useful, but I think it is more useful to understand how they are created so you can make your own recipes based upon what you have available. One of the reasons I went into so much detail in the chapter on the science of making wine is so you'd have all the tools you need to be self-sufficient.

When making a new wine for the first time, it is best to make it in a one-gallon batch. Overall, larger batches tend to come out better because they are less susceptible to temperature fluctuations, but I've made plenty of excellent wines in one-gallon batches, and the smaller amount may be less intimidating to a beginner.

In addition, even the cheapest wine ingredients are expensive at the scale of a five-gallon batch, so making a one-gallon batch is also best for experimental recipes. Reserve the larger five-gallon batches for tested recipes you know you'll be making for long-term storage or gifts. Some wine makers never make batches larger than a gallon, and they are quite happy with their results.

So let's look at the first critical decisions involved in making a wine recipe.

- Dominant and any secondary or tertiary fruits or flavors. This decision is purely aesthetic, and if you are someone with chronically bad taste you might consider consulting a friend or loved one for guidance. For example, I might want to make a wine with apple dominant, mulling spice secondary and honey tertiary. It would be rather daring as there would be little residual sweetness to balance the spice, so instead I'll make the apple dominant, honey secondary and mulling spice tertiary. Another example would be a wine with sweet cherry dominant and concord grape secondary.

- Check the tannin levels of each fruit. Any fruit that is high in tannin cannot be more than half of your must. If you want the fruit to be dominant anyway, you'll have to choose something unassertive such as generic white grape juice as a secondary. For example, if I want to make a wine with blueberry dominant, because blueberry is highly tannic, I am limited to four pounds of blueberries per gallon and will need to use adjuncts that won't overshadow the blueberry, such as white grape juice to make up the difference in volume.

- Check the acid levels of each fruit. Though the tables I've included are not a substitute for actual measurement, you can use them to get an idea that lemons are too acidic to constitute a major proportion of a wine must and that watermelon would need acid added. If the level of acid in the fruit is greater than 9g/L, then the quantity of that fruit should be limited to avoid excess acidity.

- Sugar level. Get a general idea of how much sugar will be in the major fruit ingredients, and how much will need to be added. Also, decide what form that sugar will take.

- Spicing. Look at the earlier tables when deciding how much spicing to add, if any.

- Pectic enzyme. Other than straight meads, all recipes will need pectic enzyme. Review the tables to see if the amount used is according to package directions or needs to be doubled.

- Yeast. Decide what type of yeast to use based upon its characteristics, and include yeast energizer in the amount recommended on the package.

# One Gallon Example: Cherry Wine

**Few can resist** the idea of cherry wine, so it's a good start for a recipe. I've made cherry wine during the winter months and used a combination of bottled cherry juice, frozen cherries, and other adjuncts.

- I would like my dominant flavor to be cherry, my secondary flavor to be grape, and my tertiary flavor to be vanilla.
- Checking the tables, I see that cherries are high in tannin so they can't form more than half of my must, and they are high in acid too. So I will use one quart of bottled organic 100% black cherry juice, and one ten-ounce package of frozen sweet cherries, and make up the difference with organic white grape juice. Because less than half the recipe will have the higher tannins of cherry juice and the remainder of the recipe will come from white grape juice, tannin is likely to be a bit on the low side, so I'll add a quarter teaspoon of tannin.
- The two primary acids in cherries are malic and citric in that order, so if an acid test shows more acid is needed, I'll add a 2:1 mixture of malic and citric acids.
- Because I'm using bottled juices and frozen cherries with nutritional labels, I can add up how much sugar would be in the gallon: 200g from cherry juice, 42g from frozen cherries, and 480g from grape juice for a total of 722 grams. Converted to ounces that is 25.5 ounces. Looking at the hydrometer tables, I see that I need 31.6 ounces of sugar for a starting gravity of 1.090, so I figure I'll need

about six ounces of sugar, though I will test with a hydrometer to be sure.

- Looking at the spicing table, and not wanting to overpower the cherry, I am including one vanilla bean in the primary fermenter.
- A lot of yeasts are available, but Montrachet looks like a really good match for what we're making.

So the final recipe looks like this:

## Winter Cherry Wine

1 quart organic black cherry juice

1 ten-ounce package of frozen sweet cherries

3 quarts organic white grape juice

6-8 ounces of sugar, based on hydrometer test

1 vanilla bean

¼ tsp yeast energizer

¼ tsp tannin

2:1 blend of malic/citric acids as needed

1 packet Montrachet yeast

# 16

# Advanced Techniques in Winemaking

**Some of the** techniques in this chapter truly are "advanced" in terms of difficulty or equipment, but most are merely extensions of what you already know that will help you produce wines with different characteristics.

## Making Wine Without Sulfites

**In the previous** chapter I oriented procedures around the use of sulfites, because the use of sulfites makes it easier to produce a solid product. Even before modern times, sulfites were employed by burning sulfur to create sulfur dioxide gas to purify musts, and many yeasts generate their own sulfites during primary fermentation. There is no such thing as a sulfite-free wine. The best that can be managed is to make wine without adding them.

If you don't want sulfites added to your wine, here are some tips:

- Clean all equipment using scalding (140+ degree) water. Water this hot is, in fact, scalding. Use caution.
- Though it decreases the quality of the result somewhat, you can pasteurize your must by heating to 150 degrees and holding it there for ½ hour before putting it in your primary fermenter. Add bottled water to make up any difference in volume. Make sure the temperature has dropped below 80 before adding pectic enzyme or yeast. Musts that have been pasteurized often create very hazy wines, so don't do this with fruits that require a double dose of pectic enzyme.
- When using unpasteurized must, your yeast must out-compete all other yeasts and bacteria. So instead of sprinkling the yeast on top of the must, get your yeast ready two days in advance by sprinkling the yeast into a pint jar containing bottled apple juice mixed with a pinch of yeast energizer and then cap it with several layers of cheese-cloth. Set it in a dark place at 60-70 degrees. When you add this yeast to your must, just pour it in smoothly and do not stir. Now your yeast has a head start so it can out-compete the wild yeasts and bacteria on the fruit.

# Advanced Testing of Sulfite Levels

**The sulfite test** kits you can buy through wine hobby suppliers are fine for lightly colored wines but inaccurate when testing heavily colored wines because the phenolic coloring compounds in the wine take up some of the testing reagent. Errors can be as high as 20ppm. In an earlier chapter, I advised that you could "guesstimate" by subtracting 10ppm from the test results. If you aren't comfortable with guesstimates, you can do your own testing. The following procedures work on the principle of calculating total sulfite, calculating the error, and then subtracting the error from the total. You will be working with sulfuric acid in this procedure; safety goggles and a lab apron are required.

## Equipment

50 ml     beaker

3 ml      syringe (no needle needed)

5 ml      syringe (no needle needed)

10 ml     graduated cylinder

250 ml   volumetric flask (only needed if preparing your own iodine solution)

Scale (only needed if preparing your own iodine solution)

## Chemicals

Distilled Water

.02N Iodine solution[53]

1% Starch solution

25% Sulfuric Acid solution

3% Hydrogen peroxide solution

Clean all equipment with distilled water. Put a 20ml sample of wine in the 50ml beaker. Add 5ml of starch solution, swirl to mix, then add 5ml of sulfuric acid solution to the sample and swirl to mix again. Fill the 3ml syringe with iodine solution. Add iodine solution a little at a time, swirling after each addition, until a distinct color change (it will

---

[53] This can be purchased from a lab supply company or made. To make it, mix .63g of iodine crystals and 1.3g of potassium iodide crystals together, place in a 250ml volumetric flask, and fill to 250ml with distilled water. Due to methamphetamine labs, iodine has been regulated since 2007 as a precursor. You can still buy elemental iodine, but your name goes on a list. Your name won't go on a list if you buy ready-made .02N iodine solution, but it is pretty expensive. If you aren't running a methamphetamine lab, don't worry about your name being on a list.

be dark blue) that remains for several seconds occurs. The measured amount of sulfite in ppm is:

$$(3ml-\text{reading on syringe}) \times 32$$

Write this number down as we'll use it twice in the next part of the procedure. Now we need to measure the error. To do this, we'll need to remove the free sulfite from the solution. The 3% hydrogen peroxide solution is way too strong for a sample this small, so make some 0.012% solution by adding 1ml of hydrogen peroxide solution to 250ml volumetric flask and adding enough distilled water to meet the 250ml mark. Clean all equipment with distilled water. Put a 20ml sample of wine in the 50 ml beaker. Add an amount of your prepared hydrogen peroxide solution equal to 0.14 ml for every ppm detected in the earlier procedure. So if the first procedure gave a result of 57ppm, add 0.14 x 57 or 8 ml of hydrogen peroxide solution. Swirl to mix and wait a few minutes. Add 5ml of starch solution and 5ml of sulfuric acid solution to the sample. Fill the 3ml syringe with iodine solution. Add iodine solution a little at a time, swirling after each addition, until a distinct color change (it will be dark blue) that remains for several seconds occurs. The measured amount of error in ppm is:

$$(3ml-\text{reading on syringe}) \times 32$$

The corrected amount of sulfite in the wine is: (measured sulfite)−(measured error) ppm.

# Malolactic Fermentation

**Most wine musts** will contain some lactic bacteria. These are inhibited by sulfite levels greater than 20 mg/L, by alcohol concentrations of greater than 14%, low temperatures, and active yeast. If you have ever been quite certain that secondary fermentation has completed but later found your bottled wine to be slightly carbonated, it is likely that malolactic fermentation occurred spontaneously. Sometimes it even occurs simultaneously with alcoholic fermentation and you never notice.

Commercial wineries subject a large proportion of their red wines and a lesser proportion of their white wines to deliberate malolactic fermentation for a variety of reasons. The most obvious reason is that malolactic fermentation changes sharp malic acid to smooth lactic acid. It raises the pH and reduces the acidity slightly. The formation of lactic acid in the presence of ethanol also allows the creation of ethyl lactate, an ester that gives wines a fruity character. In addition, bacteria will produce diethyl succinate, another fruity ester along with diacetyl and other flavor compounds. Malolactic fermentation also serves to make wine more self-preserving by consuming pentoses and hexoses[54] not used by yeast, as well as malic acid that would otherwise serve as food for other bacteria. Malolactic bacteria secrete bacteriocins that inhibit the growth of other bacteria, which makes the wine more microbiologically stable. Finally, by deliberately conducting a malo-lactic fermentation, you can be certain that one won't occur spontane-ously in the bottle.

There are a number of malolactic cultures available. Some are sin-gle species (usually *Oenococcus oenii*) and others contain a mix of spe-cies. Only *Oenococcus oenii* can work at pH values lower than 3.5, so all cultures contain at least that one bacteria.

Malolactic bacteria and wine yeast are often incompatible as one will inhibit the other. Therefore, malolactic culture is best introduced after the secondary alcoholic fermentation is complete unless the wine

---

[54] Pentoses and Hexoses are five-and six-carbon sugars, respectively.

has a final alcohol level exceeding 14%. Though different products will require slightly different procedures and I based the following on the use of Lalvin's malolactic culture, it's a good guideline for malolactic fermentations generally.

- Wait until secondary fermentation has completed. It can be considered complete after the wine sits for three months without dropping any precipitate at the bottom of the fermenter and it is clear.
- About a week before adding the malolactic cultures, move the wine to an area with a temperature between 64 and 75 degrees. It must remain at this temperature throughout the fermentation.
- Rack the wine into a new, clean secondary fermenter. Do NOT add sulfite in this racking!
- If you have a sulfite test kit, you can test that the sulfite is under 20 ppm. If it is above 20 ppm, you can reduce it to that level via the addition of hydrogen peroxide as described in the chapter on wine chemistry.
- Add the packet of malolactic culture directly to the wine.
- Fit with an airlock. (The fermentation generates carbon dioxide.)
- Malolactic fermentations complete in one to three months, but because they proceed so slowly, it is hard to gauge. You could assess the progress using commercially available paper chromatography kits for malic acid detection, but these cost from $50 to $200 and their shelf life is only a few months. Unless you are making a LOT of wine, this doesn't make a lot of sense.
- After three months, rack the wine into a clean secondary fermenter, adding 50ppm sulfite to the must (one Campden tablet per gallon). This will inhibit any malolactic bacteria that remain. Allow to age for at least another month, then bottle.

# Fortification

**Fortification is the** addition of distilled spirits to wine in order to increase its alcohol content. Wines are fortified for three reasons: to bring them to an alcohol level suitable for the development of what is known as a sherry flor; to arrest fermentation before all the sugar has been consumed so it retains sweetness; and to make a more biologically stable wine for purposes of long storage and shipping. Being distilled from wine, brandy is the most common spirit used for fortification.

Sherry wines are fermented to dryness, their alcohol content is assessed, and then they are mixed with brandy to reach an alcohol level of between 14.5% and 16%. This range is conducive to allowing the specific strain of yeast used in sherries to develop a cap known as a flor that protects the wine from further oxidation and promotes aldehyde production. If the wines were good but unexceptional, they are made into oloroso sherry by fortifying to a level exceeding 16% so that a flor isn't formed. If they were really bad, they are set aside to make vinegar or brandy.

Port wines are fortified to an amount of alcohol around 20% before the primary fermentation has completed. The high level of alcohol from fortification stops the fermentation very quickly so that high sugar levels remain.

Because distilled spirits are expensive (why would you use the cheap stuff?), the financially practical batch size for fortification will likely be limited to a gallon or so. Even though fortification will stop the yeast fermentation, the wine will continue to undergo small changes from aging for as long as forty years.

The first step in fortification is to assess the level of alcohol in the wine. For wines fermented to dryness, this is easy—you can just use the potential alcohol corresponding to the original hydrometer reading of the must. For wines that will retain sweetness, you will take a hydrometer reading every day or two during the primary fermentation and perform the fortification at a point corresponding to the degree of sweetness you want to retain. In general, you'll want to do this at a reading between 1.010 for slightly sweet to 1.040 for very sweet. The alcohol level level can be determined by subtracting the potential alcohol at the point of fortification from the potential alcohol at the start of fermentation.

For example, if the original specific gravity of my must was 1.093 (12.8% potential alcohol) and I perform my fortification when the must reaches 1.027 (3.7% potential alcohol), the level of alcohol is 12.8% - 3.7% or 9.1%.

Once you know how much alcohol the wine already contains, you must decide how much alcohol you want it to contain after fortification. If you are wanting a sherry flor, you'll want 15%, but if you are making a sweet wine, you'll want 20%.

Then you need to calculate how much distilled spirit and how much wine to add to make a gallon at the desired strength. Though there are tables for this, algebra is the most flexible tool, and the equation is easy enough.

A = Percentage of Final Wine as Alcohol expressed as a decimal (e.g. 20% = .2)

B = Percentage Alcohol of Starting Wine expressed as a decimal

C = Percentage Wine of Distilled Spirit expressed as a decimal

D = Size of final batch in ounces

X = Ounces of Wine for the batch

$X = D\,(A-C)/(B-C)$

So, if I want a wine with 20% alcohol, my starting wine is 9.1% alcohol and I am fortifying with brandy that is 40% alcohol to make a batch of one gallon (128 ounces):

$X = 128(.20 - .40)/(.091 - .40) = 82.8$ rounded to 83 ounces.

So now I know I will use 83 ounces of wine and 128–83 or 45 ounces of brandy to make a gallon of my sweet fortified wine.

The procedure is straightforward. You put 45 ounces of brandy in a secondary fermenter, rack wine into the fermenter until you have a gallon, and then top it with an airlock. If you are making a sweet wine you'll need to rack it in another week or so, and then treat it like any other wine. If your starting wine was already completely fermented, you can wait a month before racking and then treat it like any other wine.

# Oak Aging

**Oak aging is** traditional in wines, especially red wines. There's no question that the traditional aging of wines in oak barrels alters the flavor through the extraction of a variety of compounds from the oak. However, oak barrels are very expensive and require considerable care. Studies show that using a neutral container (such as glass) and adding toasted oak chips will impart the same compounds as aging in a barrel.[55]

Oak chips are available from both American and French oak, and in a variety of toasting levels. French oak imparts more tannin and spice notes, whereas American oak imparts more vanilla and sweet notes. Toasting oak cubes of either sort makes some of the compounds such as vanillin more available but also imparts a more charred character to the wine, especially at the highest levels of toasting.

⊗ Oak chips are easier to work with than barrels and impart indistinguishable results.

[55] A. Bautista-Ortín, A. Lencina, M. Cano-López, F. Pardo-Mínguez, J. López-Roca and E. Gómez-Plaza (2009), "The use of oak chips during the aging of a red wine in stainless steel tanks or used barrels: effect of the contact time and size of the oak chips on aroma compounds."

Oak chips impart their character quickly at first, and then more slowly over time. Once they have been added, they can be removed and the compounds they add will remain and continue to work throughout the aging process. Though they can be retained in the fermenter for as long as nine months, little is gained by keeping them for longer than a month.

Before being added to the fermenter, the chips need to be sanitized so they don't infect your wine with something nasty. All you need to do is fill a quart canning jar with water, add a quarter teaspoon of potassium metabisulfite powder, put your oak chips in the water, and then put on the lid. After twenty four hours, the chips can be added to the wine by simply dumping them into the wine in the secondary fermenter. They won't fit through the racking tube, so they'll be removed at the next racking. Just rinse them out of the fermenter when you clean it.

# Solera Aging

**A solera is** a grouping of containers (usually barrels) used to accomplish a unique blended aging technique in the production of certain vinegars, spirits, and wines. On a commercial scale, a solera is a substantial investment, but for an amateur with containers not exceeding five gallons, the larger concern in space. Though you can technically use this technique with as

**⊗ The technique of solera aging can be employed at home on a smaller scale using simple glass fermenters.**

few as two containers and with no upper limit, I am going to describe it using three.

Label three containers as A, B, and C, filling them all with wine. After the wine has aged a year, withdraw and bottle half of the contents of container C. Refill container C from container B, refill container B from container A and use new wine to refill container A. Do the same thing every year, and over time the average age of the wine bottled from container C will approach five years, even though you are bottling wine from it every year.

The average age increases with the number of containers and with bottling smaller portions according to the following formula:

Average Age = (Number of Containers−Fraction of Container Used)/ Fraction of Container Used

So if you started with three five-gallon containers and only bottled one gallon (.2 of a five-gallon container) a year, the average age would approach (3 - .2)/.2 or 14 years. If you used four containers instead of three and drew off half of a container each year, the average age would converge upon seven years.

If you have a particular type or style of wine that you like and that requires substantial aging, setting up a solera of three containers can be an easy way of having your cake and eating it too, where over time you can consistently produce well-aged wine in small quantity every year.

Of course, this exact same approach is used with the higher quality balsamic vinegars, many of which have average ages exceeding a decade. Because vinegar is consumed in smaller quantities than wine, it is entirely practical to set up an inexpensive vinegar solera using five one-gallon containers. If you drew off and replenished a half gallon annually, the aging would converge upon nine years.

# 17

# Principles and Materials for Vinegar

**There is vinegar,** and then there is vinegar. Most often, we buy vinegar as a commodity product without giving much thought as to quality. The gallon jugs of distilled vinegar in the supermarket are indistinguishable. There is no point in making your own vinegar when you can buy it for $1/gallon in bulk; so this chapter is not about making that kind of commodity product.

Really good vinegar is a complex taste sensation to be savored and appreciated. It takes on the character of the malt, cider, or wine from which it is derived. It can also be improved by aging as the complex flavor and aroma compounds meld, recombine, and change. It is truly a gourmet product, and hand-crafted examples are usually more than $20/pint.

Vinegar in general is a healthy condiment. Vinegar increases satiety[56] thereby reducing caloric intake, it reduces the glycemic index of foods with which it is consumed,[57] and may reduce the risks of certain types of heart disease.[58] And just as wine preserves many of the vitamins and antioxidants in the original fruit, homemade vinegars made from those wines will likewise preserve vitamins and antioxidants; thereby making it even more healthy than the commodity vinegars used in the studies.

So this chapter is not about duplicating commodity products that are cheaper to buy than they are to make. Rather, it is about making a uniquely healthful product with gourmet qualities that will enhance your salads, greens, dressings, and anything else you make with vinegar.

If you make wine and beer, you will already have the raw materials at hand allowing you to make gourmet vinegar inexpensively. So I will focus on using wine and beer as the starting materials in this chapter, even though vinegar can also be made using similar techniques if you use hard cider, sake, or practically any other product containing alcohol.

# Speaking of Wine and Beer

**I really enjoy** making wine and beer. I enjoy every aspect of the process, and I especially enjoy sharing my work with someone who will appreciate the results of my efforts. But sometimes my efforts result in

---

[56] Östman, E; Granfeldt, Y; Persson, L; Björck, I (2005). "Vinegar supplementation lowers glucose and insulin responses and increases satiety after a bread meal in healthy subjects." *European Journal of Clinical Nutrition* 59 (9): 983–8

[57] Johnston, C. S.; Kim, C. M.; Buller, A. J. (2004). "Vinegar Improves Insulin Sensitivity to a High-Carbohydrate Meal in Subjects With Insulin Resistance or Type 2 Diabetes." *Diabetes Care* 27 (1): 281–2

[58] Johnston, Carol S.; Gaas, Cindy A. (2006). "Vinegar: medicinal uses and antiglycemic effect." *MedGenMed* 8 (2): 61

a less-than-stellar product. The wine I made from bottled blueberry juice and brown sugar comes to mind as does the beer I made with far too much oatmeal. What on earth was I thinking? The good news is, I can use these to make vinegar. You will likely have some learning experiences of your own that will serve as excellent raw material.

Some commercial wines and beers are pretty poor. Even if wine or beer that you've purchased is pretty good, it may have sat in the refrigerator too long or be near its sell-by date. Rather than dump that effort or money down the drain, you might consider using it to make your own vinegar.

Wine that you use to make vinegar cannot have been preserved using potassium sorbate or sodium benzoate. Beer seldom has such preservatives. Any wine you use can be normally sulfited or it can be non-sulfited. The wine can be white or red, sweet or dry, and made from any conceivable edible fruit. The beer you use can be made from barley, wheat, or any other grain. And even though you will likely choose wines or beers for this process that were not optimal for drinking, it is very important that the starting material you choose be biologically sound.

Any sound wine or beer that you use, even if it isn't very good for drinking, will still yield a product far superior to the "wine vinegar" or "malt vinegar" you will find at the supermarket. The "wine" they use as a starting product was never intended for drinking in the first place, whereas yours was planned with drinking quality in mind and is hence a better material from which to make vinegar.

# What is Vinegar?

**Vinegar is a** dilute form of acetic acid, ranging in strength from 4% to 8%. It is made by the oxidation of ethyl alcohol into acetic acid through a fermentation process undertaken by acetic acid bacteria

(AAB). Just as the yeast in wine derives its energy from sugar and produces ethyl alcohol as a waste product, AAB derive their energy from alcohol and produce acetic acid as a waste product. And just as the ethyl alcohol in wine acts as a preservative against organisms that cannot tolerate alcohol, acetic acid acts as a preservative against organisms that cannot tolerate the low pH created by acetic acid. This is how pickling foods in vinegar keeps them from spoiling.

# Acetic Acid Bacteria

**There are a** great many specific strains of AAB. They are present on the surface of both healthy and damaged fruit as well as the nectar of flowers. They are also commonly transferred by the fruit flies that could have been attracted to your wine-making or brewing process.

Wine is produced in anaerobic conditions, meaning that oxygen is excluded. Vinegar, on the other hand, is produced under aerobic conditions as the AAB require oxygen to work. In the absence of oxygen, the bacteria go dormant.

Various strains of AAB[59] are present in wine must from the very beginning and remain in the wine even when it is bottled.[60] The primary factor that keeps it suppressed in wine is lack of oxygen and alcohol levels that are too high for the bacteria to process. So especially with newly-made wines, all that is theoretically necessary to turn wine into vinegar is to permit the entry of oxygen. In the presence of oxygen the bacteria would quickly proliferate as a film on the surface of the wine and turn the alcohol to acetic acid, especially if the alcohol level is under 10%.

---

[59] Acetobacter aceti, gluconobacter oxydans, and acetobacter pasteurianus predominate.

[60] A. Joyeux, S. Lafon-Lafourcade, and P. Ribéreau-Gayon (1984), "Evolution of Acetic Acid Bacteria During Fermentation and Storage of Wine," *Appl Environ Microbiol.* 1984 July; 48(1): 153–156

Beer is even more susceptible to acetification because its lower alcohol content, lack of sulfites, and higher nutritional content make it an attractive target.

Acetic acid bacteria are not the only bacteria that can take hold in wine or beer, and leaving the results to chance can result in a product that is not only unusable, but thoroughly rotten. So for our purposes, just as a specific strain of yeast is used to make wine, a specific strain of bacteria is used to make vinegar. Acetic acid bacteria are commercially available in a form called vinegar mother. Vinegar mother, also known as *Mycoderma aceti*, is a gelatinous substance containing the AAB that forms on the surface of vinegar. Though vinegar could certainly be made from *Gluconobacter oxydans* or *Acetobacter pasteurianus* among many other possibilities, all of the commercially available vinegar mothers are *Acetobacter aceti*.

*Acetobacter aceti* needs to float on top of the wine or beer you use to make vinegar so that it has access to oxygen at all times. Without access to oxygen, it will go dormant. The vinegar mother you obtain may look like crude vinegar, or it may look like jelly. If it looks like jelly, it is very likely that when you put it in your vinegar crock, it will sink and thereby go dormant for lack of oxygen. To prevent this, a piece of thin wood about the size of a playing card is floated on top of the wine or beer, and the vinegar mother is placed on it. This piece of wood is usually made of oak and is called a vinegar raft.

Vinegar mothers are available as white wine, red wine, beer/malt, and cider. All of them have the same acetic acid bacteria, and the only difference is the carrier. In small batches of vinegar—say less than a gallon—the carrier makes a difference in the flavor, but in larger batches of vinegar the carrier doesn't matter.

Some strains of acetic acid bacteria, such as gluconobacter oxydans, will go dormant once all of the ethyl alcohol has been consumed. But the *Acetobacter aceti* that you'll be using does not go dormant once all of the ethyl alcohol is used. Instead, it starts consuming the acetic acid that it produced, with the end result being just carbon dioxide. So vinegar conversions using a commercial vinegar mother must be arrested once the conversion has completed or you'll end up with no vinegar at all.

The conversion process can be stopped in two ways. For purposes of aging the vinegar, it can be placed in a canning jar with a tight-fitting lid that excludes oxygen. This leaves the vinegar alive, but dormant. For purposes of long-term storage or use in an environment where oxygen might be admitted, the vinegar is pasteurized. Vinegar is pasteurized by heating it to 150 degrees for 30 minutes with the lid adjusted as for canning to prevent evaporation. Once it has been pasteurized, it can be stored in any clean container for a nearly indefinite period of time.

# Ethanol to Acetic Acid Conversion

**If you are** using commercial beer or wine to make vinegar, the amount of alcohol (by volume) is listed on the label. If you are using your own, you should have a good idea how much alcohol is in your beer or wine from the hydrometer readings you recorded.

The chemical equation for the conversion of ethanol to vinegar is:

$$C_2H_5OH + O_2 \rightarrow CH_3COOH + H_2O$$

So ethanol plus oxygen gets converted to acetic acid plus water. Looking at the equation, each molecule of ethanol is converted into one molecule of acetic acid. The molecular weight of ethanol is 46.07 and its density is .789 g/cm³. The molecular weight of acetic acid is 60.5 and its density is 1.049 g/cm³.

This means that every gram of alcohol will result in 60.5/46.07 or 1.313 grams of vinegar. A gram of alcohol will occupy 1/.789 or 1.27 cm³. Alcohol percentages are done by volume, but vinegar percentages are done by weight. We can get a good idea of the conversion factor, that is, how much acetic acid a given amount of ethanol will create, by doing the math for a hypothetical 10% wine.

If I have a liter of 10% wine, that liter contains 100 ml of alcohol. 100 ml of alcohol has a mass of 100 $cm^3$/1.27 $cm^3$ or 78.7 grams. The mass of the vinegar produced will be 78.7 * 1.313 or 103 grams.

Therefore, a 10% alcohol by volume wine will create a 10.3% by weight vinegar. So in essence the percentages are identical. Knowing this fact will allow us to dilute the beer or wine we are adding to the vinegar mother to produce a vinegar of known strength. We'd still test it just to be sure, of course. But this allows us to make our vinegar very precisely.

# How to Safely Use Homemade Vinegar in Canning

**All canning books** tell you to never use homemade vinegar in canning. That's because pickling recipes rely upon the vinegar having a certain strength of 5%, and if you use vinegar of a lesser strength you could wind up with botulism-tainted food that could kill you. So if you don't know for sure that the strength of your vinegar is 5% or greater, you can't use it safely. Of course, if the vinegar is substantially stronger than 5% you could wind up with pickled foods that are a lot more acidic than you'd like. You can always dilute it if it is too strong.

The solution to this problem is to figure out how much acidity is in the vinegar. You can do this easily by using the ingredients in a standard acid testing kit available from all wine-making suppliers, a pH meter, and a slight change in procedure. I specify using a pH meter rather than the phenolphthalein indicator because phenolphthalein turns pink when the endpoint is reached, and such a color change may be difficult to discern in vinegar of certain colors. A pH meter won't trick your eye.

## Equipment

1 50ml   beaker
1 10ml   syringe (no needle needed)
0.2N     Sodium Hydroxide solution
          Distilled water
          pH meter

Rinsing the syringe using distilled water after each use, put 2ml of the vinegar to be tested and 20ml of distilled water in the 50ml beaker. Fill the syringe with 0.2N sodium hydroxide solution to exactly the 10ml mark. Initially, add 1ml of sodium hydroxide to the beaker each time, swirl, then test with the pH meter. As the pH approaches its endpoint of 8.3, use lesser quantities. Repeat until the solution has a pH of 8.3.

The amount of acid in your vinegar is given by the following equation:

Percentage Acetic Acid = 0.6 × (10−reading of syringe at endpoint)

# 18

# Vinegar Making Techniques

**Making vinegar is** easier than making wine or beer and requires minimal equipment or ingredients. Other than a vinegar crock and the wine or beer you'll be using, you can get everything else you need for under $30. Here are the items you'll need:

## Vinegar Crock

**Vinegar can theoretically** be made in any sort of container. Traditionally, it is made in oak barrels called vinegar casks or in ceramic urns known as vinegar crocks.

There are three important features in a container used to make vinegar. The container should have a mouth wide enough that you can insert your vinegar raft and preferably your whole hand. It should have a tap, spout, or spigot near the bottom, but far enough from the bottom that it doesn't pick up sediment. Finally, it should be made of a material that will not react with the vinegar. Vinegar is a dilute acid, so it will react with most metals given time.

Given these features, you are not constrained to only use products officially sold as vinegar crocks. Anything officially sold as a vinegar crock will quite frankly be seriously over-priced. I looked on the Internet recently and found many of them priced at nearly $100!

I use two containers to make vinegar. One is a miniature ceramic water crock that holds a half gallon. It costs $24. The other is a one-gallon plastic beverage dispenser I picked up at a department store for $4. Both of these containers have the essential features, including the spigot. Normal ceramic water crocks hold 2½ gallons, an amount which may far exceed the amount of vinegar you plan to make. That's why I got a miniature ½ gallon crock.

You could go all out and get an oak vinegar cask, but that will set you back at least $80. If you want your vinegar to be oak-aged, just add oak cubes to the sealed pint or quart jar that you are using to age your vinegar.

# Cheesecloth and Rubber Bands

**These items are** used over the mouth of your vinegar crock to allow oxygen to enter but keep fruit flies and other critters out. Not all cheesecloth is created equal. The material that is sold as "cheesecloth" at the supermarket is not suitable for making cheese, and even doubled or tripled it won't keep fruit flies out of your vinegar.

Unless you have a good gourmet shop nearby that sells real cheesecloth, you may have to order it from a supplier of cheese-making supplies over the Internet. It is a bit expensive when you include shipping, so I recommend saving on shipping by ordering a couple of

⊗ Use a doubled piece of high-quality fine cheesecloth to cover your vinegar urn. Otherwise, fruit flies will get into your vinegar.

packages. They won't go to waste because you'll need the cheesecloth for making cheese in the next chapter.

The size of the needed rubber bands will be different depending upon the size of the mouth of your vinegar crock. The only caution worth mentioning is that light and vinegar fumes will degrade the rubber, so check the rubber bands weekly and replace them if you see signs of deterioration. Otherwise you'll look at your crock one day and find more flies in it than vinegar.

# Miscellaneous Supplies

**A vinegar raft** is a small thin piece of oak that floats on top of your vinegar. Its purpose is to keep the vinegar mother from sinking because if the vinegar mother

⊗ The materials for oak-aging vinegar are simple and inexpensive.

sinks, it will stop making vinegar. These are available in vinegar kits or individually from many Internet sites. Just type "vinegar raft" into a search engine.

Some people prefer the taste of vinegar that has been aged in oak, or the astringency contributed by the tannins leached from the oak. Oak barrels are expensive and time-intensive to maintain.

An alternative is adding oak chips or oak cubes to the vinegar. Add a quarter cup per gallon, enclosed in a tied spice bag for easy removal later. The chips or cubes are added during the aging process and left in the vinegar for four to six weeks. For these purposes, you don't want to use oak from your building supply store. Instead, order it from a winemaking supplier. Winemaking suppliers can offer a range of oaks with different taste characteristics that you know aren't contaminated with anything nasty.

Canning jars are a good choice for aging and storing vinegars. They seal tightly, which will cause the vinegar mother to go dormant during aging, and they can be used repeatedly which makes them a good bargain.

One other thing you may find helpful is a funnel that you have attached to a piece of plastic hose such as the hose used for racking wine. As vinegar is being made, you need to add more beer or wine. The easy way to do this without risk of disturbing the vinegar mother is to insert the hose into the liquid in the vinegar crock, and add the liquid through the funnel.

A candy thermometer will be needed for pasteurizing vinegar, unless you plan to can it using a boiling water bath canner for long-term storage.

# Consolidated Equipment and Ingredient List

- Vinegar crock
- Vinegar mother
- Cheesecloth
- Rubber bands
- Vinegar raft
- Canning jars

- Candy thermometer
- Oak chips or cubes (optional)

# Making Your Vinegar

**The first thing** to do is pre-dilute your wine or beer if needed. At levels higher than 7% alcohol it might inhibit the AAB. You can always make it less concentrated, down to 3%, for purely culinary use or if your beer only has that much alcohol, and it isn't unusual for sherry vinegars to be as high as 7%. In general, I recommend diluting to 5.5% so the vinegar can be used with greater versatility. Always dilute with clean, non-chlorinated water. I use bottled water for this purpose.

So . . . how much water do you add to your beer or wine to get a certain percentage of alcohol? Start by dividing the current concentration in percent by the desired concentration in percent to get C. So if I have some 10% wine and I want 5.5%, I divide 10 by 5.5 to get 1.82. Next, multiply the volume of your wine (say 500 ml in a standard wine bottle) by C to get the total diluted volume: 500ml × 1.82 = 910. Finally, subtract the volume of wine from the total volume to get the volume of water you need to add. 910 ml – 500 ml = 410 ml.

This also works with beer. Say I have some beer that is 6% alcohol and I want to dilute it to 5.5%. The standard beer bottle is 12 ounces. So C = 6%/5.5% = 1.09. Multiply 12 oz × 1.09 = 13. Finally, 13 – 12 = 1, so I would add one ounce of water.

The quantity of diluted wine or beer that you use is important because it takes a while for the vinegar mother to work, and in the meantime the underlying beer or wine is vulnerable to outside infection. You want to limit the amount you put in the crock to no more than triple the volume of the vinegar mother, which is eight ounces. So your initial ingredients of the vinegar crock will be 24 ounces of beer or wine diluted as needed and eight ounces of vinegar mother for a total of 32 ounces.

# Making Vinegar, Step by Step

1.  **Clean your vinegar** crock thoroughly and sanitize it using sulfite solution. (See the chapters on wine for how to make sulfite solution.)
2.  Check the capacity of the container of vinegar mother you ordered. Usually it is eight ounces.
3.  Add diluted wine or beer to the vinegar crock. The amount added should be twice the volume of the vinegar mother. So if you have eight ounces of vinegar mother, put 24 ounces of wine or beer in your crock. The alcohol percentage cannot exceed 7%.
4.  Open your vinegar mother. If it is gelatinous, place your vinegar raft on top of the water/wine solution in the vinegar crock.
5.  Add the vinegar mother. If it is all liquid, just gently pour it into the crock. If it is gelatinous, add it on top of the vinegar raft.
6.  Cover the mouth of the container with cheesecloth and hold it in place with a rubber band.
7.  Set the container in a dark place or at least someplace well out of the sun. The ideal temperature range is 80 to 90 degrees, but it will progress fine at 70 to 100.
8.  Depending on temperature and other factors, the complete conversion of wine to vinegar can take anywhere from six weeks to three months. Check your vinegar weekly by sniffing it through the cheesecloth. It should smell like vinegar is forming.
9.  To increase the volume of the vinegar being made, you can add more diluted wine or beer starting at the fourth week and every fourth week thereafter. Add by using a sanitized funnel and tubing.

10. Six weeks after the final addition of wine, start tasting small (less than ¼ tsp) samples of the vinegar to see if it is done. It's done when all the alcohol flavor has been replaced with vinegar flavor. Your tongue and nose are amazingly sensitive and able to detect many substances in very low concentrations of parts-per-million. This is as accurate as any easily performed test in determining if the vinegar is done.

⊗ The mother in this vinegar crock is doing nicely.

11. Once the vinegar is done, it is important to remove it from the vinegar crock because with all the alcohol gone, the vinegar mother will start consuming the acetic acid, and thereby destroy the vinegar. Take out as much vinegar as you can through the spigot and then start your next batch using the same vinegar mother in that container. As long as your vinegar doesn't become contaminated, you can use the same vinegar mother indefinitely.

# Aging Vinegar

**Just like wine,** vinegar made from wine will mellow with age. Freshly-made vinegar is very sharp with a lot of pointed edges. When it is allowed to age, the compounds within the vinegar combine in various ways that make the vinegar more mellow and to bring out other flavor components.

Even though it is easy to visualize the vinegar mother as sitting on top of the wine, many of its bacteria are spread throughout the vinegar.

When you draw off a sample, even if it looks clear, it is filled with acetic acid bacteria. (These bacteria, incidentally, are totally harmless to humans.) Freshly-made vinegar is teeming with life.

When vinegar is aged, it is aged with that life intact. The vinegar is drawn from the crock via the spigot and placed in a container sealed so as to exclude air. This renders the acetic acid bacteria dormant. Vinegar can be kept in a sealed container for an indefinite period of time. In fact, genuine balsamic vinegar is aged for at least twelve years, and often for as long as 25 years. The minimum period of aging I would recommend is six weeks.

Vinegar can be aged in porcelain, glass, impervious plastic, or wooden barrels. A lot of the better traditionally-made vinegars feature oak aging. The oak aging serves to impart an astringent principle to the vinegar in the form of tannin. Tannin is not just one substance. The term "tannin" refers to literally dozens if not hundreds of related compounds formed around either a gallic acid or a flavone core. Tannins have in common not only their astringency, but also their ability to bind and precipitate proteins. This means that tannins introduced into vinegar will scavenge stray proteins left over from fermentation by combining with them to form an insoluble substance that will sink to the bottom of the container.

So over time, an initially high level of tannins is reduced and a number of protein- or amino acid-based substances are removed. This serves to alter the flavor in more ways than merely introducing astringency. In fact, the addition of tannin, through its ability to remove other substances, can paradoxically decrease the astringency of vinegar over a period of aging by removing other substances. Tannins also combine with metals in a process known as chelation. Chelation forms soluble compounds that include the metal but render it unavailable to combine with other substances. This likewise affects the flavor.

You can use oak in the aging of your vinegar by placing a quarter cup of the cubes or chips in a tied spice bag in your aging vinegar. Leave it in the container for six weeks, and then remove it using sterilized tongs and re-seal the container. The rest of the vinegar's aging will continue to be affected by the tannins imparted by the oak.

# Keeping Vinegar

**Eventually, the aging** process ends and the vinegar is ready for storage. The next step is to filter and pasteurize. Perfectly adequate filtration is achieved by pouring the vinegar from the jar in which it is aging through a funnel lined with a coffee filter into a clean canning jar.

Fill the jar with vinegar to within a quarter inch of the top, and install the two-piece canning lid. Process for 10 minutes in a boiling water bath or steam canner and pasteurization is complete.

# Making Herbal Vinegars

**I'll confess that** I have never purchased an herbal vinegar. Anytime I have seen herbal vinegar, it is usually in some sort of craft shop. The vinegar is in an ornate bottle with a sprig of some herb and has a fancy label. It also has an obscenely fancy price. The price seems crazy to me because I'm pretty certain that the vinegar they used was $1/gallon commodity vinegar and the sprig of herb cost about a penny, and the cost is $12 for six ounces. No thanks!

Herbal vinegars can be quite nice, though, and making your own is easy enough. You can make it using commodity vinegar from the supermarket or your own hand-crafted vinegar. I don't recommend using cider vinegars for herbs.

As you may know from an earlier book,[61] growing your own herbs is easy. The hard part for beginners is choosing which herbs to use (and how much). To help you get started, I suggest the following single herbs: borage, thyme, rosemary, dill, basil, tarragon, and oregano.

I recommend making your herbal vinegars from fresh herbs when possible. Using fresh herbs, I recommend ½ ounce of fresh herb per cup (eight ounces) of vinegar as a starting proportion. Because the vinegar is a preservative, the herbs won't rot. When using dried herbs, use two tablespoons of dried herb per cup of vinegar.

The procedure is straightforward. Add the cleaned herbs to the container that will hold the herbal vinegar. Heat up the vinegar to a simmer (NOT a boil!), and then pour the vinegar into the container holding the herb. Seal the container. Allow the flavors to meld for three or four weeks to develop the full flavor before using.

If you want something really impressive for making an oil and vinegar dressing for salad, I would suggest making vinegar from pear wine, and then using the pear vinegar to make a borage herbal vinegar.

# Oil and Vinegar Dressing

## *Ingredients:*

| | |
|---|---|
| 11 ounces | Virgin olive oil |
| 5 ounces | Hand-crafted wine vinegar |
| 2 ounces | Water |
| 1 Tbsp | Pulverized dehydrated sweet red pepper |
| 1 Tbsp | Pulverized dehydrated onion |
| 1 tsp | Sea salt |

---

[61] *Maximizing Your Mini Farm*

| 1 tsp | Garlic powder |
| 1 tsp | Dried oregano |
| 1 tsp | Dried basil |
| ⅛ tsp | Xanthan gum OR ½ tsp dried powdered purslane or okra (optional) |

## Procedure

Add ¼ cup of water and ½ cup plus 2 Tbsp vinegar to your container. Add the remaining solid ingredients except for the xanthan gum/purslane. Shake and allow to sit for a few minutes. Add the xanthan gum/purslane and shake thoroughly. Add 1¼ cup plus 2 Tbsp of olive oil. Shake thoroughly.

The purpose of the xanthan gum or purslane in this recipe is to keep the mixture from separating too quickly for practical use because oil/vinegar and oil/water don't normally mix. The xanthan gum or purslane helps to keep it in suspension. If you use xanthan gum, don't use more than the recommended amount or you'll end up with a jelly-like substance rather than dressing.

# 19

# Cheese: Ingredients and Equipment

**Protein is an** essential part of the human diet. Though vegetable sources can provide protein, in most cases the protein lacks crucial amino acids. The most readily available complete proteins are meats, eggs, and dairy; the latter two are the least expensive. Continuing the theme of preserving nutritive content through fermentation, we arrive at cheese. Milk contains a lot of complete protein, but it is also highly perishable.

In the ages before refrigeration was reliably available, one of the few ways to make the nutritional value of milk last longer while also making it quite portable was turning it into cheese. Hard cheeses in particular, if waxed, can last for years.

Another advantage of cheese is that many hard cheeses lack lactose. Lactose is a sugar in milk that many folks (including myself!) cannot digest. As a result, if they consume most milk products they will suffer severe gastrointestinal distress—sometimes for days. When the whey and curd are separated in the first phases of making cheese, 94% of the lactose stays in the whey. Most aged cheeses lack lactose and as a result provide lactose-intolerant people with a delicious way of obtaining the nutritional benefits of milk.

Cheese also has its own health benefits. It is rich in cancer-preventing conjugated linoleic acid and sphingolipids, fights tooth decay, and helps maintain bone strength.

Like beer making, cheese making is both art and science. If anything, there is even more art to making cheese because it requires practice to master the various steps. So this chapter is enough to get you started, but you'll likely want to branch out once you've mastered the techniques covered here.

# What is Cheese?

**Cheese is the** coagulated fat and protein from the milk of domesticated dairy animals. The fats and proteins of milk are coagulated in various ways for the manufacture of different types of cheese. In some cases, a bacterial culture is added. The bacterial culture consumes lactose to make lactic acid; this lactic acid causes the coagulation.

In other cases, rennet is added. Rennet is a complex mixture of enzymes that likewise coagulates milk. In yet other cases, an acid such as citric acid, tartaric acid, or even vinegar is used to cause coagulation. Though the products of these various methods of coagulation are markedly different, they are all cheese because they have in common the coagulation of milk.

# Milk: Where it all Begins

**In the United** States, cows are the usual source for milk; goats are utilized to a lesser extent. In other countries, the milk of bison, buffalo, sheep, horses, yaks, and other animals are also used. The nature of the milk of different species varies appreciably and this is reflected in the character of the cheese produced. Theoretically, you could make cheese using the milk of any mammal; I wouldn't attempt this until you get good at making cheese from well-characterized herbivores such as cows and goats. Not only that, trying to milk a tiger or a bear is probably more dangerous than warranted.

Likewise, the components of the milk will vary between different breeds of dairy cattle. Even the milk of a particular cow will vary with season and diet. Probably the most striking example of this was in the cream cheese my grandmother would make from cows that had been eating wild onions. The smell and taste of the wild onions was transferred to the milk and hence to the cheese. In the case of cream cheese, the results were delicious!

❷ Most organic milk is ultra-pasteurized, making it unsuitable for cheese.

It is important to know that though pasteurized milk is fine for making cheese, the ultra-pasteurized milk that you find in the store is unsuitable. This is unfortunate, because it is the organic brands that tend to be ultra-pasteurized. Ultra-pasteurization is used to extend the shelf-life of expensive milk that doesn't sell very quickly. Unfortunately, that process damages the protein in milk so extensively that it is unsuitable for making cheese.

Milk from other animals can certainly be made into cheese, but doing so would require changes in timing, temperature, quantities of ingredients, and so forth that are simply too extensive to be treated in a single chapter.

So we are going to use pasteurized, homogenized cow's milk from the grocery store as the learning medium for your first forays into cheese making. After you have mastered these skills, you can branch out from there. You can find specific types of milk suitable for your needs by finding a local dairy at www.smalldairy.com.

# About Raw Milk

**Cheese connoisseurs insist** that the best cheeses are made from raw milk that has been neither pasteurized nor homogenized. The trouble is that raw milk is not readily available and quite often there are legal impediments to buying it directly from farmers. The basis for these legal impediments is widespread recognition of the likelihood of the presence of pathogens in raw milk.

In former times the largest risks of raw milk were brucellosis and tuberculosis; today the risks are E. coli, salmonella, and listeria. Testing of vats of milk in modern times shows that even from healthy cows, anywhere from 0.87% to 12.6% of raw milk harbors dangerous pathogens.[62] How do healthy cows give pathogen-infested milk? They don't. Inadequate sanitation and cleaning of equipment introduces fecal bacteria into the milk. The reason pasteurization became a requirement in the first place was that farmers were actively falsifying their records so that tuberculosis-infected cows wouldn't have to be removed from milk production.[63]

---

[62] Position Statement on Raw Milk Sales and Consumption, Cornell University Food Science Department

[63] "Not on My Farm!: Resistance to Bovine Tuberculosis Eradication in the United States," Alan L. Olmstead and Paul W. Rhode, January 2005, *The Journal of Economic History* (2007), 67 : 768-809 Cambridge University Press, Copyright © 2007 The Economic History Association, doi:10.1017/S0022050707000307

The reason it continues to be required is because human nature hasn't changed, and maintaining sanitation on an industrial scale of a biological product created by an animal that excretes feces requires extreme levels of conscientiousness that cannot be guaranteed. In essence, because the healthiness of cows and their milk can be tested to assure a safe product without pasteurization, it is possible to sell perfectly healthy raw milk. But pasteurization is required anyway to compensate for the existence of lazy or dishonest people that will prioritize the production of a single infected cow over the health and well-being of their customers. I'm quite sure most people would do the right thing, but in an industrial system where the outputs of various farms are mixed together, it only requires one feces-contaminated vat to sicken thousands of people.

Obviously, raw milk that does not contain pathogens can be made. Humans have consumed raw milk for thousands of years before pasteurization was invented. Such milk was collected at home by the end users, so there was a direct correlation between shoddiness and adverse consequences that would result from collecting milk in a bucket that wasn't clean. The milk was used immediately rather than transported thousands of miles, so any pathogens present had less opportunity to multiply to dangerous or infective levels. It is therefore possible to obtain raw milk that will not make you sick, provided it is supplied by an honest and conscientious farmer.

How to determine if someone is honest and conscientious, I can't say. If I could write a book describing a sure-fire technique of that sort, personnel managers across the world would rejoice. In the absence of that, I would instead look at the idea of mutual self-interest. If a farmer were to sell you raw milk that made you sick, your family could sue him into oblivion. So it is in his best interest, if he sells raw milk at all, to make sure it is pristine. Many such farmers use small-scale low-temperature vat pasteurization just to be sure, and this process is less damaging to the milk proteins than standard pasteurization processes.

One other layer of protection is to only use raw milk to make hard cheeses that are aged for longer than two months. The process of cheese-making, when combined with the conditions of aging in cheese, serve to eliminate potential pathogens and render the cheese safe. This only applies to aged hard cheeses! Soft cheeses and those eaten less than two months from manufacture should be considered as risky as raw milk, and I personally avoid making cheese from raw milk, but that's an individual choice.

If you use raw milk in cheese-making, there are only two procedural changes you'll need to adopt. The first is that you can avoid using calcium chloride (described later), and the other is that when heating the milk, especially for thermophilic cheeses, you will need to top-stir the milk. Top stirring is just slowly dragging a utensil across the top quarter-inch of milk in order to keep the milk fats from separating out.

To find raw milk, I recommend the following Internet resources:

- A Campaign for Real Milk: www.realmilk.com
- The Weston A. Price Foundation: www.westonaprice.org
- Farm-to-Consumer Legal Defense Fund: www.farmtoconsumer. org

# Categories of Cheese

**Cheese can be** categorized in various ways depending upon the substances from which it is made, its appearance or consistency, whether it is aged or eaten fresh, and the procedures used to produce it. For our purposes, we will use fresh and aged cheeses as categories, as well as soft and hard cheeses, since these categories have the greatest differentiation.

# Equipment

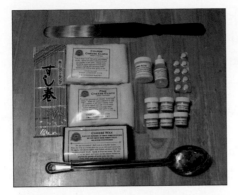

**❽ Quality ingredients and equipment will contribute to a quality product.**

**When it comes** to the equipment needed to make cheese, quality matters. The good news is that most of this equipment is a once-in-a-lifetime purchase. You will likely end up ordering most of these items over the Internet because you may have difficulty finding them locally.

## *Measuring Cups and Spoons*

You want both a large (2 ⅓ cup) and small (1 cup) Pyrex™ glass liquid measuring cups. You will also need measuring spoons, but not the ordinary cheap ones you get at the dollar store. You want high-quality stainless steel measuring spoons that measure in $\frac{1}{32}$, $\frac{1}{16}$, $\frac{1}{8}$, and ¼ teaspoon increments, as well as the traditional sizes.

I have noted by comparing volumes to my laboratory standards that cheap measuring spoons are often undersized or over-sized. This is not a critical matter when making a cake; when making cheese it can spell the difference between success and failure.

## *Large Double Boiler*

With batches of cheese starting with a gallon of milk or less and that use a mesophilic starter culture (more on starter cultures later), you can get by with a standard large pot that you set in a sink of hot water. For batches of cheese requiring more than a gallon of milk or using a thermophilic starter culture, you will need a double-boiler. In cheese-making, this double-boiler is also called a "cheese pot." For very small batches of cheese starting with a quart of milk, you can improvise by setting a smaller pot into a larger one as long as the handles on the smaller pot will sit on the lip of the larger pot so the smaller one is surrounded by water.

Again, depending on the size of your largest intended batch of cheese, you may be able to use a double-boiler as small as eight quarts. But because it takes a large amount of milk to make enough curd to yield very much hard cheese after pressing, you won't go wrong with a boiler as large as 20 quarts. No matter what size you use, make sure it is stainless steel because acidified milk will leach aluminum or iron into your curd and impart metallic flavors.

If you don't already have a double-boiler, this is probably the most expensive item you'll need to get. Searching the Internet, I found prices ranging from $88 to $130 for a 20-quart model. It won't come cheaply, but you'll be thankful that you got it. You can use it for batches of cheese starting with anywhere from one gallon to four gallons of milk, and its configuration will help to hold temperatures steady while preventing scorching.

## Colander

You'll need a large eight-quart colander that will fit into the cheese pot with the handles resting on the edges of the pot. You'll use this to separate the curds from the whey, with the whey going back into the pot.

## Special Utensils

You need a large stainless steel slotted spoon, a stainless steel skimming ladle, and a stainless steel curd knife. This latter utensil is specialized so you will probably have to get it via an Internet source.

## Cheesecloth

You want high-quality coarse (20 thread count) and fine (60 thread count) cheesecloth. The fine cheesecloth is used for making soft cheese such as cream cheese; the coarse cheesecloth is used to hold harder cheeses during the pressing or curing process.

Cheesecloth is packaged in two-yard increments, so you get a piece that is three feet wide and six feet long. Cut off pieces as needed with good scissors. Before use, cheesecloth must be sterilized. Put it in a pan of water, boil for five minutes and then dump the cheesecloth and water into a colander in the sink. Cheesecloth can be re-used. Rinse it under cool running water, work a few drops of dish liquid into it, rinse it thoroughly, and boil it for five minutes. After boiling, hang it up to dry, then store the dried cheesecloth in an airtight bag. Don't forget to sterilize it before using it again.

## Bamboo Sushi Mats

These allow good air circulation for cheese that is either draining or aging, and is essential in making hard cheeses. Luckily, they are inexpensive at $4 each or less. They can't be sanitized and should be discarded after use.

## Cheese Wax or a Vacuum Sealer

Cheese wax is used to protect the cheese from air while it ages. This is a special kind of

⊗ Two types of cheese press.

wax that melts at a low enough temperature that it won't hurt the cheese when you brush it on. Don't try to substitute canning wax for this! Another alternative is to use a vacuum sealer to seal the cheese in an airtight bag from which all air has been evacuated. That's what I do because it is more convenient than waxing.

## Cheese Press and Mold

A cheese press is used to knit the curds together into a solid mass while expelling excess whey. There are a variety of designs of varying expense and complexity. A search on the Internet will even reveal many free design plans for making your own.

For most of the batches of cheese I've made, I have used a simple plastic press and mold that only cost $21. The downside is that you have to use external weights with it. Still, you can't beat it for the price and ease of use. Recently, I have acquired a stainless steel press made by Wood Lab that works very well.

## Instant-read Digital Thermometer

Temperatures are critical when making cheese. Some types of cheese require gradually raising the temperature or holding at a certain temperature for a specified time. The best thermometer for such purposes is one that gives you an instant and accurate reading. A good digital thermometer is not expensive.

I have a "Norpro electronic digital read thermometer/timer" that cost $16 and a hand-held Hamilton Beach instant-read digital thermometer. Both cost under $20, have stainless steel probes that are easy to sterilize, and can be found at cookware stores.

## Dedicated Small Refrigerator

Traditionally, many styles of cheese were quite literally aged in caves. Caves maintain a constant temperature and humidity throughout the year. Most of us don't have access to a suitable cave, and we don't have an area in the house that will reliably maintain a certain temperature for months on end.

If you decide to make cheeses requiring aging, you will find a dedicated refrigerator indispensable. A second-hand dormitory-sized refrigerator and an external thermometer set up to turn it on and off as needed will work perfectly for such an endeavor. A refrigerator dedicated to cheese-making is called a "cheese cave."

# Ingredients

**Not all of** these ingredients are needed for all cheeses, but you'll want them on-hand. Some of these you may already have from your excursions into wine, beer, and vinegar making.

## Vinegar, lemons, and tartaric acid

These common acids are used to make soft cheeses via the direct acidification method. In this method, the milk is heated to a certain temperature, a measured amount of acid is added and stirred into the milk, and then the milk clots after a period of time. This clotted milk is poured into a colander lined with cheesecloth; the cheesecloth is tied into a bag. The bag is hung in a warm place for the whey to drain out of the soft curds. These are among the easiest cheeses to make, and they work especially well as dips and spreads.

# Calcium chloride, 30% solution

When milk is pasteurized, the calcium ion balance is upset in the milk, which can impede proper curd formation. A small amount of calcium chloride solution diluted further in distilled water and mixed into the milk can correct this imbalance.

You can order food-grade calcium chloride and make the solution yourself (percentages are by weight!), or you can order the pre-mixed solution from various Internet stores specializing in cheese making supplies.

Calcium chloride, incidentally, is also an ingredient in some ice melting pellets used to melt the ice on sidewalks and driveways. This is a very crude product that isn't suitable for human consumption, so make sure you get food grade calcium chloride.

# Flaked or canning salt

Salt is used as a flavor enhancer, a bacteriostatic preservative, a modulator for enzymatic action, and it helps expel water from cheese curds through osmotic pressure. Special "flaked" cheese salt is available, but canning salt or Celtic sea salt will do as well.

The important thing is to avoid the ordinary salts in the grocery store because not only do many of them contain iodine, they often contain anti-caking agents and other chemicals that could interfere with cheese-making. So anything you use should be purely salt.

# Starter Culture

You can buy starter culture in packets from a supplier, or you can make your own from buttermilk and yogurt. Starter cultures are either mesophilic (meaning "medium heat-loving") or thermophilic (meaning "high heat-loving"). Starter culture is an inoculant containing a mix of bacteria that eat the lactose in milk and excrete lactic acid. The first purpose of these bacteria is to lower the pH of the milk in order to encourage curd formation. The second purpose is the continuing development of flavor characteristics during the making and aging of the cheese. The nature of the starter culture strongly influences the flavor of the cheese.

Mesophilic starter cultures work best at room temperature—around 72 degrees. They usually contain at least *Streptococcus lactis*, and many also contain *Streptococcus lactis* var. *cremoris* along with other lactic acid bacteria such as *L. delbrueckii* subsp. *lactis*, *L. lactis* subsp. *lactis* biovar *diacetylactis*, and *Leuconostoc mesenteroides* subsp. *cremoris*.

*Streptococcus lactis* is used to make cultured buttermilk; therefore fresh buttermilk with active live cultures can be used to make a mesophilic starter culture for cheese-making. Cheeses that begin with a mesophilic starter include farmhouse cheddar, edam, stilton, and Monterey Jack, among others.

Thermophilic starter cultures work best at temperatures above 80 degrees and below 130 degrees. A specific recipe will dictate the best temperature within this range for the particular cheese being produced, but the culture works best at 110 degrees. Exceeding 130 degrees may kill a thermophilic culture. This culture may like heat, but it doesn't want to be scalded or boiled. Thermophilic starters are used to create Swiss and Parmesan cheeses among others. *Streptococcus thermophilus* is a common bacteria in thermophilic starter cultures, but *Lactobacillus delbrueckii* subsp. *bulgaricus*, *L. delbrueckii* subsp. *lactis*, *L. casei*, and *L. plantarum* are all used.

Yogurt is made with thermophilic bacteria. One prominent brand of organic yogurt uses six live cultures that include *Streptococcus thermophilus, Lactoba-cillus delbrueckii* subsp. *bulgaricus,* and *L. casei.* This means that plain yogurt can be used to make more yogurt, and it can also be used to make a thermophilic starter culture for cheese.

If you opt to buy starter cultures from a cheese-making supply store instead of making your own, there are only two important things you need to know: You want the sort of culture called a "direct vat" culture, and you should put it in the coldest part of your freezer the very second you get it. Keep it in the freezer until ready for use.

## Rennet

Rennet is an enzyme that was originally derived from the stomachs of suckling animals. It is a proteolytic enzyme that breaks protein bonds in such a way as to turn liquid milk into solid curds. All infant mammals produce rennet. This turns milk into a solid form that stays in their digestive tract longer. That's why when a baby spits up milk, it has mysteriously turned into a clumpy solid. Babies of all mammals have miniature internal cheese factories.

In practice, animal rennet is a byproduct of veal production. Animal rennet of this sort is extremely perishable and has to be kept refrigerated. It's also pretty expensive.

Rennet can also be made from certain fungi and plants. The sort made from plants has to be made fresh on the spot, which may not be feasible during winter or if you can't find the plants. For our purposes I am recommending vegetable rennet, which is actually made from fungi. It is inexpensive and if you put it in the freezer it will stay good for about six months. It comes in tablets that can be divided into halves and quarters; this must be done carefully as it has a tendency to disintegrate.

Rennet is an extremely powerful enzyme. Tiny quantities will clot gallons of milk. When adding rennet, dissolve the required amount into a quarter cup of distilled water over a period of 20 minutes, then sprinkle it over the surface of the milk. Mix it into the milk using up-down and back-and-forth motions rather than swirling because swirling doesn't mix as efficiently. It's important that rennet be mixed efficiently because otherwise the curd it forms will be of uneven consistency.

## How to Make Rennet from Nettles

In a pinch, you might need to make your own rennet from nettles. This rennet works, but it doesn't give as clean a break or as solid a curd.

Put a pound of stinging nettle tips in a large pot and cover with water. Bring to a light boil and boil until the volume has been reduced by half. Filter through cheesecloth into a clean container. You can keep this in the refrigerator for up to two weeks. You use one cup per gallon of milk to be curdled.

## Other Cultures and Enzymes

As your cheese-making expertise increases, you'll want to try to make specific types of cheese. Toward that end, you will need different cultures and enzymes.

Lipase is an enzyme that splits milkfat into free fatty acids. It develops a characteristic picante flavor in the manufacturing of feta, blue, mozzarella, and provolone cheeses. Like rennet, it is extremely powerful. Unless a recipe directs otherwise, use between $\frac{1}{16}$ and $\frac{1}{8}$ tsp of the powder per gallon of milk. Dissolve the powder in a half cup of cool water for 30 minutes prior to use. Lipase is added immediately before rennet by sprinkling it on top of the milk and mixing it in using an up-down and back-and-forth motion.

Propionic Shermanii culture is used to create the characteristic holes and flavor of Swiss cheeses. As it ferments, it creates carbon dioxide that expands to create the holes. This is added to thermophilic starter culture at the rate of ⅟₁₆ tsp per gallon of milk.

Not all mesophilic or thermophilic starter cultures are created equal. The specific varieties of bacteria make a difference in the ultimate flavor of your cheese. As you learn more about cheese, you will want to try other starter cultures.

# 20

# Practical Cheese Making Techniques

**In this chapter,** I am going to progress from the easiest and least time-consuming techniques to the more involved, using a few examples. By mixing, matching, and varying these techniques you can make a wide array of interesting cheeses. Buttermilk and yogurt are an ideal starting place because both can be used to make other cheeses while saving money on starter cultures.

## How to Have a Lifetime Supply of Buttermilk and Mesophilic Cheese Starter

**I have always** loved cultured buttermilk. Its thick consistency with sweet-tartness is irresistibly delicious, and it makes wonderful pancakes as well! Buttermilk costs 70%

more than regular milk, so if you like it, you can save money by making your own.

Start with cultured buttermilk from the store that uses live cultures. You can make any amount of buttermilk you'd like from this by re-culturing. To re-culture, put the amount of milk you would like to turn into buttermilk into a stainless steel container. Either use a double-boiler or put the container of milk into a sink of hot water, and raise the temperature to 86 degrees.

Hold at 86 degrees for ten minutes, then add ¾ cup of buttermilk per quart of milk. (1½ cups of buttermilk for a half-gallon and 3 cups of buttermilk for a gallon.) Remove the milk from the heat, cover with cheesecloth to keep out bugs but allow oxygen, and allow it to sit at room temperature undisturbed for twelve hours.

That's it. Really. If you refrigerate it after the twelve hours are up, it will keep in the refrigerator for up to two weeks. Anytime you want more buttermilk, just repeat this procedure using a bit of the buttermilk you already made and you can have buttermilk forever unless your supply becomes contaminated.

Anytime a cheese recipe calls for "mesophilic starter" you can use your buttermilk at the rate of four ounces of buttermilk per one gallon of milk that you'll be turning into cheese. It is possible to freeze buttermilk for use later to make cheese, but I don't recommend that as the viability of the culture becomes spotty. I recommend using only unfrozen buttermilk to make cheese.

# How to Have a Lifetime Supply of Yogurt and Thermophilic Starter Culture

**Yogurt is a** bit more difficult to make than buttermilk because it requires the yogurt-in-progress to be held at a higher temperature for a long time. A yogurt-making machine can help, or make the yogurt on a weekend. If your family uses a lot of yogurt, it may be worthwhile to purchase a yogurt machine for less than $100. Yogurt costs anywhere from 300% to 400% more than milk, so if you eat a lot of yogurt you can save a lot of money by making your own.

You can make yogurt successfully from plain yogurt from the store, or you can buy a starter culture for the specific type of yogurt you wish to make. Viili culture produces a thick but mild yogurt similar to what you you mostly see in stores, whereas Piimä culture makes a thinner, drinkable yogurt. There are many other cultures available, but no matter how you start your first batch, yogurt cultures are serial cultures, meaning that you can continue to propagate them indefinitely simply by using a quantity from the last batch to make the next.

If you decide to use plain yogurt from the store to make more yogurt, please read the ingredient label carefully to make sure you are buying a product made only from milk and cultures. There are some yogurt brands whose "plain" yogurt contains adulterants and other ingredients that won't be helpful. Pectin is often used as a thickener and this is okay.

First, heat your milk to 185 degrees in a double boiler while stirring often. This is to kill off competing organisms. Then, remove the milk from the heat and allow it to cool to between 105 and 122 degrees. Once it is between these two temperatures, add either your starter culture according to package directions or ¾ cup of live yogurt per gallon of milk. Pour the mixture into cleaned and sterilized quart canning jars, and adjust the two-piece caps for a seal. Keep the temperature of these containers at 105 to 122 degrees for the next eight hours. The temperature can be maintained by filling the sink with water at 120 degrees, and then adding a bit of boiling water to the water in the sink whenever the temperature drops below 110 degrees. After eight hours, put your jars in the refrigerator where the yogurt will keep for two weeks.

Maintaining this temperature for so long will be difficult, but the bacteria have a better sense of humor than most regulatory agencies, so as long as you keep the temperature above 98 but below 130, your yogurt will still be fine. To maintain this temperature you can use the sink method already mentioned, a mattress heating pad or an electric blanket; be sure you keep an eye on things and check frequently so it doesn't overheat. Or, use your oven if it can maintain temperatures under 120. A slow-cooker with water on the lowest setting may also work by setting the jars in water in the slow-cooker and watching the temperature. The key is to improvise creatively.

The yogurt you create is plain yogurt. You can mix anything with it you'd like—fruit, nuts, granola, sweeteners, etc. If you decide to use it as a thermophilic cheese starter, use four ounces of your fresh plain yogurt per gallon of milk that you will be turning into cheese.

# Okay, Let's Make Some Cheese!

**There are literally** hundreds of types of cheese, all of which require differences in procedure, technique, or ingredients. Rather than try to cover all of it, I am going to illustrate how to make four representative cheeses that are easily made at home using the ingredients and equipment described. Between these four cheeses, all of the basic techniques will be covered, and you will gain enough experience to experiment and branch out.

I am going to cover a direct acidification soft cheese. Using the same principle, you could make a soft cheese using a different acid. Then, I will demonstrate a soft cheese using a starter culture. Next, I will demonstrate a minimally-aged hard cheese using both starter culture and rennet. Finally, I will describe making an aged cheddar cheese and most importantly the cheddaring technique.

# Soft Cheese by Direct Acidification: Queso Blanco

**Using a double** boiler, raise the temperature of one gallon of milk to 180 degrees while stirring so the milk doesn't precipitate protein. Add ¼ cup of vinegar by slowly dribbling it into the milk while stirring. (You can use distilled vinegar or some of your homemade vinegar. For a different taste, you can use the juice of 3-5 lemons.) Continue to stir for ten to fifteen minutes until the milk is completely clotted. If the milk doesn't clot, add up to four more tablespoons of vinegar while mixing for another ten to fifteen minutes.

Meanwhile, prepare cheesecloth by boiling in a pan of clean water. After boiling, use the cheesecloth to line a colander. Pour the clotted milk into the cheesecloth-lined colander, allowing the liquid to go down the sink. After the cheese has cooled, form the cheesecloth into a bag, and hang it over a bowl until liquid no longer drains out of the bag. (This works best at standard room temperature.

⊗ Raising the temperature to 180 degrees before adding the vinegar. Notice the cheesecloth boiling on the right.

⊗ The clotted milk draining in the colander.

⊗ I have a hidden hook under my cabinets for hanging cheese to drain.

⊗ This easy cheese is great on bagels or mixed with herbs as a vegetable dip.

If the temperature is too cold, the cheese won't drain well. This process should complete within five to seven hours.)

Scrape the cheese out of the cheesecloth into a clean, covered container. Add and mix salt, dried herbs such as garlic powder, dill, or basil into the cheese as desired. This is what is called a "fresh" cheese and it should be refrigerated promptly after making. Use within a week to avoid spoilage. Because of all the different things you can mix with this, it is a very versatile cheese that can be used for bagels, dips, and dressings.

# Soft Cheese using Yogurt Starter Culture: Farmer's Cheese

**Add ½ teaspoon** of 30% calcium chloride solution to ¼ cup of water, and mix thoroughly with one gallon of milk in a double boiler. Using the double-boiler, raise the temperature of the gallon of milk to 105 degrees. While the milk is heating, dissolve ¼ of a rennet tablet in ¼ cup of cool non-chlorinated water. Once the milk has

❷ I'll add the yogurt once the milk reaches 105 degrees. You could also use commercial thermophilic starter culture for this step.

❷ Here I am adding the dissolved rennet by pouring it slowly through a slotted spoon for better distribution.

reached 105 degrees, keep it there for five minutes and then add one cup of plain yogurt, stirring it in thoroughly. Keep the temperature at 105 degrees for ten minutes, then turn off the heat.

Once the temperature has dropped to 95 degrees, add the rennet by sprinkling it over the milk and mixing using a gentle up-down and back-and-forth motion. Remove the pot and cover it with the lid. Allow the mixture to set for about an hour and then check for the development of the curd. Check the curd by inserting a clean and sterile blunt object (such as a glass candy thermometer). If it can be withdrawn cleanly without anything sticking to it, and the hole it makes doesn't immediately fill with liquid, the curd is ready and you have what is called a clean break. If the curd isn't ready, allow the pot to set while covered for another fifteen minutes and check again.

Now that you have a clean break, you need to cut the curd. The purpose of cutting the curd is to allow for uniform drainage of the milk liquid (known as whey) from the curd. (Yes, this is the famous "curds and whey"—a primitive predecessor to cottage cheese—likely eaten by Miss Muffet in the nursery rhyme.)

Your goal in cutting the curd is to cut the curd into uniform-sized curds for even drainage of whey. In general, the smaller you cut the curds initially, the harder the style of cheese you are making; though there are practical limits. In this case, you are cutting the curd into one-inch cubes. Do this by using your curd knife to first cut a grid at right-angles the entire depth of the

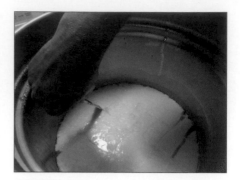

⊗ The horizontal cuts are being made by tracing the grid with the knife held at a 45 degree angle.

curd so you end up with a one-inch checkerboard pattern. Then, make horizontal cuts by positioning your curd knife at a 45 degree angle and cutting along one row of parallel lines in your grid. Though there are all sorts of other ways to do this and special gear you can buy, it is really that simple.

Once your curd is cut, cover the pot again and allow it to sit for another fifteen minutes so some whey can gather at the bottom of the pot. Then, put your pot back into the double boiler and slowly, over a period of 30 minutes or so, raise the temperature of the curds to 110 degrees. As the curds are heating, gently—very gently so you don't break them—use your slotted spoon to stir the curds in such a way as to exchange those on the top with those on the bottom in order to promote even heating. Once the curds have reached 110 degrees, keep at that temperature for thirty minutes while gently

⊗ The curds will release whey and shrink. The metal device is the temperature probe.

⊗ The cheese is being mixed with flaked cheese salt.

mixing every five minutes or so. You will notice the curds getting smaller and the amount of whey increasing. While this process is ongoing, prepare a large piece of cheesecloth by boiling.

Line your colander with a double-layer of cheesecloth, and gently pour the curds and whey into the colander. You can save the whey for baking later, add it to your compost pile or let it go down the sink. (If the whey is greenish, do not be alarmed—this is normal!) Let the curds drain in the colander for an hour or so, then put the curds into a bowl and salt to taste, turning the curds evenly for uniform distribution. I prefer sea salt for this, but you can also use cheese salt or canning salt. Do *not* use regular table salt (iodized or not) because it will make your cheese taste bitter.

Prepare some more coarse cheesecloth by boiling, and then use a double layer to line your clean cheese mold. Add the curds to the mold, fold the cheesecloth over top of the curds, and put the top of your mold on top of the cheesecloth. Put your mold in a shallow pan (a disposable pie plate

⊗ I used a 2.5 pound weight on the cheese press, and it worked fine.

would be ideal) to catch whey that is expelled. Add two pounds of weight on top of the mold, and place the whole works in the refrigerator.

Once the cheese and press have been allowed to work in the refrigerator for four or five hours, turn the cheese out of the mold, unwrap it, and place in a closed container in the refrigerator. Use within a week.

❸ The completed cheese before wrapping it in plastic and storing in the refrigerator.

# Hard Minimally Aged Cheese Using Mesophilic Starter: New Ipswich Jack

**Mix one teaspoon** of 30% calcium chloride solution into a quarter cup of water, and mix with two gallons of milk in a double-boiler. Bring the temperature of the milk up to 85-90 degrees, and add either ½ tsp of powdered mesophilic starter or one cup of fresh cultured buttermilk, mixing thoroughly. Cover the mixture and allow it to ripen for 30–40 minutes while maintaining the temperature between 85 and 90 degrees.

While the mixture is ripening, prepare your rennet solution by mixing ½ tablet of rennet with ¼ cup of cool non-chlorinated water. You'll know the mixture has ripened by the fact 30–40 minutes have passed and it smells like buttermilk or yogurt. Once the mixture has ripened, add the rennet solution by dripping it around the milk and mixing it gently but thoroughly using up-down and back-and-forth motions. Continue to maintain a temperature of 85 to 90 degrees while allowing the mixture to sit covered for an hour. At this point, the curds should give you a clean break.

Use your curd cutting knife to cut the cubes into 1/4-inch cubes. Continue holding the temperature at 85 to 90 degrees for another 40 minutes while gently stirring the curds every five minutes or so. Keep the curds covered while not stirring or checking the temperature. You'll notice the curds shrinking and the volume of whey increasing.

Slowly increase the temperature to 100 degrees over a 30-minute period while stirring every five minutes or so. This amounts to about two degrees every five minutes. Hold the temperature at 100 degrees for another 30 minutes while stirring every five minutes.

Now, very gently so as not to damage or lose curds, pour off as much of the whey as you can. This may be easier to do with a helper holding back the curds using the slotted spoon while someone else tips the pot over the sink.

Put the pot back into the double boiler and continue to stir for another 30 minutes while maintaining the temperature at 100 degrees. Meanwhile, prepare a double-layer of course cheesecloth by boiling first, and use it to line a colander. Pour the curds into the cheesecloth-lined colander. Add two tablespoons of cheese salt and mix the curds gently.

Line your cheese mold with cheesecloth, and then pack the mold closely with the curds. Fold your cheesecloth over top of the curds, install the top of your mold, and put your mold in a shallow pan to catch the whey that will be expelled.

Put a ten-pound weight on top of the mold to press the cheese for fifteen minutes. Then, remove the cheese from the mold, take it out of the cheesecloth, flip it over within the cheesecloth, and put it back in the mold.

This time, press the cheese for 30 minutes with a thirty-pound weight. (I recommend stacking three 10-pound dumbbell weights as these are easier to handle.) Then, take the cheese out of the press, take it out of the cheesecloth, flip it again within the cheesecloth, re-cover it, and put it back in the mold. Press it this time with 40 pounds for twelve hours.

After this, take it out of the mold and cheesecloth, and lay it on a bamboo sushi rolling mat. Flip it on the mat once a day so that it dries evenly. After three to five days, it should be dry to the touch. Once it is dry to the touch, it is ready for aging.

This cheese should be aged at temperatures of from 50 to 60 degrees for anywhere from one to three months. Maintaining such temperatures is a tall order in most homes, but any temperature range from 45 to 68 will do. Luckily (at least in this respect) my house is old and drafty so I can age cheese in a kitchen cabinet anytime from November to April without need of maintaining a special environment.

If, however, you happen to either live in a warmer climate or have a more energy-efficient home, you will likely need to create a cheese-cave from a dorm refrigerator as described earlier in this chapter.

Larger cheeses will form a natural rind that will protect them from invasion; smaller cheeses (like the size that we have made in this example) will need to be protected by either wax or plastic.

If using plastic, first wash the cheese using vinegar on a clean paper towel to reduce bacterial counts, then seal it in plastic using a vacuum sealer.

If you are using cheese wax, melt it by putting a small stainless steel bowl in a pot of boiling water and adding wax to the bowl. (This bowl will be almost impossible to clean after, so you might want to get a cheap bowl at a department store for this purpose.) After you have washed the cheese with vinegar, use a natural bristle brush to dip in the melted wax and then paint it onto the cheese. Once the wax has hardened on one side of the cheese, turn the cheese over and coat the other side. Check the cheese over thoroughly to make sure you haven't missed any spots and that the cheese is coated uniformly, and then set the cheese aside to age.

After this cheese has aged for a month, it is safe for people who are lactose intolerant; after it has aged for two months, it is safe even if made from raw milk.

# Monadnock Cheddar

❷ Despite a couple of imperfections in uniformity of coating, this waxed cheese is aging nicely.

**This cheese starts** off identically to the New Ipswich Jack cheese, and the primary variance starts with the cheddaring process. Mix one teaspoon of 30% calcium chloride solution into a quarter cup of water, and mix this with two gallons of milk in a double-boiler. Bring the temperature of the milk up to 85-90 degrees, and add either ½ tsp of powdered mesophilic starter or one cup of fresh cultured buttermilk, mixing thoroughly. Cover the mixture and allow it to ripen for 45-50 minutes while maintaining the temperature between 85 and 90 degrees.

While the mixture is ripening, prepare your rennet solution by mixing ½ tablet of rennet with ¼ cup of cool non-chlorinated water. Once the mixture has ripened, add the rennet solution by dripping it around the milk and mixing it gently but thoroughly using up-down and back-and-forth motions. Continue to maintain a temperature of 85 to 90 degrees while allowing the mixture to sit covered for 45 minutes. At this point, the curds should give you a clean break. If not, allow to sit for another 15 minutes and test again.

Use your curd cutting knife to cut the curd into 1/2-inch cubes. Slowly increase the temperature to 97 to 100 degrees over the next

40 minutes while gently stirring the curds every five minutes or so. Keep the curds covered while not stirring or checking the temperature. You'll notice the curds shrinking and the volume of whey increasing. Hold this temperature for another 30 minutes while stirring periodically to prevent matting or clumping. During the last five minutes, don't stir so the curds can settle on the bottom.

Line a colander with boiled cheesecloth and put the colander over a large pot to collect the whey. Pour the contents of your double-boiler into the colander and put a lid on top to retain heat, and allow to sit for one hour. (Make sure that the level of the whey in the pot isn't high enough to actually touch the curds. Any excess whey can be drained or put in your compost pile.)

Here is the the distinctive process that makes cheddar cheese and it is called "cheddaring." At the end of an hour you'll notice that the curds have amalgamated into a solid mass. Cut the mass of curd into slabs about ¼ inch thick. Stack the curds like dominoes and cover with the cheesecloth. Every fifteen minutes, rearrange the stack so the slabs that were outside are now inside, and those that were on the top are now at the bottom. After four or five rounds of this, the texture should resemble very firm tofu or turkey breast.

❷ The cut curds are starting to release whey.

After the cheese slices have reached the desired texture, they need to be milled. That just means you need to cut these slices up into chunks about the size of a pea. Put the milled curd in a bowl and sprinkle with 1½ teaspoons of flaked salt while gently rolling the curds around for uniform distribution.

Line your cheese mold with cheesecloth, and then pack the

⊗ The slabs are cut and being stacked.

⊗ Cheese in the process of milling.

⊗ The cheese slabs are stacked. You can
see the liquid draining from them.

mold closely with the curds. Fold your cheesecloth over top of the curds, install the top of your mold (also called the follower), and put your mold in a shallow pan to catch the whey that will be expelled.

Put a ten-pound weight on top of the mold to press the cheese for fifteen minutes. Then, remove the cheese from the mold, take it out of the cheesecloth, flip it over in the cheesecloth, and put it back in the mold. Press with the ten pounds of weight for another 45 minutes. The reason we use a light weight at first is to prevent expelling fat with the whey.

Then, flip over the cheese in the cloth, and increase the weight to 40 pounds for 24 hours. The next day, flip the cheese again, and continue to press with 40 pounds for another 24 hours. So in total, the cheese has been pressed for two days and an hour.

Now, remove the cheese from the cloth, wipe it down with either vinegar or a brine solution using a clean cloth, and place it in a protected room-temperature place on a bamboo mat for a day or two until a rind starts forming. (You can make brine solution by mixing as much salt into water as the water will dissolve.) What I do to keep insects away is put a wire scaffold over the cheese and drape some cheesecloth over it. Once the rind has started to form, either coat the cheese with cheese wax or seal it in a plastic bag using a vacuum sealer.

Mature the cheese from one to three months. The ideal temperature for aging cheddar is 50 degrees. During the winter, this is the temperature of my porch so I'm lucky. You can age it at temperatures ranging from 45 to 60 and it will come out fine.

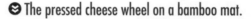

⊗ The pressed cheese wheel on a bamboo mat.

⊗ A wire scaffold will hold the cheesecloth away from the cheese and keep flies away.

# Tip for Maintaining Temperatures

**Reading books about** cheese making, you'd think everyone owns a precisely controlled stove that allows maintaining temperatures within a single degree for hours on end. In the real world, maintaining temperatures is somewhat difficult. Using a double-boiler keeps the milk from scorching. Unfortunately, when you raise the temperature of the milk to, say, 90 degrees using a double boiler, if the inner container is left in the outer container the temperature will continue to rise well beyond that of the culture you are using even if you turn off the heat.

Once the milk has reached the higher end of the temperature range, simply remove the inner container from the outer container and set it on an unused burner on the stove. Check the temperature once in a while and if it seems to be going too low, just set it back in the outer container for a few minutes, and take it back out once the temperature is in the proper range. Because the amount of milk and water involved has a substantial thermal mass, usually this need not be done more than once for a particular waiting period.

# Experiment and Keep a Log

**A lot of** times people want to make cheeses like those that they buy at the store. If you want to do that, there are a host of sites on the Internet that give specific recipes. But what I recommend instead, is that you experiment and keep a log. I have covered all the fundamental principles you need to know in order to make your own unique cheeses. Fresh cheeses have to be refrigerated to be safe and should be used in less than a week. Cheeses made from raw milk have to be aged for at least two months to be safe. Hard cheeses need to be pressed with increasing amounts of weight. But now, from just the four cheeses I have given in this chapter, you can think about the variations.

The Queso Blanco recipe was a direct acidification cheese made with vinegar. What would happen if, instead of adding vinegar, you added a mesophilic starter and held it at 88 degrees for an hour before pouring into the cheesecloth? It would certainly taste different!

The soft Farmer's Cheese described earlier used a yogurt (thermophilic) starter culture. What if you used the same technique, but instead used a buttermilk (mesophilic) starter and varied the temperature accordingly?

The Jack cheese recipe is pretty interesting. Don't you wonder what would happen if you used a thermophilic starter and some lipase instead of a mesophilic starter? How would it come out? What would it taste like? What would happen if you added a pint of heavy cream and a tablespoon of wine vinegar to one of the recipes?

So rather than copying other recipes, what I am encouraging you to do is follow the general principles I have described here to make your own and keep notes. I think you will be very pleasantly surprised at how easy it is to make astonishingly good cheese that is uniquely your own and can't be bought anywhere at any price. This is ultimately what will make cheese-making a worthwhile thing for a mini-farmer.

# 21

# Introduction to Composting

**In general, compost** can be described as organic matter that has decayed to a point of biological stability, but such a generalized definition doesn't tell us much. The reason generalizations fail is because compost can be made from practically anything that was once alive, and it can be made using a vast array of methods. Every variation produces something different, so no two batches of compost are the same.

Compost can be made both aerobically (using oxygen) and anaerobically (without oxygen). It can be made at relatively high temperatures (thermophilically) or at moderate temperatures (mesophilically). You can even make it using earthworms as digesters. Though doing so is inefficient, it can be made entirely from a single starting ingredient, or from any mixture of ingredients. All of these approaches can be combined at various stages, and each has benefits that are balanced against shortcomings. The potential for confusion can seem insurmountable, which may be why anytime I go somewhere to speak, I get questions about composting.

The happy reality though, is that nature is on your side. It's really hard to mess up compost so badly that you get no compost at all. Nature loves compost and will turn anything that was once alive (or produced by something living) into compost all by itself. Biological materials will naturally degrade, and composting those materials is simply a way of accelerating or controlling the process. Though there are many ways of composting, each with its own trade-offs, nature will ultimately have its way and organic materials will rot with or without your help. The end product will be compost. So the most important thing you need to do when approaching composting is to not worry.

In the chapters ahead I'll take you through the nutrient cycle, explain the role of compost in soil microbiology and plant health, and delve into the various methods of composting. Even though I will stress a lot of points as being important, if you keep coming back to the fundamental concept that *organic materials will all eventually turn into compost with or without your help,* you'll realize that you can just dig right in and your end results will be a tremendous benefit no matter what.

Nearly all books that cover compost concentrate only on aerobic composting with a special emphasis on thermophilic composting. But this is not, in my opinion, enough to make someone self-sufficient. For example, maybe you have noticed that you need compost for soil blocks when you are starting your onion seedlings in January, but your outdoor compost pile is going to be frozen until April so it won't do you any good. Or maybe you have a back or leg injury, and turning a two-ton thermophilic aerobic compost pile is simply not feasible.

Because nature is on your side, there are a lot of different ways to create compost, and all that is really necessary is an underlying under-standing of the nature of the processes at work and an eye toward safety to adapt numerous methods to your situation. I personally use many methods both indoors and outdoors, and this book will help you do the same.

# Why Use Compost?

**If you are** looking at this book, you're probably already sold on the idea of composting. If you aren't already sold, then I am going to convince you.

Whether you garden using chemical fertilizers, pesticides and fungicides, or using organic methods, there is abundant and compelling scientific proof that compost will improve the fertility of your soil so that less fertilizer is needed. It will also reduce the incidence and severity of diseases that reduce your crop yield. The math is straightforward: using compost means your garden will be more cost-effective because you will have to spend less money on fertilizers, insecticides, and fungicides for a given harvest of any crop. That means *money*. A lot of money.

Compost induces resistance to a wide array of bacterial and fungal diseases.[64] Induced resistance (as opposed to acquired immunity) is a form of epigenetics. That is, how a plant or animal expresses its genes is not controlled simply by the genes themselves, but also how various environmental factors affect that expression. Plants were not intended to be grown in sterile soil. Rather, they were intended to be grown in living soil. Compost creates and sustains a living soil, so when grown in the proper environment as nature intended, the gene expression of plants is optimized for their health.

This concept also applies to humans. Humans were never intended to be sedentary bumps on a log. Studies show that proper exercise

---

[64] Vallad, G., Cooperband, L., and Goodman, R., "Plant foliar disease suppression mediated by composted forms of paper mill residuals exhibits molecular forms of induced resistance.", *Physical and Molecular Plant Pathology* 63 (2003): 65–77

literally turns certain genes on or off and thereby affects our vulnerability to a host of diseases to a substantial degree.[65] So the fact that environmental factors such as the presence of compost can have a large effect on the well-being of plants is not at all surprising. When humans eat right and get their exercise, the aggregate cost of health care is reduced. When plants eat right, the cost of their health care is also reduced. Just as a human in optimal health is more productive, a plant grown in soil amended with compost has greater yields.[66]

According to the Washington State University Cooperative Extension Service (along with dozens of other sources), compost helps soil retain fertilizers better, and also reduces or even eliminates the need for fertilizer altogether. Fertilizer, like fungicides, costs money. WSU also states that the beneficial microorganisms in compost can help protect crops from pests, thereby reducing the need for pesticides. That's even more money.

So right there, if you garden and your intention in gardening is to save money over buying an equivalent product at the grocery store, the case for using compost is open and shut—done. If you aren't using compost, you are throwing money away.

Another reason to use compost is human health. Depending on which experts you ask, humans need anywhere from twenty-two to fifty elements in their diet for optimal health. I am not speaking of vitamins and other complex molecules, but rather basic chemical elements that we need in order to catalyze the synthesis of cellular enzymes or even as core constituents of structures such as bones. Though a person can survive and even thrive for a time with an ongoing deficiency in some of these elements, over time deficiency takes its toll, and some USDA researchers have come to believe that most cancer and as many

---

[65] Agus, D., *The End of Illness*, (New York: Free Press, 2012)

[66] Edwards, S. et al., *The Impact of Compost Use on Crop Yields in Tigray, Ethiopia*, 2000-2006 Inclusive, ISBN 978-983-2729-91-4.

as 50 percent of all deaths globally are caused directly or indirectly by insufficient intake of important trace elements.[67]

Though this information has not been widely disseminated in an environment where other branches of the USDA continue to push nutritionally vapid commodities as "healthy", it is available for those who care to search. In fact, long before the USDA researchers came along, Dr. Maynard Murray conducted numerous experiments demonstrating dramatically reduced risks of cancer and many other chronic diseases in animals fed foods grown in such a way as to contain as many elements as possible.[68]

Many find it puzzling that in an era where preventable causes of cancer and heart disease are in decline, many other forms of cancer and heart disease are increasing. But taken with the information above, it might not seem so surprising once we realize that the elemental content of agricultural soil has declined by 85 percent over the past 100 years[69] and the nutritional content of commercially available foods has declined by anywhere from 30 percent to 81 percent over the past thirty years.

So the elements in the soil you use for growing food are important. The full complement of elements is certainly important for the well-being of your crops, and assists them in fending off pests and diseases through their own robust immune systems. But the elements in your soil are also important for the well-being of the people who eat those crops, including you.

Standard agricultural methods can be described as having mined all the nutritionally necessary minerals out of the soil. Those methods return a handful of elements in the form of fertilizer, but only thirteen

---

[67] Banuelos, G., and Lin, Z.(eds), *Development and Uses of Biofortified Agricultural Products* (CRC Press, 2008)

[68] Murray, M., *Sea Energy Agriculture* (Acres USA, 2003 (reprint))

[69] Marler, J. and Wallin, J., Nutritionsecurity.org "Human Health, the Nutritional Quality of Harvested Food and Sustainable Farming Systems"

elements are generally required to grow a good-looking and marketable food commodity in a competitive market that doesn't distinguish one tomato from another. All of the other elements needed for human health—elements that were abundantly present a century ago—are either absent or severely depleted.

Compost contains and preserves these micronutrients that are so important to human health. So if you grow a garden for your health, you really need to use compost otherwise you are largely wasting your time.

# Why Make Your Own Compost?

**If you weren't** already convinced of the value of adding compost to your garden soil, I hope I have convinced you. But the next question is: why should you make compost yourself rather than just buying it?

Cost-effectiveness in a home garden requires different methods than those employed in large commercial farms. Substantially enhanced nutrition and major cost savings can only be achieved in a home garden through the use of sustainable and organic methods,[70] and the primary practice that enables these methods is *composting*.

If you have read *Mini Farming: Self Sufficiency on ¼ Acre*, you know that I put a great deal of emphasis on compost. That emphasis is not misplaced, because composting is the primary method that will help to retain the elemental content of your soil in a biological matrix that will make it available to plants as needed, without being washed out of your soil.

Keep in mind that there is no such thing as a perfectly sustainable system because, if you eat the food you grow, part of that mineral content is retained in your body and some is discarded as waste. But even then, the mineral conservation achieved through composting

---

[70] My books *Mini Farming: Self Sufficiency on ¼ Acre* and *Mini Farming: Maximizing Your Mini Farm* cover cost-effective and sustainable methods.

substantially reduces the amount of minerals you will need to supply via outside sources.

Likewise, for a variety of reasons, few soils available to homeowners and renters already contain an optimum mineral content, and they will need to be supplemented with the required minerals. But once those minerals are in the soil, conscientious composting practices will help to retain them, so that fewer will need to be added in the future.

Fewer additives equates to less money being spent for the value of the produce you raise. So composting will allow you to raise more sturdy plants that provide superior nutrition for less money. If self-sufficiency or health are your objectives, composting is not optional—it's necessary.

Though you may need to buy bagged compost when you start gardening, bagged compost is extremely expensive. Though it varies from crop to crop, in general you may need to add anywhere from two to eight cubic feet of compost for every thirty-two square feet of garden. At the time of writing, bagged compost costs anywhere from $5 to $8 per cubic foot. It wouldn't take a very big garden for this to run into hundreds or even thousands of dollars. And what you get for all that money may not be what you expect.

When you buy bagged commercial compost, you have no idea what went into it. Though the regulations for USDA Certified Organic agriculture prohibit the use of sewage sludge on crops labeled as "USDA Organic", there is no such prohibition on the labeling of bagged compost, and many types of compost labeled as "organic" contain sewage sludge.[71]

In theory, composting human waste is just fine, provided it is done in a fashion that eliminates pathogens. Even drug metabolites in human waste are often effectively destroyed or rendered biologically inert as part of the composting process. But sewage sludge is *not* a result of such

---

[71] Arnell, N., "Many types of organic compost are really packaged human sewage", Natural News.com, May 6 2011

a composting process, and large-scale waste treatment systems are not equipped to remove many harmful chemicals. Humans consume a vast array of chemicals in the form of medications, artificial colors, preservatives and so forth. The levels of drug metabolites in our waste stream are so high that pharmaceuticals such as Prozac have shown up in water supplies.[72] Sewage sludge also contains more than merely human waste. Sludge contains the chemicals, hair dyes, heavy metals, paint, degreasers, detergents and motor oil people wash down their drains, drugs that are not detoxified by the sewage treatment process and more. An EPA survey of sludge samples conducted in 2009 found detectable levels of a dozen drugs, flame retardants and even endocrine disruptors.

So if you DO wind up buying bagged compost, please pay attention to the fine print and ask about its contents.

As previously stated, bagged compost is pretty expensive. If when you start your garden you have to buy compost because you have made none of your own, it will be more cost-effective to have it delivered by the truckload if such an option exists for you. Compost delivered by truck is measured in yards. As a point of reference, a yard of compost is twenty-seven cubic feet. I have had compost delivered on a couple of occasions. In both cases the compost was not yet finished and couldn't be used until the next season. In one instance the compost contained asphalt rocks and even hypodermic syringes. (Yikes!)

So remember, just as food you grow yourself is superior because it is grown with your own well-being as a priority, so is compost that you make yourself. *It is in your best interests to start making your own compost* because it is far less expensive and because you control its ingredients and how it is made.

Making your own compost is easy, and I have written this book to show you how.

---

[72] Townsend, M., "Stay Calm Everyone, There's Prozac in the Drinking Water", *The Observer*, 7 August 2004

# 22

# Starting with the Soil

**Though this book** is about composting, compost is intended to conserve or augment the soil in your garden. As the nutrient cycle starts with your garden soil, and any nutrients conserved through composting started out in the soil of your garden, a comprehensive examination of your soil and the ways it might be improved is a good place to start.

As a gardener you want soil that will hold adequate moisture without becoming so waterlogged as to exclude oxygen from the roots. You also want soil rich in organic matter that will hold nutrients and release them to the roots as needed. Soil should also be within the ideal pH range of most plants you'll grow, and your soil should have adequate levels of the nutrients plants need most, such as nitrogen, phosphorus, and potassium. Ideally, you want soil that doesn't crust over so seeds can sprout. Finally, you want soil with a broad spectrum of micro-nutrients both for the optimum health of the plants and the health of those who eat them.

In practice, few gardeners start with such ideal soil. Soil either has too much sand, too much clay, too high or low a pH, or lacks fundamental nutrients including nitrogen, phosphorus and potassium. To say that the soil most homeowners have to work with is less than ideal would be an understatement, considering that in many cases their yards are composed of sand and filled with only enough loam to start grass. Just under the grass mat what passes for soil looks awfully sterile. How do you start the rehabilitation process?

# Analyzing Your Soil's Water Characteristics

**Soil has three** important characteristics pertaining to water: infiltration, percolation and available water-holding capacity.

Infiltration is a measure of how quickly water is absorbed into the soil. Quicker infiltration means less water is either lost or runs off. Percolation is how quickly water that is in excess of what the soil can hold leaves the soil. Available water-holding capacity is how much water the soil can hold. In practice, if you can get the infiltration and percolation rates within reasonable ranges, your water holding capacity will take care of itself.

Analyze percolation rate by digging a hole 1' deep and 6"–8" in diameter, and keep it topped off with water for at least four hours on the day before you test. The day you test, adjust the water level in the hole to 6" from the bottom (use a plastic ruler). Next, set a timer for ten minutes. At the end of ten minutes, use a ruler to measure how many inches the water fell. Bring the water level back up to 6", repeat the process, and average the two distances. The percolation rate in minutes per inch (MPI) is: MPI = 10/Distance. You want an MPI of between 60 and 30. If it is greater than 30, use raised beds to prevent waterlogging. If it is less than 6, increase the level of compost you would add based on biological activity by 50 percent. Do this with each compost addition until you have an MPI of 6 or greater.

Infiltration rate is tested two days after a thorough (e.g. equivalent to 1" of rain) watering. It is measured using a "double ring infiltrometer". This fancy sounding gadget is two pieces of PVC pipe, each 8" long, one being 4" in diameter and the other being 6" in diameter. Use a rubber mallet to drive the larger ring 2"–3" deep into the soil, and then drive the smaller ring the same depth in, as close to the middle of the larger ring as is practicable. Fill both the inner and outer rings with water to a 4" or 5" depth. (Use a ruler.) Now, set your timer for ten minutes. At the end of ten minutes, measure how much

⊗ Testing the soil's percolation rate.

the water level has decreased in the center tube. Refill both rings and repeat twice more, then average your results. Your infiltration rate is: Infiltration = 10/Distance. If your infiltration rate is less than 2, your soil is too sandy and you can help with compost or by adding the same amount of peat moss as you would compost. If your infiltration rate is greater than 10, your soil likely has too much clay. Add gypsum with your other soil amendments at the rate of 10 lb per 100 sq. ft. Test annually, and continue to add gypsum with your other amendments until the infiltration rate is greater than 10.

While it is recommended that gardens be watered at a rate that approximates 1" of rain weekly,[73] the amount and frequency of watering is determined to some degree by soil variables. Though these can be tested, it is far easier to just observe. Start off by checking to see if your crops look like they need water in less than a week. If they do, then you know you should be watering more often. Watering more in a given session likely will not help because the excess water will simply drain, but watering more frequently will supply what is needed. Over time, additions of compost will improve water-holding capacity. If the water-holding capacity seems seriously lacking, you can amend with vermiculite at the rate of two cubic feet of vermiculite per thirty-two square feet of garden soil. Vermiculite is mica that has been heated and popped like popcorn, and it does well at taking up and releasing water.

# Analyzing Your Soil's Biological Activity

**A very important** factor that should be measured in soil is its biological activity. This is the quantity and activity of microorganisms in

---

[73] I explain how to do this with a standard watering attachment, bucket and timer in *Mini Farming: Self Sufficiency on ¼ Acre.*

the soil. The health of microbes in the soil is important because it is the interaction between microbes and the roots of plants that converts nutrients from an organic form useless to the plants into an inorganic form that plants can readily assimilate. Such a measurement reflects many underlying factors of soil fertility, as healthy microbes indicate a healthy soil. Furthermore, microbes tie up certain nutrients and make them available as needed. Thus, the amount of supplementation for nitrogen that a soil test indicates is required can be reduced if biological activity is high. This is because a soil test for nitrogen only tests for inorganic nitrates, and can't take the nitrogen available in microorganisms into account. Likewise, the biological activity of a soil can be used to determine how much compost needs to be added.

There are two ways to measure the biological activity of soil: respiration testing, and counting the number of earthworms. Both methods

⊗ Counting earthworms is the easiest and least expensive method of assessing your soil's biological activity.

are best used in mid-spring or mid-fall because either extremely hot or extremely cold weather will falsely suppress the results. The earthworm method is the easiest: a couple of days after a good rain, using a flat spade, dig up a 1' x 1' x 1' cube of soil from your garden, dump it into a wheelbarrow or onto a flat piece of wood and count the earthworms.

Earthworm testing is the easiest (and least expensive) method available, but there are some areas where the soil is perfectly fine but earthworms have simply never been introduced[74] or don't thrive for some other reason. In those cases, soil biological activity can be measured via respiration testing, which measures the amount of carbon dioxide generated by microbes in the soil.

Because respiration testing is expensive, I have searched for cheaper methods. The problem is that the amount of carbon dioxide generated by a practical amount of soil is measured in millionths of a gram, so such methods aren't practical for home use.

One method would be to make a liter of saturated lime water solution, and inject the air trapped over a section of soil into the lime water. (Lime water is 1.5 g of calcium hydroxide dissolved in a liter of distilled water.) As carbon dioxide combined with the calcium hydroxide to form calcium carbonate, the calcium carbonate would precipitate out of solution. It could be caught on filter paper and weighed. The weight of the calcium carbonate could then be used to determine how much carbon dioxide had been captured. The trouble is that the amount of calcium carbonate created would be so small that weighing it would not be practical on scales that are generally affordable. This problem could possibly be solved by collecting air over a fairly large area (e.g. a square yard), but this becomes logistically difficult.

---

[74] Earthworms became extinct in North America during the past couple of Ice Ages and were re-introduced by European explorers.

The two generally available methods that will accurately measure such small quantities of carbon dioxide are the Solvita Basic Soil Respiration Test ($120 for material to perform six tests) and the USDA Soil Quality Test Kit, which costs over $800 from Gempler's in Iowa. Thankfully, you can use only a subset of the latter kit in order to perform the soil respiration test. Even so, the initial cost will be somewhat high, but ongoing costs (i.e. a new Draeger™ tube for each test at $6.50 each) will be more reasonable in the long run. Again, let me point out that if you can count earthworms in your soil, this isn't needed.

## Biological Activity Measurement

### Materials Needed

- 1 x 6" diameter piece of 1/8" thick aluminum pipe 5" long, a clearly scribed line should be marked 2" from one end and the edge of the other end should be beveled—contact a local welding shop.
- 1 x 6" stove-pipe cap, with two 1/2" holes drilled in it. The holes should be 1" from the edges, opposite each other.
- 2 x #00 rubber stoppers
- 8" long piece of 2"–4" lumber
- 2–4 lb rubber mallet or mini sledgehammer
- Soil thermometer
- 2" x 6" long sections of latex tubing, 3/16" outside diameter, 1/8" inside diameter
- 2 x 18 to 22 gauge 1.5" hypodermic needles
- 140 cc syringe
- Pack of 10 x Draeger tubes, 0.1% $CO_2$
- Timer that will time up to 30 minutes

## Procedure

- The day before you plan to conduct the test, water the soil thoroughly, to the equivalent of 1" of rain.
- Place the beveled edge of the pipe against the dirt. Lay the 8" long board across the pipe, and use the mallet or hammer to bang the pipe into the dirt until it is level with the inscribed line.
- Cover the pipe with the lid and wait for 30 minutes. If the lid doesn't form an airtight seal, use some duct tape to tape the bottom edge of the lid to the pipe.
- While you are waiting, insert the soil thermometer 2"–3" into the soil immediately adjacent to the pipe.
- Also while you are waiting, assemble the measurement apparatus as follows:
    - Use nail clippers to break the nipples off both ends of a Draeger tube.
    - Note that the tube has an arrow indicating direction of airflow.
    - Make sure the syringe piston is fully depressed, and connect a piece of tubing from the syringe to the end of the Draeger tube where the arrow is pointing.
    - Connect the other piece of tubing on the opposite end of the Draeger tube, and attach one of the needles to the far end of the tubing.
- After 30 minutes, insert the needle in the measurement apparatus through one of the stoppers into the head space inside the pipe, and insert the other needle (which is attached to nothing) through the other stopper to provide for airflow. Draw air through the Draeger tube by pulling back slowly on the plunger at the rate of 5 cc per second until 100 cc of air has been drawn into the syringe.
- Read the color change on the Draeger tube. If the color change has not reached the 0.5 mark in the column labeled "n = 1", take 4 additional samples. Expel the air from the syringe before each sample by

| Amount of Compost to Add Based on Measurements | | | | |
|---|---|---|---|---|
| *Earthworms per Cubic Foot* | *Grams CO$_2$/ m$^2$/Day* | *Solvita Test Result #* | *Cubic Feet of Compost to Add per 32 ft$^2$* | *Biology Level* |
| 20 or more | 2.9 or more | 3.5+ | 1.5 | A |
| 10–19 | 1.4–2.9 | 2.5–3.5 | 1.5–2.5 | B |
| 5–10 | 0.85–1.4 | 1.0–2.5 | 2.5–3.5 | C |
| <5 | <0.85 | <1.0 | 3.5–5.5 | D |

first disconnecting it from the tubing and then reconnecting it to the tubing before the next draw. Do all 5 draws at the rate of 5 cc per second until 100 cc of air has been drawn into the syringe. Read the results from the "n = 5" column on the Draeger tube.

You can calculate the amount of $CO_2$ (and hence the soil respiration and its biological activity) through use of the following formula:

T = Soil temperature in degrees Celsius. If your thermometer reads in Fahrenheit you can convert from Fahrenheit to Celsius:

$$\text{Celsius} = \frac{5 \times (\text{Fahrenheit} - 32)}{9}$$

P = Percent $CO_2$ as reported in the appropriate column on the Draeger tube

Grams of $CO_2$ – C per Square meter per Day
$$= ((T - 273)/273) \times (P - 0.035) \times 10.4$$

# Analyzing Macro-nutrients and pH

**If you have** ever seen a series of numbers on a bag of fertilizer, such as 10-10-10, 5-10-5 or even 45-0-0, those numbers are the NPK rating of the fertilizer. They mean that 100 lbs of that fertilizer will supply the stated number of pounds of nitrogen, phosphorus or potassium. So 100 lbs of 5-10-5 fertilizer will provide 5 lbs of nitrogen, 10 lbs of phosphorus and 5 lbs of potassium. Because other macro-nutrients such as calcium, carbon and water are supplied as part of liming, watering or simply from the air, these three major nutrients are the ones described on the bag.

Depending upon the type of fertilizer, the rest of the product may be utterly inert, or it may contain other nutrients as well.

Soil analysis is a very complex field and there are two major competing schools of thought regarding what is important. The sufficiency method is used by most laboratories and commercial farms. It tests for the major macro-nutrients: nitrogen, phosphorus and potassium, along with pH and a handful of micro-nutrients The analysis is accompanied by recommendations for additions. You can test the first four of these yourself using home testing kits available at home and garden stores.

The Albrecht method measures the amounts and ratios of positively charged bases (such as calcium, magnesium, potassium, sodium, ammonium and several trace minerals) in the soil. Albrecht's base saturation theory then recommends amendments in proportions that will both raise the saturation level of bases as needed and adjust their relative proportions for optimum conservation of organic matter and soil fertility. The only comparative study undertaken to date, however, concludes that using the Albrecht method gives no significant improvement in crop yield, but costs more.[75]

I therefore recommend the sufficiency method, which has the added bonus of also being something you can do yourself with at-home soil testing kits. Though I use the LaMotte Soil Testing Kit, the other commonly available kits (such as Rapitest) work just as well

---

[75] Exner, Rick, "Soil Fertility Management Strategies – Philosophies, Crop Response, and Costs" (Iowa State University, University Extension, 2007)

⊗ Readily available soil testing kits are entirely sufficient for the home gardener's needs.

so long as you follow the directions precisely and use bottled water (rather than tap water) for mixing with the soil. (A lot of tap water has a substantially "off" pH. My uncorrected tap water, for example, has a pH of 4.8, which is low enough to alter soil test results.)

When you gather soil for a soil test, clear the top inch of soil away and then gather your sample. Do this in several places, collecting a heaping tablespoon from each location. Mix them all together in a jar. I happen to use raised bed gardening, so I test each bed, gathering my sample from several places within each bed. If you are using a tilled plot, just gather from several sites in the plot if the soil is reasonably uniform. If the soil is obviously variable within the plot, test the different areas separately.

Each soil test has its own instructions which will vary with manufacturer, so I'll leave you to perform the tests. As the tests rely on comparing the color of a solution to the color of a chart, the one piece of advice I would give is to view the tests in the shade on a sunny day as that will give the most true color comparison. If you can't do that, fluorescent lighting is your next best bet. I put a sheet of white paper behind my solution and color comparison chart to aid in interpreting the colors.

# Interpreting Soil Test Results

**Except for pH,** the results of home soil tests are not given in absolute numbers. Instead, they are reported broadly as "depleted", "deficient", "adequate", or "sufficient". If the test indicates sufficient

## Nitrogen Needed in Ounces per 100 ft²

|                | *Depleted*    | *Deficient*   | *Adequate*      |
| -------------- | ------------- | ------------- | --------------- |
| **Biology Level A** | 3 leaf/2 root | 1.5 leaf/1 root | 1 leaf/0.5 root |
| **Biology Level B** | 4.5 leaf/3 root | 3 leaf/2 root | 1.5 leaf/1 root |
| **Biology Level C** | 6 leaf/4 root | 4.5 leaf/3 root | 3 leaf/2 root |
| **Biology Level D** | 7.5 leaf/5 root | 6 leaf/4 root | 4.5 leaf/3 root |

## Phosphorus Needed in Ounces per 100 ft²

|                         | *Depleted* | *Deficient* | *Adequate*   |
| ----------------------- | ---------- | ----------- | ------------ |
| **Phosphorus Required** | 5 ounces   | 3 ounces    | 1.25 ounces  |

## Potassium Needed in Ounces per 100 ft²

|                        | *Depleted* | *Deficient* | *Adequate* |
| ---------------------- | ---------- | ----------- | ---------- |
| **Potassium Required** | 5.5 ounces | 3.5 ounces  | 1.5 ounces |

levels of a nutrient, then nothing need be added, but if the test indicates anything less than sufficiency you'll need to supplement the soil.

The reason why I detailed testing biological activity before discussing analysis of macro-nutrients is because, with regard to nitrogen, the amount of nitrogen you need to add is modified depending upon the amount of biological activity. DNA and other proteins present in soil microbes contain nitrogen that will be made available to plants throughout the course of the season, but won't show up in a soil test because a soil test only shows inorganic nitrogen. The amount of nitrogen to be added according to soil test assumes a certain level of biological activity, but if your level of biological activity is greater than the assumed level, you should add less nitrogen than the test recommends. Conversely, if your biological activity is less than the assumed level, you should add more nitrogen than the test recommends.

In general, I recommend using at least two sources of a given macro-nutrient. This will distribute a greater variety of accompanying micro-nutrients and because the sources will break down at different rates, they will provide nutrient availability throughout the season. The following tables show the amount of a given organic fertilizer to use given a certain soil test result. In the case of nitrogen, the table takes biological activity into account. Because the amount of nitrogen needed is lower for root crops, the results are shown with a slash between them, with leaf and fruit crops as the first number and root crops as the second number.

# Compounding Your Own Fertilizer

**The foregoing numbers** are interesting, but not very useful by themselves because you can't go down to the store and buy five ounces of phosphorus or three ounces of potassium. In fact, in their pure forms, phosphorus is poisonous and incendiary and potassium will explode on contact with moisture. Instead, you'll need to figure out a mix of natural substances that will give you what you need. I have never found a book or website that goes beyond listing the NPK values of various natural substances and actually teaches you how to combine them to get what you need. All it takes is a little math, which, in an era of scientific calculators and computerized spreadsheets, isn't really a problem. First, here is a table listing the NPK values of various substances used as natural fertilizers. Keep in mind that this table is an average of various brands, whose composition varies. If you buy a bag of bone meal and it lists different numbers, use those numbers instead of those in the table. The table is most useful for things that don't usually have numbers—such as wood ashes or alfalfa meal.

| NPK Values of Common Organic Nutrient Sources | | | |
|---|---|---|---|
| | *Nitrogen* | *Phosphorus* | *Potassium* |
| *Substances in Which Nitrogen Predominates* | | | |
| Alfalfa meal | 3 | 1 | 2 |
| Soybean meal | 2.5 | 0 | 2 |
| Dried blood | 12 | 3 | 0 |
| Cottonseed meal | 7 | 2.5 | 2 |
| Bat guano | 11 | 2 | 2 |
| *Substances in Which Phosphorus Predominates* | | | |
| Bone meal | 2 | 21 | 0 |
| Rock phosphate | 0 | 39 | 0 |
| Seabird guano | 11 | 11 | 2 |
| *Substances in Which Potassium Predominates* | | | |
| Wood ashes | 0 | 1.5 | 8 |
| Greensand | 0 | 1.5 | 7 |
| Seaweed, dried | 1.3 | 1 | 5 |
| Kelp meal | 1 | 0 | 2 |

There is an easy way to use the tables in this section to make fertilizer, and it is entirely close enough that your plants won't know the difference. There is also a more difficult way that gives you very tight accuracy, which I'll explain after I've demonstrated the easy way.

I will demonstrate the easy way with an example. Pretend you have tested your garden soil, found it is biology class B, has deficient nitrogen, adequate phosphorus and deficient potassium. You will be growing a root crop. Looking at the tables, this means that you need to create a fertilizer that provides 2 oz. of nitrogen, 1.25 oz. of phosphorus and 3.5 oz. of potassium per 100 sq. ft.

The equations for the number of ounces of an organic source you need in order to get a certain number of ounces of nutrient are:

Nitrogen Source Ounces = 100 x (Nitrogen Ounces Needed/"N" Value from Table)

Phosphorus Source Ounces = 100 x (Phosphorus Ounces Needed/"P" Value from Table)

Potassium Source Ounces = 100 x (Potassium Ounces Needed/"K" Value from Table)

The table of organic nutrient sources is divided into three sections according to which nutrient predominates. Pick whatever you have or can readily acquire from each category. For example, I will pick soybean meal for nitrogen, bone meal for phosphorus and greensand for potassium.

The N number for soybean meal is 2.5 and I need 2 oz. of nitrogen, so:

Ounces of Soybean Meal Needed = 100 x (2/2.5)
= 80 oz.

The P number for bone meal is 21, and I need 1.25 oz. of phosphorus, so:

Ounces of Bone Meal Needed = 100 x (1.25/21)
= 6 oz.

The K number for greensand is 7 and I need 3.5 oz. of potassium, so:

Ounces of Greensand Needed = 100 x (3.5/7)
= 50 oz.

Based upon these calculations, in order to make a complete fertilizer for 100 sq. ft, I need to combine 50 oz. of greensand with 28 oz. of soybean meal and 6 oz. of bone meal.

This fertilizer is a bit off from precisely what you need, because soybean meal also contains a substantial amount of potassium, and bone meal also contains some nitrogen. In practice, this isn't a problem because the ingredients, being organic, aren't instantly available to plants so a bit of an overabundance won't hurt as much as it would if you were using chemicals such as ammonium nitrate as fertilizer.

But if you were to use alfalfa meal and dried seaweed as ingredients, keep in mind that they contain almost as much of one nutrient as another, so using the easy technique could lead to an overabundance of fertilizer. Though it might not be an immediate problem, over the course of a season an overabundance of some nutrients (such as nitrogen) can lead to undesirable outcomes such as plants making all vegetation and no fruits or tubers. Other nutrients in excess can block the absorption of micro-nutrients. So a little bit of over-fertilization is okay, but you don't want to go too far. If you are using fertilizer components that contain substantial amounts of more than one nutrient, then you'll be better off using the more difficult method.

The solution is to use algebra to solve a system of equations. The number of equations and variables is the same as the number of ingredients. For a fertilizer composed of three ingredients, the equations would be:

$$(F_1 \times n_1/100) + (F_2 \times n_2/100) + (F_3 \times n_3/100) = N$$
$$(F_1 \times p_1/100) + (F_2 \times p_2/100) + (F_3 \times p_3/100) = P$$
$$(F_1 \times k_1/100) + (F_2 \times k_2/100) + (F_3 \times k_3/100) = K$$

Where:

$F_1$ = Ounces of the first fertilizer (this is unknown)

$n_1$, $p_1$, $k_1$ = The NPK values for that fertilizer from the table (or the bag)

$F_2$ = Ounces of the second fertilizer (this is unknown)

$n_2$, $p_2$, $k_2$ = The NPK values for that fertilizer from the table (or the bag)

$F_3$ = Ounces of the third fertilizer (this is unknown)

$n_3$, $p_3$, $k_3$ = The NPK values for that fertilizer from the table (or the bag)

N = Ounces of nitrogen needed per 100 sq. ft

P = Ounces of phosphorus needed per 100 sq. ft

K = Ounces of potassium needed per 100 sq. ft

This looks far more complicated than it really is. Repeating the prior example, using a combination of soybean meal (fertilizer 1), bone meal (fertilizer 2), and greensand (fertilizer 3) to provide 2 oz. of nitrogen, 1.25 oz. of phosphorus and 3.5 oz. of potassium, the equations look like this:

$$(F_1 \times 2.5/100) + (F_2 \times 2/100) + (F_3 \times 0/100) = 2$$
$$(F_1 \times 0/100) + (F_2 \times 21/100) + (F_3 \times 1.5/100) = 1.25$$
$$(F_1 \times 2/100) + (F_2 \times 0/100) + (F_3 \times 7/100) = 3.5$$

The system of equations can be solved via the substitution method or using matrices and determinants. Or, because we live in a wonderful age, you can literally type the equations right into a web site and it will solve them for you. The website www.solvemymath.com has such a calculator at the time of writing, but there are several others that show up via Internet searches.

Solving the system of equations shows that, for every 100 sq. ft, 77 oz. of soybean meal, 4 oz. of bone meal and 28 oz. of greensand would be needed to provide the necessary elements. These numbers differ from those obtained using the easy approach because they take into account the fact that most organic fertilizers supply more than one nutrient. If the solution to the system of equations gives you a negative number for the amount of one of the ingredients, then come up with a different set of ingredients because that combination won't work.

Using these methods will allow you to mix a custom combined fertilizer to meet any likely need for nutrient augmentation.

# Micro-nutrients

**Micro-nutrients can be** broadly divided into two categories: those needed for the optimal health of crops and those needed for the optimal health of humans. The latter category is much broader and, depending upon which expert is consulted, can include as many as fifty elements, whereas only thirteen are needed for plants to look marketable. The categories overlap, so supplying the elements needed for humans would include those needed for plants.

I advocate a three-tier approach to micro-nutrients The first tier is to use compost, and to add other soil amendments from a variety of sources so that many micro-nutrients are naturally present and conserved. The second tier is to specifically add micro-nutrients that are generally required by plants. The third tier is to include a small quantity of a broad spectrum micro-nutrient additive that will include everything humans need so it is available for uptake by the crops.

The micro-nutrients generally required by plants are boron, copper, iron, magnesium, manganese, molybdenum, sulfur, and zinc.

**Boron:** Boron is critical to practically all life processes in a plant, ranging from regulation of water uptake to the generation of hormones. You can add boron in the form of borax (from the cleaning aisle at the supermarket). You need three teaspoons per 100 square feet of garden annually. Boron is toxic to plants in excess, so don't exceed the recommended amount. Boron deficiency gives different symptoms depending on the plant. In general, root crops suffering from boron deficiency develop tubers that either have hollow cores or cores that are very prone to rotting. In vegetable crops, you may find hollow or roughened stems, stunted growth, and yellow tips on the leaves.

**Copper:** Copper is important for root metabolism, photosynthesis and enzyme activation. It is only needed in small amounts, and excess amounts can kill plants, so don't exceed the recommended amount. If you use copper-based fungicides, you don't need to add it as a micro-nutrient because you already have at least enough and probably too much in your soil. I recommend adding copper in the form of copper sulfate crystals. These are bright blue and unmistakable. Use four tablespoons per 100 square feet of garden annually. Suspect copper deficiency if newer leaves are wilted and older leaves have a pronounced tendency to curl inward on themselves.

**Iron:** Iron is crucial for the chlorophyll cycle in plants. Without it, they will take on a bleached-out appearance and their growth will be stunted. Plants self-regulate their iron uptake, so a slightly excess amount won't hurt anything. If, like me, you use blood meal in your garden, iron deficiency isn't an issue. But if you don't use blood meal, you can add iron in the form of iron (ferrous) sulfate. I recommend six ounces per 100 square feet of garden.

**Magnesium:** Magnesium's primary benefit is that it helps your soil bacteria, but it also plays a role in carbohydrate motility within the plants. Magnesium coexists naturally in dolomitic lime. If you substitute a portion of dolomitic lime with regular lime in your garden, you don't need to supplement magnesium. If you don't use dolomitic lime, you can get magnesium sulfate (a.k.a. Epsom salt) at the grocery store and add it to your garden at the rate of between twelve and twenty-four ounces per 100 square feet annually. Magnesium deficiency will cause the spaces between the veins of the leaves to look bleached-out at first, and then some of the tissue will die and turn brown. In brassicas, the bleached-out areas may include other pigments such as orange or violet.

**Manganese:** Manganese is necessary for photosynthesis and improves the yield of root crops. It is very rare to need manganese unless your soil pH is naturally higher than 6.5, which is also rare. Soils that are over-farmed can be deficient, but this is unlikely to apply to your garden. If manganese deficiency symptoms occur anyway, as manifested in a uniform yellowing of *new* leaves,[76] you can add manganese sulfate at the rate of twelve ounces per 100 square feet. Only add this once every three years as it tends to remain in the soil. Slight manganese deficiency is hard to spot because it looks like an extremely mild case of iron deficiency. In more severe cases, leaves develop a definite grayish metallic sheen and spots of dead tissue appear along the veins.

**Molybdenum:** Molybdenum is needed for practically every cellular process in a plant. Most soils are deficient in molybdenum. In excess, it is extremely toxic to plants. Furthermore, a slight excess of molybdenum will exacerbate any existing problems with manganese deficiency. Sufficient levels of copper will mitigate the adverse effects from an excess of molybdenum. For this reason, I recommend that if molybdenum is added, it should be added in conjunction with copper and manganese. If you add molybdenum, I recommend using sodium molybdate or ammonium molybdate. Ammonium molybdate or sodium molbdate should be added at the rate of one-and-a-half ounces per 100 square feet. Molybdenum deficiency looks like

---

[76] Yellowing of *old* leaves is a sign of nitrogen deficiency.

nitrogen deficiency, except the underside of the leaves doesn't look red as they usually will with nitrogen deficiency. (This is because plants need molybdenum to process nitrogen.) In severe cases, leaves will also cup upwards and develop spots of dead tissue.

**Sulfur:** Sulfur is a component of the amino acids that make the DNA, proteins and enzymes within a plant, and it is therefore critical. Any compound that includes the phrase "sulfate" contains sulfur. So when you add magnesium sulfate (Epsom salt), copper sulfate or calcium sulfate (gypsum) to your soil, you are adding sulfur along with the primary desired nutrient. Sulfur is usually added in the form of plain elemental sulfur, known as flowers of sulfur, at the rate of twenty-four ounces per 100 square feet annually. It tends to lower the pH, so adding it with an equal amount of lime is prudent. Sulfur deficiency shows itself as an overall chlorosis with a distinct pinkness in the veins of the leaves.

**Zinc:** Zinc is key for seed production and regulation of water equilibrium in plants. It is rare for soils to be deficient in zinc, but if they are deficient it will show up as chlorotic bands within the leaves of plants. The pH of the soil affects how available zinc is to plants. A soil could have plenty of zinc, but still give symptoms of deficiency in alkaline (pH greater than 7) soils. So I would recommend getting the pH down to 6.5 before supplementing zinc. When needed, zinc is used in the form of zinc sulfate at the rate of twelve ounces per 100 square feet annually. A deficiency in zinc manifests in yellowed younger leaves that also show pitting between the veins. Continued deficiency results in the tissues between the veins dying while the veins remain green.

That takes care of the needs of the plants, but what about the nutritional needs of people? What I use and recommend is evaporated ocean water. Such a product is usually called "sea solids," "ocean minerals," or "sea mineral solids."

⊗ Common sources of trace elements include wood ashes, sea solids and borax.

Over the ages, rain and erosion have moved a great many minerals that would ordinarily be on land in abundance into the sea. Over-farming without replenishment and farming practices that lose topsoil to erosion have exacerbated this problem. Though I am able to go to the seashore and collect kelp from the beach for my own compost, this is seldom practical for most people.

In essence, sea water contains, in varying amounts, every known element save those made artificially in nuclear reactors. In 1976, Dr. Maynard Murray published a book entitled *Sea Energy Agriculture* in which he highlighted the results of numerous studies he had made from the 1930s through 1950s on the addition of ocean minerals to agricultural land. Though his book was published some time ago, I have discovered that in growing beds side by side, those treated with sea minerals do, in fact, produce obviously healthier plants.

The big problem with using ocean water directly is obvious: it's really heavy and you can't grow plants in salt water because it kills them. In fact, one of the practices of ancient warfare was to sow your enemies' fields with salt so they wouldn't be fertile. Fortunately, only a small quantity of sea solids is required, and when package directions are followed not only is there no harm, but plants become more healthy and more resistant to insects and diseases. The process is also cost effective as, on a mini farm, the amount of sea minerals required is tiny; so even a ten-pound bag of sea minerals from various sources will literally last for years. (I use five pounds annually when I haven't been able to supplement my compost with seaweed.) There are a number of companies offering sea minerals such as GroPal, Sea Agri, Sea

Minerals from Arkansas and others. The key is that each offering is a bit different, so be sure to scale the package directions appropriately.

Do not use "sea salt" in place of these products. Why not? Because most sea salt sold for culinary use is this beautiful crystalline white stuff from which all of the valuable trace nutrients have been removed. There are a few unrefined offerings of culinary sea salt out there, such as Celtic Sea Salt, but these are very expensive for agricultural use.

Now before I go further, I want to discuss the effect of composting on micro-nutrients. In all likelihood, your soil will start off with some degree of deficiency. But when you add nutrients to your soil, they will end up in your plant materials. Then, when you compost the materials and add them back to the soil, the elements will have been conserved. Furthermore, the humic acid will chelate and microorganisms in compost will hold these nutrients, whether the compost is in the pile or has been added to your soil. If you use biochar, that will help the minerals stay in the soil as well.

In commercial agriculture, these elements are often an annual addition. That is because extensive tillage depletes organic matter in the soil, and composting is not usually done on a sufficient scale or with a diversity of ingredients. Thus, the soil doesn't have sufficient ability to hold onto the micro-nutrients and they are washed out with rain, or shipped away with the crops.

If, on the other hand, you are managing your soil fertility with cover crops, crop rotation, using organic soil amendments and diligent composting plus even adding some biochar, micro-nutrients will have a greater tendency to stay in your soil. This means that you should not add micro-nutrients annually once your garden is established and compost operations are underway. With the exception of molybdenum which should only be added once, add the other micro-nutrients as recommended for the first three years. But after that, you can do just fine by adding ocean minerals every other year, and the only individual micro-nutrient you'll need to add annually is boron.

When adding micro-nutrients, thoroughly mix them with some other amendment that you will add in larger quantities. It is essentially impossible to evenly distribute an ounce and a half of some powder over a 100 square foot area. So these nutrients should be added to materials such as wood ashes or bone meal that are used in larger quantities, thoroughly mixed, and added. That way, and especially for nutrients that could be toxic such as boron, copper or molybdenum, you don't end up with "hot spots" in your garden that won't grow anything.

I have received a number of emails asking where to get these substances, so I am going to give you some sources with the understanding that none of these companies has paid me, that I don't know anyone who works for them personally, and that my listing of them as a source doesn't mean I endorse or even know everything about their political positions, business practices or anything else.

Epsom salt (magnesium sulfate) and borax (sodium tetraborate) are available at any grocery store. Copper sulfate is a common agricultural chemical and should be available at any comprehensive "feed and seed" or agricultural store, as should flowers of sulfur. Iron sulfate is also a common chemical and if you can't find it at your local feed and seed store, you can find it ubiquitously on the Internet via a search for it. I got mine at Kmart, a national department store chain.

Manganese sulfate is also an agricultural chemical, but harder to find via local sources. I ordered mine from Star Nursery (www.star-nursery.com) because they sold five pound bags, but there are a lot of other sources. Sodium molybdate is pretty expensive, at over $20 for eight ounces at www.customhydronutrients.com. This is a much better deal than the reagent grade material from a chemical company which will run you $200 to $300 for a similar quantity.

# pH

**pH is a** measure of how acidic or alkaline the soil is. It is important because plants generally have a certain range of pH preference for optimal growth and because the pH of the soil actively affects which microorganisms will thrive in the environment and how readily the nutrients contained in the soil can be used by plants. pH is measured on a scale from 0 to 14. 0 is highly acidic, like battery acid; 14 is highly basic like lye, and 7 is neutral.

Many sources list a pH preference range for each plant, but these sources often differ in the details. For example, one source will list the preferred pH for tomatoes as 5.8 to 6.5, whereas another will list it as 6 to 7. The simple fact is that you don't need to be that detailed because most plants grown for food in gardens will grow well with a pH ranging from 6 to 7. True, a cucumber can grow at a pH as high as 8, but it will also grow at 6.5.

pH corrections can take months to show results and the constant rotation of beds between crops makes it impractical to customize the pH of a bed to a given crop. It therefore makes sense to test each bed individually, and correct the beds to a uniform pH of between 6 and 6.5. The exceptions are that the beds used for potatoes should have the pH lower than 6.5, and the beds used for brassicas (such as cabbage) should have extra lime added to the holes where the transplants are placed.[77]

The cost of pH meters for home use has dropped considerably in recent years, with accurate units selling for as little as $13. Simply follow the directions that come with your individual meter for measuring each bed. You don't need a pH meter, however, because the soil testing kits you use for measuring macro-nutrients also have a test for pH.

---

[77] This practice prevents the appearance of a disease called "club-foot".

(The pH meter used for testing soil is not the same type of meter used when testing the pH of beer wort.)

In most of the U.S. the soil pH is too low and needs to be raised to be within an optimal range. Correcting pH using lime can be problematic in that it takes several months to act. Though the gardening year should start in the fall along with any soil corrections, the reality of life is that the decision to start a garden is generally made in the late winter or early spring. Thus, the farmer is stuck trying to correct pH within weeks of planting instead of months.

However, with a bit of creativity and use of alternate materials, both short and long term corrections can be made to pH.

There are many liming materials available for this purpose, but only four I would recommend: powdered lime, pelleted lime, dolomitic lime, and wood ashes. Others such as burnt and hydrated lime act more quickly, but are hazardous to handle and easy to over-apply. If you choose to use these products, please follow package directions closely.

Pelleted lime is powdered lime that has been mixed with an innocuous water-soluble adhesive for ease of spreading. It acts no more or less quickly than the powdered product, but costs more. Lime can take as long as a year to take full effect, but will remain effective for as long as seven years.

Dolomitic lime contains magnesium in place of some of the calcium. In most soils in the U.S. (excepting clay soils in the Carolinas), its use for up to 1/4 of the liming is beneficial to supply needed magnesium with calcium. It is used at the same rate as regular lime, takes as long to act, and lasts as long.

Wood ashes are a long-neglected soil amendment for pH correction. They contain a wide array of macro-nutrients such as potassium and calcium; but also contain elements such as iron, boron and copper. They act more quickly in correcting soil pH, but do not last as long. Wood ashes are applied at twice the rate of lime for an equal pH correction; but should not be applied at a rate exceeding five pounds per 100 square feet. So, in effect, wood ashes are always used in conjunction with lime, rather than on their own.

The pH scale is a logarithmic value, similar to a decibel. As such, the amount of lime needed to raise the pH from 4 to 5 is greater than the amount of lime needed to raise the pH from 5 to 6. Furthermore, the effectiveness of lime is strongly influenced by the type of soil. So the following table reflects both of these factors. The numbers represent pounds of powdered limestone per 100 square feet. For wood ashes, double that number, but never exceed five pounds per 100 square feet in a given year. Wood ashes can seldom be used exclusively as a pH modifier. Rather, they are best used when mixed with lime. For example, if the table says I need 5.5 lbs of lime, I can use 5 lbs of wood ashes in place of 2.5 lbs of lime, plus 3 lbs of lime.

One further note about lime. A lot of sources say you shouldn't apply fertilizer at the same time as lime because the lime will react with the fertilizer and neutralize it. To some extent, this is true. However, lime stays active in the soil for as long as seven years, so the fertilizer will be affected anyway. As long as both are thoroughly incorporated into the soil, don't worry. In addition, these concerns largely pertain to inorganic fertilizers such as ammonium nitrate. When the fertilizers are organic, and composed of such substances as blood meal or alfalfa meal, the adverse effect of the lime is considerably reduced.

Though excessively alkaline (e.g. a pH higher than 6.5) soils are rare in the U.S., they exist in a few places such as the Black Belt prairie region of Alabama, and can be accidentally created through excessive liming.

Correcting an excessively alkaline soil can be done using a variety of substances, including elemental sulfur (known as flowers of sulfur), ammonium sulfate, sulfur coated urea and ammonium nitrate. These substances are seen to be ideal in industrial agriculture, but they are

| Pounds of Lime per 100 Square Feet to Correct pH of Acidic Soil | | | | |
|---|---|---|---|---|
| Measured pH | Sandy | Sand/Loam | Loam | Clay and Clay/Loam |
| 4 | 5.5 | 11 | 16 | 22 |
| 5 | 3 | 5.5 | 11 | 16 |
| 6 | 1.25 | 3 | 3 | 5.5 |
| 7 | None | None | None | None |

excessively concentrated and can hurt the soil biology, so they aren't recommended for a mini farm aiming at sustainability.

Some authorities also recommend aluminum sulfate, but the levels of aluminum (if the pH ends up changing) can be taken up by the plant and can become toxic to both plants and animals. I recommend either straight flowers of sulfur (if growing organically), or ammonium sulfate (if you don't mind synthetic fertilizers). In practice, the amount of ammonium sulfate required to lower soil pH a given amount is 6.9 times as much as straight sulfur, so you'll likely use sulfur for cost reasons.

Sulfur works by combining with water in the soil to create a weak acid. This acid reacts with alkalies in the soil to form water-soluble salts that are leached from the soil and carried away by rains. Because it creates an acid directly, it is easy to over do sulfur. It should be measured and added carefully, and thoroughly incorporated into the soil. It takes about two months to reach full effectiveness, but results should start to manifest in as little as two weeks.

Ammonium sulfate works by virtue of the ammonium cation (a positively charged ion) combining with atmospheric oxygen to create two nitrite anions (negatively charged ions), two molecules of water, and four hydrogen cations. These hydrogen cations are the basis for acidity; and they will then acidify the soil.

| Sulfur Needed in Pounds per 100 Square Feet to Correct an Alkaline Soil | | | |
|---|---|---|---|
| *Measured pH* | *Sand* | *Loam* | *Clay* |
| 8.5 | 4.6 | 5.7 | 6.9 |
| 8 | 2.8 | 3.4 | 4.6 |
| 7.5 | 1.1 | 1.8 | 2.3 |
| 7 | 0.2 | 0.4 | 0.7 |

# Index

# B

# C

# Notes

## ALSO AVAILABLE FROM BRETT L. MARKHAM:

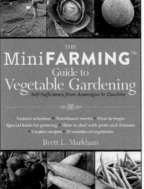

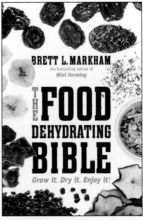